LIZZ
FREE
OR
DIE

RIVERHEAD BOOKS   *a member of Penguin Group (USA) Inc.*   *New York*   *2012*

LIZZ FREE OR DIE

[ESSAYS]

LIZZ WINSTEAD

RIVERHEAD BOOKS
Published by the Penguin Group
Penguin Group (USA) Inc., 375 Hudson Street, New York,
New York 10014, USA · Penguin Group (Canada), 90 Eglinton Avenue East,
Suite 700, Toronto, Ontario M4P 2Y3, Canada (a division of Pearson Penguin Canada
Inc.) · Penguin Books Ltd, 80 Strand, London WC2R 0RL, England · Penguin Ireland,
25 St Stephen's Green, Dublin 2, Ireland (a division of Penguin Books Ltd) · Penguin Group
(Australia), 250 Camberwell Road, Camberwell, Victoria 3124, Australia (a division of Pearson
Australia Group Pty Ltd) · Penguin Books India Pvt Ltd, 11 Community Centre, Panchsheel Park,
New Delhi–110 017, India · Penguin Group (NZ), 67 Apollo Drive, Rosedale, North Shore 0632,
New Zealand (a division of Pearson New Zealand Ltd) · Penguin Books (South Africa) (Pty) Ltd,
24 Sturdee Avenue, Rosebank, Johannesburg 2196, South Africa

Penguin Books Ltd, Registered Offices: 80 Strand, London WC2R 0RL, England

Library of Congress Cataloging-in-Publication Data

Winstead, Lizz.
Lizz free or die : essays / Lizz Winstead.
    p.   cm.
ISBN 978-1-59448-702-6
1. Winstead, Lizz.   2. Comedians—United States—Biography.   I. Title.
PN2287.W525A3   2012   2012006441
        792.702'8'092—dc23
            [B]

Printed in the United States of America
1   3   5   7   9   10   8   6   4   2

BOOK DESIGN BY NICOLE LAROCHE

While the author has made every effort to provide accurate telephone numbers and Internet
addresses at the time of publication, neither the publisher nor the author assumes any
responsibility for errors, or for changes that occur after publication. Further,
the publisher does not have any control over and does not assume any
responsibility for author or third-party websites or their content.

Penguin is committed to publishing works of quality and integrity.
In that spirit, we are proud to offer this book to our readers;
however, the story, the experiences, and the words
are the author's alone.

For Wilbur and Ginny

CONTENTS

LIZZ
FREE
OR
DIE

PREFACE

This is a book of essays about life. *My* life.

It's not a memoir, per se, as I decided to write about some specific moments that will give you some insight into the people, places, and experiences that propelled me forward. (With a few steps back in the process.) I think of these pieces as "messays," because they are a collection of stories that put my somewhat complicated life into perspective—or at least a kind of perspective.

I have been through a lot of the same stuff that you have dealt with, are dealing with, or will deal with in the future. From the struggle of being a young girl trying to find her voice, to the unlikely places she found it, to the realities and heartbreak of watching an aging parent die, this book gives you (I hope) permission to be honest with yourself, to laugh, to cry, to bitch, and to scream. And maybe if you come across any of those emotions while reading, you will realize that you, too, at some point in your life had been told to "restrain yourself" because you needed to be "appropriate."

I hate the word *appropriate*.

And I hate people who think they can define *appropriateness* as an absolute, especially because they are usually the same people who try to shove toeing the line down my throat most aggressively—proselytizing politicians and preachers and prosaic comedy producers, all who specialize in prematurely adjudicating without an appropriate leg of their own to stand on.

I hope this book redefines the word *appropriate*, or shoves it into obsolescence with other meaningless words, like *refudiate*, *jiggy*, and *Tea Party*.

So what kind of juicy details about my life are included? Well, let me be clear up front: First, this is not a book full of dark family secrets.

My father wasn't one of those horrific memoir dads. You know what I mean. He was not the kind of dad who did "things" to me that led to a social worker, which led to a judge, which led to an attorney asking in a closed hearing, "Where on the doll did he touch you?"

And my mother wasn't one of those memoir moms, either. She was not some kind of emotional gorgon who scrubbed this poor author's secret garden with Borax and Brillo pads or made her children eat their own feces in the crawl space under the basement stairs because her cult leader or the voices in her head told her to. She was more subtle than that.

At this point it should be noted that because these messays aren't chock-full of the aforementioned themes, Lifetime Television won't be clamoring for the TV rights to this book. Although I will share some woman-in-peril anecdotes, my woman-in-peril stories don't involve deadly estrangement, deadly deception, or my mom and me sleeping with our deadly pool boy. So I offer my sincere apologies right here to the careers of Missy Gold, Tracey Gold, and any other members of the Gold family who will not be employed in some made-for-TV movie incarnation of my life.

Second, I will not regale you with gag-inducing details about spontaneous sex in a Porta-Potty or how I blew some bass player from an indie band in the back of their Leinenkugel-soaked van. This is not to say I don't weave a few tales of sexual stupidity. I did lose my virginity to a mediocre high school hockey player. I grew up in Minnesota; there were a lot of girls like me, who grew up in a wintry archipelago and gave it up to a right-wing left wing with a mullet. It was 1978; there weren't a whole lot of options. Just ask Sarah Palin.

Third, it is not one of those mea culpa books. Those books always make my brain explode because more often than not they are less *mea culpa* and more *everyone else is culpa*. Themes like "I heroically sat idly by and watched as the administration I worked for subverted the facts to justify war and ordered torture and illegal imprisonment, but I'll blame everyone who was around me for that."

If you want to read one of those books, put this back on the shelf and walk over to the Your Taxes Used to Pay Me to Do a Crappy Job

Running the Country and Now I Am Making Millions Lying to You About How Great I Was at It section. It's right behind the Crafts and Hobbies aisle. Or you might want to check the How to Start Your Home Business area.

And last, it's also not a revenge book. I am not a public laundry kind of gal, unless it's my dog Buddy barfing up my thong on a busy Brooklyn street. I do share experiences that some involved may not like, and I have changed some names of people and establishments because either they have private lives that don't need to be dragged through the public mud, even though they happened to be standing in it with me, or I would rather not give free advertising to them, as I think the services they provide suck.

I also feel awful because I could not include all the fantastic people in my life (blame my editor), but as this is not a memoir, I didn't cover every special moment with all those who mean a lot to me so I hope I will be forgiven.

And as for the less fantastic people who have come across my path: I didn't include too many of them for the simple reason that I remember them all too well.

Also, I sometimes lump together chunks of my life to serve as a composite of a given time period, rather than go through a linear play-by-play. I may occasionally have a date or a month wrong, but the experiences all happened within the same general time. Finding specific dates from my life way back on the Internet proved very unfruitful. My Wikipedia page is proof of that. So when I had to estimate, I based some of my timelines on the material that went into my shows, knowing I had an accuracy window based on a certain news cycle.

In short, I can say that all this shit happened, but I may be a bit off in the exact order in which it appears here. It just means I should never be counted on to remember when your birthday is. (Mine is August 5. It is one of the few items on my Wikipedia page I will actually confirm.)

Having said all of this, these messays are stories from a brain that fluctuates from fun to fucked up and back, sometimes midsentence. They're the adventures of how I evolved from a girl who just wanted to explore her dreams to a woman who came to understand that my dream was finding a way to use humor to speak truth to power—and ultimately realized that humor is a most useful tool to help put even the most painful moments of life into perspective.

So if you want to learn some shit about me and have a laugh, quit reading this part and get to the good stuff. The sooner you get started reading about my life, the better you will feel about your own.

THIS IS NOT A GAME

I am the youngest of five children, four girls and a boy, and was raised in a Catholic family in Minnesota. The sister who's the closest in age to me is six years older, and the eldest is thirteen years older.

And that is just my immediate family. If I count just my mom's side of our extended family, I am the twenty-sixth of twenty-seven grandkids. The age gap was even greater with my cousins: The older ones were having babies before I was born. Some of my cousins attended my parents' wedding. There were always babies around—

sometimes there were so many, it seemed they came in bulk, like our family was the Costco of procreation.

As far back as I can remember, it seemed like every weekend my mom pulled the copper dessert mold off the kitchen wall, mixed up some lime Jell-O, shredded some carrots and threw in some pretzels, let it set in the refrigerator, then dragged this inedible blob and my sisters and me to another celebration of some relative's new baby.

The parties were made up of about fifteen women and were a combination of my sisters, aunts, grandma, and cousins. They sat in a big circle on flimsy folding chairs, most of them trying to balance a baby or toddler of their own on their laps while simultaneously gobbling up plates full of "the egg dish," a bready/eggy casserole lathered in cream of mushroom soup. This was the food of choice at every family gathering that started before noon. Cream of mushroom soup, however, was the ingredient of choice for every recipe ever created in the 1960s and 1970s, no matter what time the gathering or what the main dish was. I like to think of it as America's binder. And it's a fitting metaphor for baby shower conversations: thick and bland.

I have never been into babies—I didn't and still don't have the mommy gene—yet these women talked of nothing else.

My mother insisted I sit with my cousins and aunts and "visited." I knew that if I defied her I would be denied cake later—there was always cake—so I held up my end of the bargain, traveled from woman to woman, and stood with an awkward anonymity and listened as they talked endlessly to one another about all things infant. Having them, feeding them, changing them. And I really didn't care how they were made or where they came from. Why would I? I was eight. That would be like my wanting to know where vegetables came from. (By the way, until I was nineteen, I thought the answer to that one was "a can.")

And I never bought that stork story. If the stork brought them, surely I would have seen at least *one* flying around with a baby in its bill at some point in my life. The fact that grown-ups made up that lame story told me that however making babies really happened, it must be too gruesome for a child to be exposed to. Like those creature feature movies on channel 9 that played every Saturday at midnight. I just assumed babies hatched inside huge floral dresses, since every woman in my family seemed to wear one when they were pregnant. I imagined they grew in a way that was so gory and awful that it had to be hidden in a lump under a big Midwestern muumuu. I guess my conclusion came because after me, my mom was done having kids. When I was very small she had a "histo rectum tummy," as I thought it was called, so I never saw her pregnant except in pictures, wearing one of these floral dresses.

To be fair, these ladies occasionally changed the subject to husbands, but that's when they leaned in close to one another and lowered their voices, so I could only catch bits of those conversations. From what I gathered, husbands were always late, very forgetful about where they were, and slept on the couch a lot.

I gathered husbands got in trouble all the time.

I was glad I didn't have one.

When the secret husband talk started, the women didn't want me around anyway. "Why don't you go play outside, Lizzy?" one would say as she patted me on the head. It was the out I was waiting for. I smiled obediently and raced to freedom, staking out a piece of grass to perfect my cartwheels for hours on end, until my mom angrily came and found me. "I told you to visit."

"I tried, but they started whispering about Uncle Bud sleeping in the den again, and I—"

That was when Mom cut me off. She realized where the Uncle Bud conversation probably went, and if I kept talking I might ask for details about Uncle Bud, and that's not something anybody wanted. So she created a necessary diversion, plopped me onto an uncomfortable dining room chair behind this hootenanny of hormones, and rewarded me with a piece of that delicious white sheet cake, the only thing that made these parties bearable for me. I think she figured if she gave me the biggest pink frosting rose, I would forget anything I had heard about Uncle Bud and his boozy love affair. Or was it a love affair with booze? I can't quite remember. But that was okay—I had cake!

See how it worked? I already forgot.

While the cake distracted me, it couldn't make up for the boredom these baby-focused orgies always seemed to offer. So I found ways to stay sane.

Even when I was young I had a vivid imagination, so I was pretty good at entertaining myself. What I was not so good at was navigating the boundaries of appropriate behavior. (There's that ugly word: *appropriate*.)

My body was like a Slinky: unbelievably flexible. I was a human rubber band. In one of my favorite games, I curled up into a ball, made myself very tiny, and pretended I was invisible. So that's what I did. I sat up, pulled both my legs over my head, and set my cake plate on my chair.

As I sat wrapped around myself on this armless Queen Anne perch, I saw people peering at me. They looked confused. I imagined that was because all they saw was a chair holding a plate with a piece of cake on it and were mesmerized as they watched a disembodied fork spear a bite from the plate, then rise away from the plate, and *poof!* The cake disappeared from the fork into thin air.

But usually after about three slow bites, my game was shattered. The second Mom spotted me from across the room, she raced over in horror, like I had just reenacted that scene from *The Exorcist* when Regan walked into the party and peed on the floor. She jolted me out of my fantasy by poking me hard in the ribs, which acted like a pin in a balloon, and I quickly deflated, literally and figuratively, as I sat limply upright and ate my cake like everyone else.

According to Mom, sitting in a sundress on some relative's Broyhill dining room chair while eating cake with both legs wrapped behind my head as I exposed my little girl bits was "unladylike."

It seemed everything I liked was unladylike.

I was an unlady.

Then came the worst part of these parties. Inevitably, minutes after I became visible, just as I began to shove the entire delicious, waxy rose into my mouth, some adult, with an infant hanging off her hip, sipped from a plastic cup full of anger fuel, then snatched my cake plate from me and gleefully announced, "Lizzy, it's your turn to hold the baby!!!"

I was never asked if I *wanted* to hold the baby; it was always just dumped into my lap before I could say anything, so I never assumed that holding a baby was in any way fun. Why would I? Adults never let me in on their fun. They never shared that brown stuff they loved to drink. They never said, "Lizzy, have a cigarette with us." If holding that baby was soooo fun, why did they palm it off on me whenever they had the chance?

Before I knew it, a baby was in my arms. And I was right: It was about as much fun as holding a bag of charcoal.

So there this baby and I sat, uncomfortable and disconnected, like two strangers on an elevator.

The baby felt it, too.

Have you ever seen a baby scowl? Of course not. That's because you like babies. Of course they don't scowl at you. Me? They sense my resentment. I have had many a baby look at me with knowing contempt because I didn't treat it with the proper amount of adulation it had become accustomed to. Every photo of me as a kid holding a baby looks like a poster promoting a heavyweight championship fight.

As an adult, I am fully aware that a lot of this may come from my being the baby in my family, no longer getting all the attention, and (if you ask me, but nobody did) giving it to someone who has not really earned it. Couple that with the fact that I probably have some form of attention deficit disorder, which boils down to if you are not interesting enough to hold my attention, I will consider you useless.

And let's face it, babies don't hold attention, they hold court. As a kid, I looked at them as takers. Takers that offer nothing. They can't sit up, feed themselves, or tell jokes. For creatures with zero skill set, they suck 100 percent of the attention.

Me, on the other hand, I had skills. I taught myself gymnastics. I did no-handed cartwheels. I knew all the words to "Aqualung." I could put my whole fist in my mouth, and on command I contorted myself from the inside out. And yet at these parties, I was overlooked for this toothless mass that couldn't even roll over without barfing. So don't try to toss one in my lap like it's fun.

I suppose the difference between baby people and me is that I do not consider smiling while farting "holding up your end of a conversation."

But I must clarify: It's not always hostility that babies and I felt toward each other. Sometimes our dislike manifested itself with a bored indifference, like one of those bad Internet dates that you struggle through and quickly realize that just because he was cute in a picture doesn't mean the two of you are going to make a connection.

But whatever the detachment, the bottom line was we were stuck with each other until the random aunt or cousin who gave me the baby in the first place finished her brown liquid.

My attitude toward babies made it hard for most adults and even my friends to figure out how to play with me. Whenever we gathered, without fail, they gleefully showed up with at least one baby doll.

A baby doll!

Knowing how I felt about moms and babies, can you imagine how I felt about pretending to be one of them with a fake baby? For fun?

A baby doll is a toy that comes with a built-in chore. In fact, that one chore is the only thing it does. You feed it—water from a bottle— it pees; you change its diaper. Game over.

That is not fun; it's an apprenticeship. For a job I never wanted.

Add to that the accompanying accessories of baby clothes, toy ovens, strollers, and washing machines, and you have forced me into playing Mail-Order Bride. "Hey, Lizz, let's play cook and clean and take care of a baby and not get paid." What an inspiring intro- duction to the endless possibilities life offered girls in 1968.

If you're going to make little girls play house, be honest and take it to its natural conclusion. When you're done playing Doing Shit for Everyone Leaving No Time for Yourself, move on to the game Now Have Loveless Sex with Your Husband and Drink Lots of That Brown Liquid to Drown Out the Pain.

I remember thinking, *There must be something fun about this. Everyone thinks this is great but me. Maybe I just didn't give it enough of a chance.* So once again I feebly attempted some kind of doll nurturing. I made a cape with the baby blanket, or inserted its bottle in the pee hole and watched the water shoot out the mouth. "Look! The baby barfs, too!" No one liked Baby Barfs-A-Lot. Within ten minutes I grew bored, dropped the doll baby on top of the fake stove, and went outside to do cartwheels. This set off my friends, and they shrieked as though I just set a real baby on fire.

That was normally when I was told it was time to go home.

A lot of moms thought I wasn't good at playing. But that wasn't true. I just wasn't good at playing house. As I said, I *was* good at creating fantasies. I just always came up with scenarios that transported me somewhere else, like Paris or New York City, not merely a place that was forty feet away from the playroom, usually the kitchen in one of my friends' houses.

My imagination often put me on some kind of stage, and my two favorite roles to play were rock star and priest. They were the people in my little world who had all the power and attention.

My fantasies went to great lengths, and I imagined I held an audience captive with my riveting talents. I was independent and influential. And maybe the biggest fantasy of all: People paid attention to me.

So did I reject all things girly? No. It just seemed that as a little girl who daydreamed a lot about speaking my mind and exploring life, there were not a lot of female role models mentoring me to be all that I could be.

But there was one woman who had a big influence over me.

Barbie.

I worshipped Barbie. In fact, I would say Barbie was my twelve-inch-tall plastic life coach.

She had it all, a camper, a dune buggy, even a dream house. Part of why it was a dream house to me was that she was the only one who lived there. Her boyfriend, Ken, came to visit when she—er, I decided. She had a sports car and would bounce from job to job as she—er, I saw fit.

Barbie owned zero floral baby-making dresses.

I craved that independence.

And her weird-ass boobs? So what? She still reached the steering wheel of her royal blue sports car.

Some people thought that the fact that her feet were fucked and she couldn't stand was a problem. But to me, it meant she was free. Free from standing at a stove, or a washing machine, or with a baby hanging off her hip. She has no hips. Plus, she didn't have to walk; she drove her convertible everywhere.

God, I loved Barbie.

She was free in every way I knew how to define freedom.

But even as a kid, I knew there was one big detail that differentiated all my fantasy freedoms from the real ones.

Money.

As an eight-year-old I was lucky. I didn't need a lot of cash to meet my needs. I earned an allowance for cleaning my room and pulling weeds from the garden. Plus, I always got bonus coin when I fetched cigarettes for my parents. (Yes, it was a simpler time when I just biked down to the Tom Thumb convenience store in our neighborhood with a note from my folks, picked up a pack of Pall Malls, and with the money that was left over got a sheet of those candy acid tabs for myself. It was more than enough. A Clark Bar, Charms Pop, and an ample stash of Bub's Daddy, the foot-long powdered tube of bubble gum that, if you could put the entire stick in your mouth, earned you a lot of street cred with the boys.)

But as the years went by and I started reaching puberty, my tastes became more sophisticated. I no longer needed candy; I needed candy-flavored lip gloss. That addictive strawberry- or green apple–flavored lacquer applied with a rolly ball was the rite of passage to junior high school womanhood. Plus, it was the only thing we were allowed to apply to our faces in seventh grade at a Catholic school in Minneapolis in the 1970s, so it was a must-have for the fashion forward.

As I grew, I knew I needed to up my income-generating game to fulfill my new habit. So I started on my quest for some serious monetary emancipation.

The sad irony? I quickly discovered the only clear revenue stream immediately available to me was—you guessed it—babysitting.

What a cruel joke. I had developed expensive tastes, and yet my income opportunities were abysmal, unfulfilling, and let's just say not in my skill set.

I would have to find another way to earn some cash, or some poor baby would end up with a bottle in her butt because I was bored.

IN DOG WE TRUST

As a kid, my wondering about God happened more and more as He messed with my direct happiness.

At around age ten, I made the mistake of telling Mom some of my concerns, and from that point forward any question I had put my salvation at stake.

A salvation defined for me by Mom.

A salvation defined for my mom first by the Catholic Church, and much later amended by the Catholic Channel and Fox News.

Honestly, I have never felt more in need of salvation than when, as an adult, I sat in front of the TV with her, forced to watch a picture-in-picture of Sean Hannity as he flapped his yap, while in the smaller box on the screen a bevy of cloistered nuns prayed the Rosary.

At first my ten-year-old questions were not particularly alarming to my mom. They weren't profound and had all the heft of a Wolf Blitzer probe. The first one came out of a lesson taught in religion class; when my teacher (let's call her Sister Saint Invective) announced that dogs and Jews didn't go to heaven. I was appalled. It seemed so cold and unreasonable. Dogs didn't go to heaven? It was unacceptable to me that my dog, my best friend Susie, would be denied entrance into the Kingdom of God.

And I was confused why Sister Invective even brought up Jews. I thought Jews were just fictional characters in that *other* Bible, make-believe creatures like hobbits or Argonauts. I didn't even meet a Jew until I went to public school many years later.

But, I was told, they were real.

And controlled the media.

And never mind that Jesus was a Jew. That *never* came up.

When I got home and told my mom Sister Invective's story of unimaginable horror, Mom backed up the nun.

"Lizz, Susie has no soul," Mom explained. "She is here for our enjoyment on earth. That's why God put all animals here."

Yikes. It was the nun/Mom wall of truth. Now nothing could put me at ease.

Till that moment, I never thought about Susie dying. Once Mom explained how ruthless God's salvation was, it became an obsession.

Susie would one day just croak. Dead. Gone. Never to be seen again. And everyone was okay with it.

I developed fear headaches as my imagination created her ugly fate, usually just as I was about to fall asleep. It was the same scenario over and over: She got hit by a car in front of our house. I ran to her, and as she lay in my arms in the middle of the street, before I said my good-byes, crows from that movie *The Birds* swooped in, pecked at me, and then picked her flesh apart until the biggest bird snatched her from me. Nothing was left in my lap except a bit of an ear and some fur.

And that would be the last I saw of Susie.

Every time the king crow snatched her away, if I didn't open my eyes right away, reached for Susie and made sure she was still breathing next to me, it felt like my bedroom ceiling was closing in on me and would crush my face. It got so bad that I taught myself to fall asleep on my back, resting the back of my forearms on my cheeks, palms up. I figured if the ceiling hit my hands first, it wouldn't crush my skull.

This information also factored into my fascination with the priesthood. If I were a priest, I thought, then *I* could fix this problem with God myself. I could persuade God to let Susie into heaven.

In the hierarchy to God, nun trumped Mom, and priest trumped nun, so priest trumped Mom. Yep, Father Lizz was the goal. Plus, I liked the way it sounded.

When I delivered the news about solving the Susie problem to Mom, she did what she always did: half listened as I explained.

"If I become a priest, I could get closer to God than you are, and then maybe I could get Susie into heaven; maybe more dogs than just Susie. Imagine if I were the person that got all dogs into heaven. I would surely be invited to be on *The Mike Douglas Show*."

My mom agreed. Mike Douglas would be lucky to have such an imaginative girl on his show.

Mike Douglas was the half she heard in that round of half listening.

But a few years later, the questions got harder when I ventured into a territory I'll call "the Taboondocks."

Taboondocks: /tä'bün-däks/ n. *A topic of conversation so unexpected and uncomfortable, very few people ever go there.*

I was stumped by the story of Adam and Eve. There were some loose ends I needed to have tied up. It wasn't the whole "God created the world in six days" thing or the talking serpent stuff that I needed clarified. No, all of that was somehow plausible to me. It was when we learned the facts of life; it contradicted some of that creation stuff we learned, and things didn't add up for me.

First there was that requisite menstruation/sorta sex-ed movie that Sister Saint Invective showed us in Catholic school health class, which was religion class every other day. From what I remember, the film used a ridiculous metaphor of a yellow dress (interspersed among all the clinical parts) to tell the story of "becoming a woman." Some blond girl who was my age wanted a yellow dress she saw in a store window, but her parents felt she was just too girlish to have it. Then once she started her period, her body "changed," and as a reward for starting forty years of monthly triage, her parents bought her the dress. Because along with the blood, you grow boobs, so she had "matured" enough and could now "fill out" the dress.

I paid zero attention to anything other than how beautiful that yellow dress was. Lemon chiffon with white trim and a slight dip in the neckline to show off your "fill out."

In fact, I took a page from Mom's half-listening book and tuned in and out as needed. As a result, my synopsis of the movie: First you bled, then you grew Barbie boobs, then you got a cool dress. At least you got a dress.

Oh, and I did kind of remember an animated portion called "Sexual Intercourse." It showed wormy things with tails that shot out of a cartoon man's wiener and somehow got inside the cartoon woman. They swam up some organ in her body that looked like a ram's skull.

Or something. I half watched. I mostly gazed out the window and watched the boys play street hockey, and when I turned back to the movie, something must have happened, because the next thing I knew a baby hatched inside the woman.

I think I learned that if you didn't hatch a baby, I guess you bled for a week instead.

It was a terrible movie.

The boys were so lucky they didn't have to watch this. They got extra recess. Boys got all the good stuff.

I went home that day, freaked out at how gross all of this was. I asked Mom if she knew anything about this movie, and she confirmed that everything in it was true. Even the part where I would start bleeding for a week and yet not die.

I asked her if I would get a yellow dress if I started bleeding. She said no.

I was not happy about this. What was in it for me?

I had to become a priest to talk God out of this bleeding idea, too. Especially if I am not getting a yellow dress in the end like the girl in the movie.

"Now you have learned where babies come from," Mom said.

"And you believe everything in that movie?" I asked.

"Of course I do. I had all five of you kids just like they explained in the movie."

"And it always takes a man and a woman to make a baby, right? No exceptions?"

She upped the ante. "Yes, a husband and wife."

And that was where my trek into the Taboondocks started.

"Mom, I'm confused."

I think she thought my next question would be "How do I work the complicated beltlike contraption and minifuton we were each given after the movie?" But that wasn't it.

"About what?" Mom asked.

"About how this works with Adam and Eve. So God made Adam and Eve. Eve was made of Adam's rib."

"That's right."

"So this stuff from the movie between the naked man and naked woman started with Adam and Eve?"

Mom was very sure of herself on this one. "Yes. Adam and Eve made three sons: Cain, Abel, and Seth, just the way they showed you in that movie."

I was impressed by how much Mom knew about the beginning part of the other Bible.

So was she.

"So, if Adam and Eve had three sons, and they had kids—"

"Too many to name," Mom said, trying to preempt my quizzing her on that.

Now came my unintentional curveball.

"So if you always need a man and a lady to make a baby, and Adam and Eve had three boys, did Eve have sexual intercourse with her sons?"

Mom stopped for a second, then responded with that tone you invoke when you are very proud you have just pulled something out of your ass that seems plausible: "My mistake. God took more ribs from each boy and created wives for them. And *they* went on to have lots of girls and boys, like in the movie."

"So they married their cousins, then?" I asked, not understanding there would be any shame in that. I was confused. Mom just said you had to be husband and wife to have babies. I just wanted clarification.

"No, Elizabeth, you are not cousins if you come from ribs," Mom, the world's foremost DNA expert, said defiantly. Then she resorted to her standard line for ending all hard conversations: "It's very confusing."

This time I agreed with her.

Then she started vacuuming to make sure this rib incest talk would not continue.

It didn't.

DECORATE TO MANIPULATE

Reminders we lived in a Catholic home hung in every room of our house. In fact, to the day she died, Mom had more pictures of Jesus hanging on her walls than she did of me.

Sure, we had some of that harmless but odd stuff, like Virgin Mary on the Half Shell, or the regionally acceptable portrait of the Scandinavian-looking Jesus who could have been in an ABBA tribute band.

But when it came to Jesus on the cross, Mom didn't put up just any crucifix. Oh, no. On the left side of the front door hung an eighteen-inch cross-shaped wooden box with a six-pack-abbed metal Jesus Christ nailed to the lid of another cross-shaped wooden box. It was a cross on a cross on a cross, in case you were ever to forget the original story of Easter. (It wasn't until the twentieth century that the corporate hog farming and processed sugar industries added ham and Peeps to the celebration, as I understand.)

This holy container had a name: a sick call box. The contents were a small white candle and a clear glass bottle of holy water with a white cross painted on it. And it had a *very* specific purpose. If you were dying at home, a priest came, took the kit off the wall, lit the candle, sprinkled the blessed water on you, and said the last rites, and then when you died you went to heaven or something.

I once asked Mom, "Doesn't the priest carry that stuff with him? Why do we have to hang it in our house?"

"Well, what if he forgets to bring it?"

The answer was obvious. *Then he is a crappy priest,* I thought to myself. Instead I said, "So it is like a holy spare tire?"

"Yes, I guess it is."

In keeping with that analogy, we were lucky that we never had to use that sick call box, because the Winsteads' salvation spare tire had a flat the whole time it hung there. Mom never replaced the candle after she used it one year to light up a Halloween pumpkin, and I don't think the bottle of holy water was ever filled. In fact, over time, the glass clouded up, and eventually the bottle became a final resting place for a few unlucky mosquitoes that somehow managed to penetrate the wood *and* glass. How they ended up there was truly a mystery.

The sick call box had a companion piece that hung on the other side of the front door, the wildly popular creepy disembodied praying hands plaque. I would argue that its prevalence in so many homes in the Christ the King parish made it the Farrah Fawcett swimsuit poster of '70s Catholic wall art.

When I was a kid, the hands freaked me out more than any other religious symbol. Whose hands *were* they? These creepy disembodied hands belonged to someone. Just like the bronzed baby shoe that sat on our coffee table once belonged to my sister Linda.

There was no Internet back then, but even now when I Googled "Whose praying hands are on the religious plaque?" I just got vague results about where to buy them, not whose hands I would be buying or what they symbolized.

I had so many questions about them. Were they meant to give comfort? If so, then why weren't they open hands, palms up, welcoming all who entered our home? You know, imagery that gives off an "Everyone is welcome" or "How can I help?" vibe. These hands weren't in any way comforting or welcoming. They were tightly pressed together, exclusionary hands. Hands that looked like they were trying to suffocate a butterfly.

I asked Mom about whose hands they were. It was obvious that this question confused her, so she gave me another one of her brilliant answers that forced me to drop the issue.

"Lizz, were you not listening in religion class?"

What was I going to say? "No"?

Mom won again.

I am sure, however, that I was never taught whose hands they were or what they represented. You never forget anything you learned in Catholic school. You can't. Catholic school was a manipulative branding iron that seared into your brain its one true gospel that you are, and always will be, fatally flawed. One of the first things Catholic school taught me is that babies were born sinners.

You sucked before you took your first breath. (Okay, I think babies suck, too, but not in an eternal damnation kind of a way.)

Since no one gave me any information about the amputee associated with the praying hands, my nine-year-old imagination was forced to make up my own story, a dark and gruesome tale whose details made me grow up to hate and resent them.

2I decided these were not loving, praying, "symbolic" hands, but the anonymous hands of a real kid who did something bad. Maybe the same kind of bad stuff I did. The only difference? This kid got caught.

Yes, I decided the sole purpose of these eerie-ass hands was actually to terrify children into obedience. Children like me.

I stared at them and went over in my head the story of how these particular hands got to our house. These were the hands of a girl who got caught stealing Big League Chew from a drugstore in a faraway land, like Hawaii or Des Moines. And I had created a very detailed scenario of how the punishment was implemented.

When she was caught, (I always imagined a girl, when in hindsight the hands were clearly old man hands) the Catholic authorities were contacted. (At nine, all the adults in my life were "Catholic authorities.") A pair of henchmen in friar getups were deployed to fetch the girl. When they arrived, they put a black hood over her head and hauled her off to a super-secret room in the basement of the rectory of some church. The place looked like Dr. Frankenstein's laboratory.

The friars put the girl on a slab, tied her down, and—*WHACK, WHACK* with two swift ax wieldings—her hands were severed, put in a Styrofoam picnic cooler, and shipped to the dipping and mounting facility, which was at the Vatican, wherever that was. (All I knew was that was where the Pope lived. I was nine; I didn't know if Minnesota was north or south of Wisconsin. It's west.) After the hands cooled, they were packed up in a box with the return address of a lady named Lillian Vernon and were sent to our house.

I scared the crap out of myself with this story.

I was convinced if *I* got caught stealing Big League Chew from the drugstore on 50th and Xerxes, my hands would be sawed off, too, then sent to the Holy Dipper to be shipped off to some *other* Catholic family's home to scare the piss out of some *other* kids, who won't know who the fuck the hands belong to, either. It was a vicious Catholic cycle.

How could I be wrong? Could there be a more perfect reminder of the consequences of bad behavior than a pair of mounted severed hands? It was a befitting punishment for almost any crime.

Caught stealing? Hands chopped off.

Caught smacking sister? Hands chopped off.

Caught masturbating? Hands chopped off. (Small caveat: Should you go blind while masturbating, mounted chopped-off hands would be rendered useless as a visual deterrent.)

Well, the years went by. After a few minor thefts and having put some time in touching my vajeeper, my hands are *still* attached to my wrists. Add to that the fact that there were never rashes of kids with hooks for hands who ran around in packs, I rested easier realizing my theory was probably slightly off base.

But I still wondered how Mom knew that just the sight of unexplained symbolism could be so powerful. Did she learn that in some kind of feng shui class she and her pals took over at the Pax Learning

Annex that taught Catholic moms to "Decorate to Manipulate"? Or maybe the hands came with instructions on how to strike fear in the heart of your youngest daughter to get the biggest bang for your terror buck.

I can see them now:

HOW TO ACHIEVE THE OPTIMUM PERFORMANCE OF YOUR NEW "SCARE PAIR"® PLAQUE

1. Make sure your "Scare Pair"® plaque is placed near the most commonly used exit in your home. It should be the last thing your child sees before leaving the house, keeping him or her obsessing about the "Scare Pair"® plaque instead of participating in sinful behaviors like obsessively masturbating and obsessing about obsessively masturbating.

2. Gaze reverentially upon your "Scare Pair"® plaque whenever your children are in the room. This gives the "Scare Pair"® plaque a secret power that will paralyze your children with fear.

3. Whenever children are within a one-foot radius of your "Scare Pair"® plaque, all adults should mumble a short nonsensical word combo, throw in a few Latin words, then reverently and gently touch the "Scare Pair"® plaque. This will give the hands extra secret power and encourage children's minds to create the most dreadful and vivid scenarios.

4. For optimum effect, hang something Jesusy close to your "Scare Pair"® plaque. An old head shot of Jesus, the cruci-

fix, anything Son-of-Godlike will do. This will ensure the children think Jesus himself is enforcing the fear.

5. Washing your "Scare Pair"® plaque in an automatic dishwasher is not recommended. Always clean the "Scare Pair"® plaque by hand with a mild soap and hand dry immediately with a soft cloth to avoid damaging the finish.

E xploring fear as a commodity is not a new idea. I just never understood why it worked.

If the idea of God is such a good one, why keep selling me on the bad parts? I don't see McDonald's ads trying to entice me by saying, "If you eat here every day, you will slowly clog your entire arterial system with a sludge that will lead you to morbid obesity and premature death." No, the McDonald's executives are apparently smarter than the leaders of a centuries-old religion. They show me hot, glistening fries, and I succumb.

Truth be told, I am not inspired to embrace beliefs that terrify me. The hands, the crucifix, the deep red bleeding heart embedded with thorns that hung next to the kitchen door—none of these symbols motivated me to do one good thing in the name of anyone.

And, really, why would I? I won't even go back to a store if the clerk treats me like shit.

Show me a Jesus I can relate to. What about a statue of Jesus pulling hair out of my tub drain? Or what about a painting of him picking up the dog poop in my yard for me? And, praise heaven, how about the Jesus who takes my mom to Target? Now that would be my personal savior.

Sign me up for that Jesus, because the startling savior images people kept pushing on me did nothing more than make me scream, "If God is awesome, quit showing me the bloody monster version of him who hates me!"

You want me to spend my time on earth worshipping a God who thinks I am a shrew right out of the womb, when I still weigh less than a decent-sized Thanksgiving turkey? No, thank you. I am looking for a God who at least lets me learn a few words before I am damned to the fiery pits of hell for all eternity.

And doesn't have Michele Bachmann on speed dial.

But if the plan is to scare the bejesus out of me, then mission accomplished.

GET ME TO
THE ALTAR

I sat in church one Sunday, going about my business, doing what I always did: lip-synching along with Father Hansen, our dreamy young priest. "This is the cup of my blood, the blood of the new and everlasting covenant. It has been shed for you and for all men so that sins may be forgiven. Do this in remembrance of me." He was so handsome. A strawberry blond Adonis in his midthirties with a perfect mustache that made him look like the Sundance Kid. I made sure I went to the masses he said because he was as close to a movie star as we had in Southwest Minneapolis at the time. (Years later, a Miss America was crowned who went to my high school, and Tiny Tim married a girl who lived across the alley.)

Then he took a sip of the cup and handed it to Paul Anderson, the altar boy to his right. As I watched Paul wipe Father Hansen's spit off the chalice, I suddenly saw dollar signs. I remembered that these altar boys raked in money serving funerals and weddings. Five, sometimes ten bucks a pop. This was more than lip gloss and record money. This was ice skates and bike money.

Yes! I, too, would make my fortune being an altar boy.

I couldn't believe I'd never thought of this. *I can't believe not one other girl ever thought of this.*

It was everything I wanted. It was a stage, it was a performance, it had costumes, there were no little kids, and it paid. Huge.

Not to mention, this was my stepping-stone to the priesthood.

Dream. Realized.

I was a genius.

After mass, as we stood in the "make sure Father Hansen knew you were in church" line, I told Mom about my brilliant idea of becoming an altar boy. She replied as she always did when she heard my big ideas.

"Oh, Lizz, you exhaust me."

When we got to Father Hansen, Mom shook his hand and thanked him for his sermon.

I was a little shy in his presence because he was so breathtaking and nice. But this new job idea was so important, I used this opportunity and turned on the charm.

"Hi, Father Hansen," I said, because that was the only icebreaker I knew.

"Hi, Lizz. You seem to get taller every time I see you."

"I am taller than most of the boys in my class!" I exclaimed.

"So I have noticed!" He noticed. He said he noticed.

Bingo! "Say, Father, I wondered if I could come and talk to you about an idea I have for Mass."

"Sure. Sister Carmella says you are getting pretty good on the guitar. I have office hours from three to six Tuesdays and Thursdays, so set up an appointment with Mrs. Pennington."

So I did.

I came prepared with a list of my skills. I would be the best altar boy ever. So good, in fact, that he would only need one. Just Father Hansen and me, on stage. Blowing everyone away.

Our meeting was in the rectory study. Wood paneling, leather chairs, even more Jesus pictures than we had, as I recall. It looked like one of those libraries that rich old vampires had on *Dark Shadows*.

"So what did you want to talk to me about today, Lizz?" he asked, gesturing for me to sit in the matching wingback chair.

I thought I would hit him with some of my background first. I opened strong: "Well, I love performing." Then I told him how much I loved playing my guitar and singing for my family and friends. He seemed to be enchanted.

I knew I had him in the palm of my hand. So I pulled out my trump card: my love of reenacting Sunday Mass. I explained in great detail about how I played the priest—so convincing that I sometimes had as many as four friends who acted as parishioners. I emphasized that I recited the entire Mass by heart. I knew all the parts: his part, the congregation's part, and most important, the altar boy's part.

As I talked, he seemed to lose a bit of enthusiasm as I described how I even methodically pressed Wonder Bread rounds into hosts and served them as communion. And when I asked if he wanted me to show him any or all of my performance, he politely said no, he didn't think so.

But I knew I had impressed him.

"Well, you sold me!" he said, slapping his knees. "I think you are just about ready to play with Sister Carmella at the guitar Mass."

"Cool, yes!! Wait . . . what?" I didn't come to talk about the guitar Mass, but what a bonus. If he thinks I am good enough to play at mass, I could be the singing altar boy!

I was a bit cocky now, so I just cut to the chase. "And I would really like to start serving Mass as an altar boy! I think if I'm look-ing at being a priest, I should start right away."

His face turned white. The white that is really gray, the color skin turns right before you barf up fish sticks.

He had not expected this.

He was quiet for a second, then said, "Lizz, we just don't have girls as altar boys. It's not allowed."

I didn't understand. I quickly went through all of my qualifica-tions in my head.

Age 12: Check.

Ability to hold big cup: Check.

Light napkin folding: Check.

Bell ringing on cue: Check.

Why wouldn't I be allowed? It's not like part of the job was haul-ing around anvils, and those dresses the boys wore were pretty much unisex. It didn't seem like the penis came into play. (Don't go there.)

It just did not make sense, so I simply asked, "Why isn't it allowed?"

Clearly he was used to most Catholics who just took his word as, well, gospel, so he had to think of an answer pretty quickly. And after a minute that seemed like an hour, he gave me the lamest excuse I had ever heard in my life, before or since.

"Well, because it's called altar *boy*, not altar *girl*."

Really? I said to myself. *That's all you've got?* No way was he this pathetic. Father Hansen was supposed to be the cool young priest.

Then I realized: This was a fixable problem. I helped him out with the perfect rationale.

"But aren't they called that because there're only boys doing it? Couldn't you just call the boys *altar boys*, and the girls *altar girls*?"

The ball is in your court, Padre.

He did not seem at all bowled over by my solution. He started that adult rubbing-palms-on-the-pants thing that meant he wanted this to be over.

I didn't really like *this* Father Hansen. It seemed like he didn't want to help me. He did not see how I was head and shoulders above these stupid boys. And he didn't give me any good reason why it needed to be a boy to wipe his loogies off a wine cup or carry candles. It was pretty much an outrage.

I thought priests were trained to see greatness and that they had special connections to God so they were able to fix anything. He knew he just offered up a bill of goods, and he knew that I didn't buy it. I didn't really think he bought it, either, so he did what all adults do: He made this someone else's problem.

"Maybe you should write a letter to the bishop and see if he can help," he suggested.

Ugh. This was just like at home when Mom didn't want to be the bad guy so she said, "Go ask your father." Except now it was Father Hansen who said, "Go ask my father."

All adults were the same. Lame.

Of course, it never occurred to me that women couldn't be priests. I just thought they all wanted to be nuns. I was oblivious. My twelve-year-old goals were of the moment: wowing the crowds with my mad altar boy skills and making money so I could buy stuff. I had no idea that if this conversation continued, it would lead to the eruption of a shit volcano of questions Father Hansen did not want to answer. That's why he passed it on to someone more powerful.

And though I knew *this* battle was lost, the war was not. I would write to Bishop Roach.

Yes. Roach.

I left the rectory and raced home to work on my letter. I blasted through the kitchen past Mom.

"So how'd it go?" she asked

"Father Hansen suggested I write Bishop Roach and ask him for help!"

She smiled a huge smile and said, "Ahhh, you go ahead and do that, then."

Wow, I thought. *Mom is not confused? Cool. Weird, but cool.*

But Mom and Father Hansen knew a little something about Bishop Roach that I didn't: He had a great love of the drink. As part of Mom's dedication to the church, she used to make lunch at the rectory and had served the bishop a few lunches in her day, and he had served himself a few too many cocktails. His alcoholism was one of the worst kept secrets in the archdiocese, and it all became very public when, years later, he was arrested for DUI after he ran into a 7-Eleven with his car.

So unbeknownst to me, I was pouring my heart and soul into a letter to a man who was pouring his heart and soul into a highball glass.

The Roach never wrote me back.

And even though I did get to play "Turn! Turn! Turn!" on my guitar at a few masses, I never got to be an altar boy. I held my guitar and watched how John Marsh or Pete Peterson dropped that napkin or missed a crucial bell ring and thought, *You blew it, Father. I would have hit that bell every time.*

I think it was my first real taste of injustice. I was so frustrated as I watched the boys week after week on the altar. They went through the motions like zombies, with no flair or style—no presence. I sat in the pew and fumed as I observed, relegated to sit back as the boys got the audience they somehow automatically merited. Because they were boys.

But because I was twelve then and performing was a driving force behind my altar boy crusade, I redirected that angst in a more positive way when later that same year I was presented with a new opportunity for the spotlight. The seventh grade class of Christ the King mounted a production of *Heidi*. And I was cast as one of the leads.

Shockingly, I did not immortalize the role of the endearing Heidi, or even the enchanting invalid Clara. I was bestowed the role that fit my mood: the evil governess Frau Rottenmeier. I had a lot of emotion to pour into that role.

It was exciting. I liked playing the mean old woman even more than I liked playing a priest. I created a persona that was believable and sold it. Just like a priest. But the costume was better.

My performance was met with rave reviews, if "You are a natural" counts as a rave.

But alas, good press didn't count as currency. I still needed to make that lip-gloss money. I played songs from *Godspell* on my guitar to do it.

For a quarter of what the altar boys made.

IF YOU ARE TRAVELING WITH A CHILD OR SOMEONE WHO REQUIRES ASSISTANCE, SECURE YOUR MASK FIRST

My curiosity is not a choice. It's always been part of me. I think of it as a vital organ.

New experiences and ideas kept—and keep—me alive. Even when I was a kid, I didn't just sulk when adults said no; I panicked. And when they said no, my questions became more frequent and demanding. The kind of questions that threatened the most close-minded or the laziest of adults, whose reasoning either made no sense to me, was incomplete, or impossibly condescending. Reasons given so they could shut me up or shut me down. But I demanded to know the reason they wanted to do that. I am sure this made me unbearable.

But the most horrible adults thought they could preempt my inquisitiveness with declarative pontifications about what they had decided I was capable of.

One I'll never forget came from a psychology teacher I had my senior year of high school. We had taken our final exam, which was essay based. As the teacher passed back the graded papers, he started to tell a story about how there was one person who took this final who had wisdom beyond their years, who indicated through the final that they truly understood the psychology of human nature and knew how to deal with people, and who showed they had a tremendous instinct into what makes people tick.

He had passed out all the finals as he kept yammering about this Einstein of intuition, but he had not handed me mine. I waved like I was trying to get the attention of the last bus of the night before it pulled away, nonverbally flailing *Excuse me, I didn't get my paper yet.*

He stopped at my desk and dropped my final in front of me, on it written *A++ Beyond impressed! You really know about the psychology of people!* just as he said, "And that person is Lizz Winstead." I was stunned, then I was elated. I really thought I *could* read people. I *knew* I was a good communicator. *I show a natural ability, it says it right here on my paper!* Then came the punch to the gut. After all that praise, he laid it out: "Lizz, with a paper like this, you showed you have all of the skills of becoming a great mother one day."

"Or how about a psychologist?" I said with a tad of incredulity.

Some in the class laughed.

He ignored me and walked back to his desk as the bell rang.

Fuck you, I thought to myself. *You get an F++ in reading people.*

I ignored him as I walked out of the classroom.

Simple comments like that pegged me as a rebel. I didn't believe that I had a rebellious streak in me back then. I considered it a bad reaction to cases of belittlement, boredom, and rejection.

And since I grew up the youngest child trying to get a word in edgewise, I knew about belittlement, boredom, and rejection. When you were low man on the family totem pole, the tiniest slight felt profound; nothing rolled off my back because I didn't have enough life experience to prioritize the big stuff from the small stuff. It was all big stuff. Add to that long winters of being trapped inside the house for months on end, where I constantly endured a plight from which every young girl thought she would never recover: teenage sister rejection.

One episode in particular illustrated my little sister pest/big sister evil dynamic. It was after school on one of Minnesota's infamous thirty-five-below-zero days. We were housebound for probably the tenth time in a month. Mom had just finished cleaning (for this particular day; she was never really ever finished cleaning) and had moved on to ironing Dad's dress shirts in the living room so she could watch her stories at the same time. We were not allowed to bring toys into the living room after she had cleaned it, and the temperature of the basement playroom—a cheery windowless gulag that was decorated in an eclectic motif of chipped wicker furniture and asbestos—hovered at a balmy fifteen degrees, and I was not allowed to use the space heater without adult supervision. (It was the 1960s, and at the time, space heaters were actually exposed toaster ovens that when fired up were about as safe as walking through a metal foundry in a G-string.)

And I was banished from the bedroom I shared with my sisters, Ann six years older and Mary eight years older. Why? Because they were having friends over. I was never allowed in the room when they had friends over. Why? Because they were older. So I sat quietly, as I often did, on the floor outside our bedroom door and listened to them as they laughed and talked in hushed tones, convinced they were saying things that were profound and life-changing. I pretended I was a spy. It was dangerous and sneaky and I was very proud of myself that I had figured out there was just enough space between the wall and the door that when they opened it to use the bathroom, I was hidden.

The part that I loved the most was listening to the music they played. I lost myself in the music. Even through the door I managed to memorize all the song lyrics. I whispered along to "Factory Girl" by the Rolling Stones and "Femme Fatale" by the Velvet Underground and Nico, and taught myself to harmonize to Small Faces' "Itchycoo Park." I fantasized as I sang that I was at a concert when suddenly, Nico got a stomachache and couldn't sing. Then Lou Reed spotted me in the crowd and invited me to replace her. I held my own on "Stephanie Says" and "Heroin." Lou was so impressed that after the concert we hung out and listened to records in my bedroom, and when my sisters tried to horn in on me and *my* friend Lou, we laughed at them, slammed the door in their faces, and talked about things that were wondrous to us both, like Barbie's camper or how cool it was to fit the whole green apple Bub's Daddy into your mouth. My sisters would be sorry about all the times they shut me out.

But this day, I let my guard down. And that was the day that my spying career came to an end.

I got a little carried away as I took the high harmony on "It's all too beautiful, it's all too beautiful." I broke the first rule of good spying: I got too comfortable. The music took over and I subconsciously went from my murmurings into a full-on Fillmore East performance, and my body position went from the stealth knees-to-the-chest position to a cross-legged, arm-flailing bit of theatrics. Then suddenly, without warning, Mary threw the door open, which smacked my knees and jarred me back into reality, and screamed, "How long have you been there? Mom, Lizzy is ruining everything!"

Then she bent down and with her frosted pink lips an inch from my face she started interrogating me like a scene from *Marathon Man*.

"What did you hear?"

"Everything."

"Wrong. What did you hear?"

"Nothing."

"You are damn right you heard nothing."

"Mom, Mary swore at me!"

And with that, Mom came up the stairs, grabbed me, and pulled me down into the living room. "Mary, did you swear at Lizzy?"

"No."

"But she did! She said—"

"Do not bother your sisters," Mom said, interrupting me. *No* was the answer my mother wanted to hear, because it required the least amount of action on her part.

As I was being dragged away by the ironing maiden, I turned to Mary and screamed, "Lou Reed hates you and thinks you're stupid!"

"If you can't find something productive to do with yourself, then you will just sit with me," Mom said.

But I *was* being productive. I was a spy. A singing spy. Who knew Lou Reed.

Now I was back to being a nobody, relegated to the living room, forced to watch Mom press my dad's shirts as she watched *As the World Turns*, a TV show where other women ironed and had conversations like the ones at those awful baby showers. The walls started to close in a little. I would open and close my eyes very wide, trying to reset my reality.

It didn't work. I was still there, staring at my future. I didn't want to grow up and do chores while I watched people on TV do chores. I wanted to be a singing spy. Or Nico. Or fourteen.

All my crazy dreams for the future were always a source of bewilderment to Mom. I think because she simply loved being a mom, so she couldn't imagine why her youngest daughter wanted to complicate her life by fantasizing about something else. She never discouraged me from pursuing the things I was interested in, like becoming an altar boy on my way to the priesthood, for example, but when I hit the roadblocks that slammed into my psyche, she never really understood how bad my internal injuries were. Because they weren't *her* roadblocks, and because she loved *her* life, it baffled her when I couldn't find comfort in her world. She saw my pain as an unnecessary burden—on me and on herself.

Yes, she always hugged me during the disappointment, but she couldn't fathom why I chose things that seemed so hard. So confusing. So exhausting. Why didn't I take that energy and play house, then when I got older, find the right guy, get married, have some kids, and channel my creativity through them?

She was completely comfortable with the power structures she had in her life. The certainties of marriage, and family, and the church imposed clear roles on her, because none of those roles blocked her from her path.

That was her path. And even decades after I spied on my sisters at our bedroom door, she still worried about me, because I chose a life of great unknowns. Being a wife and mother, the fallback Ginny Winstead hoped her youngest daughter would eventually embrace, was no longer an option for me. I would not watch my kids in school plays, watch them play basketball, or watch them dance at halftime at a football game.

The key word here is *watch*.

Mom loved being an observer. She beamed with joy at her kids' accomplishments. To her, they were *her* accomplishments, too. But the disconnect was that she never really understood that my drive to participate was the core of who I was. It wasn't a childhood phase or a teenage phase; the goals changed, but the drive was who I am. I think she expected I would one day fall in line, get married, and have kids, then pass the desire to be seen and heard on to them and transition from participant to observer and derive the same joy she did from the proverbial bleachers.

For some women, that is possible, even preferable. But for me, it is death.

I love to observe, don't get me wrong. But the joy I get from experiencing another person's talents is the chance to listen, to learn from them, and to bring them into my own life. I want them to inspire me to explore my own voice. A voice that I was looking for outside my bedroom door all those years ago.

I remember the first time I flew on an airplane: I was five, and when the stewardess (she was a stewardess back then) gave the oxygen mask speech ("If you are traveling with a child or someone who requires assistance, secure your mask first, and then assist the other person"), it made perfect sense to me. Mom had to put on that mask first so she had the strength to help me.

I think about that a lot. As I grew up, it seemed like the perfect analogy for life. Get your shit together so you can help others. It's all I really ever wanted to do: figure out what I'm good at and put it out into the world. It's astounding how so many people fought me on it.

But I fought back. And won. The prize? Learning I had the balls to stay in the fight.

IT WAS SO NEW YORKY

My high school experience was a reflection of my insatiable curiosity. People couldn't really pigeonhole me, because the second they tried, I did something that threw them off.

It wasn't intentional; it was just the way I was and the way my mind worked. For example, during high school I was on the dance line, which performed Rockettes-type numbers at basketball games. Yet I choreographed a routine to Joan Armatrading's "Show Some Emotion." I was nerdish in my love of *The Lord of the Rings*, but I read it between periods at hockey games. Wearing Gloria Vanderbilt jeans, Candies, and an old Rolling Stones *Sticky Fingers* T-shirt I stole from one of my sisters.

And the only reason I was on my high school student council was those kids had the best pot in school but were perceived as the "good kids." Even then, I understood that in politics, it's all about access and perception.

Music, movement, and dialogue drove me—really any activity that involved losing and regaining control I wanted to try. I gravitated to people who tested their own boundaries and told stories about their adventures rather than recounted the adventures of others. They inspired me to indulge my own curiosities.

At the time, people's perception of me was that I was well-rounded. The reality was that my nagging fear of being suffocated by boredom drove me to dive into my obsessions without thinking. Often I couldn't keep up with myself, and there were times when I nearly drowned under the weight of my own enthusiasms. Fortunately, passion is an amazing flotation device.

By the time I reached high school, my sisters were long out of the house, but they left behind two important items: their crappy Magnavox stackable record player and a subscription to *Rolling Stone* magazine. (For years one of them renewed it for me every year on my birthday.)

That was when I developed my own musical tastes: the Talking Heads, Elvis Costello, and the Ramones. And I endlessly daydreamed that I lived in New York City, but mixed up all that I had learned about it, which was mostly from magazines, movies, and TV. I made up a whole life for myself. I lived in some *That Girl* kind of apartment close to St. Marks Place on the Upper East Side, and hung out at the Odeon or Max's Kansas City with only the coolest people, like Woody Allen, Gilda Radner, and of course Lou Reed. Sometimes, if I got downtown early enough before gymnastics lessons (oh yeah, I was on varsity gymnastics, too, and my nickname was Winspread—fuck you), I would stop at Shinders, the downtown newsstand at my bus stop, and scour the ads in *the Village Voice* for clubs like CBGB and the Peppermint Lounge just to see the acts they had booked there. I bought records based on that.

It was as divorced from reality as just about any dream I ever had. But despite that, I knew that one day I would live in New York.

In fact, under *Future Plans* in my senior yearbook, I wrote, *Move out and live somewhere in Manhattan*. Once I accomplished that, I'd figure out the rest.

Now, it's not as if we were totally without cool in the Twin Cities. We had a downtown. It had fancy stores like Dayton's and Schlampp's. Even Mary Tyler Moore pretended to live there.

We even had nightclubs, like Uncle Sam's. Uncle Sam's was a disco, and at sixteen I imagined it was our version of Studio 54 or the Mudd Club or one of those places I read about in *Rolling Stone* where glamorous people went to be glamorous with one another. You know, like what happens every day in New York.

Like any club worth a shit, Uncle Sam's was located in the not-so-nice part of downtown Minneapolis, surrounded by a few establishments frowned upon by many in this Lutheran-occupied territory.

It was in an area with a few strip joints that featured a wide variety of dancers, from the blond pigtailed junkie to the really tall blond pigtailed junkie.

There were also a few flophouses, a pinball arcade, and head shop.

And, of course, a McDonald's.

But the cornerstone of the area was a bar called Moby Dick's. The sign read MOBY DICK'S: A WHALE OF A DRINK. It was the perfect name for a bar fifteen hundred miles from an ocean. Its patrons ran the gamut of stereotypic ne'er-do-wells: bikers, pimps, hookers, and a lot of other folks with lesser ambitious career aspirations, many whose livers were probably the color of Chris Matthews.

Moby's had a big, clear jar on one end of the bar filled with AA chips, because at Moby's if you came in and dropped your AA chip in the jar, you drank all day for free. It was all part of that "Minnesota Nice" you've heard so much about.

My mom declared that part of downtown a morality-free zone.

Naturally, I was drawn to it.

I knew every inch of that area, because the Shinders bus stop was right across from Moby's. I had gymnastics practice every Saturday morning, and every Saturday morning when I would leave the house, Mom instructed me, "Walk on the Chinese side of the street" (because there was a Chinese restaurant next to Shinders), "walk very fast, and act like you have a purpose."

I supposed acting like I had a purpose was more on her mind than the fact that her sixteen-year-old daughter paraded around a sketchy neighborhood in a leotard and tights with far too much interest in the world around her. Her priorities on my safety needed to be fine-tuned; sticking close to the Chinese restaurant wasn't necessarily going to keep a girl out of trouble. Pimps also enjoyed an egg roll. No, this isn't the dramatic part where I become a hooker.

One spring Saturday morning, as a few of us robotically went through our mat warm-ups in the studio, some of the girls started talking about going dancing on Sunday at teen night at Uncle Sam's.

I sat straddled and leaned into my left leg so no one could see my reaction to this amazing news. *There's a teen night?* I said to myself as my face got closer to my inner knee. I didn't want to ask for more information because I couldn't bear it if these girls knew *I* had never heard about teen night.

How did *they* know about teen night? Or even know about Uncle Sam's? They didn't take the bus. Their parents drove them to gymnastics.

I always thought of my social status as "What I lacked in money, I made up for in cool." But it was clear that I had some catching up to do.

I moved to stretch over my right leg and asked, "So, how did *you* hear about teen night?" like I had gone for years and was bored that she had just discovered it.

"My dad knows the owner, so I can get in for free. It would be cooler if it were one of the places out on the Strip where all the Minnesota Vikings hang out."

The Strip was a string of bars out in the suburbs famously known as the place professional athletes often partied and made news when their blood alcohol levels landed them into bed with a woman who was not their wife, or in a ditch.

Ugh. No. It wouldn't. She had no idea about cool.

But Oh My God! Teen night!

This was too good to be true. Dancing at a real nightclub, like in the movies. Like in New York.

I rang up my two most "adventurous" friends, Greta and Joan. These were my go-to gals for talking music and dreaming of Manhattan.

It wasn't long before we were teen night bound.

We told our parents some lie about going bowling, then we drove a few blocks, changed in the car from our 501s into our New Yorky outfits—or *slutfits*, as I call them now—and headed downtown.

I was so excited. I was convinced teen night was the chance to dress and dance in a way that a thousand trips to the confessional wouldn't forgive.

With boys from other schools.

Read: Punk boys.

Read: Black boys.

And gay boys.

Some of the gay boys, it turned out, were actually from our school. And it wasn't long before we had an unspoken agreement with them. We kept our yaps shut about them grinding on the dance floor with other boys, and they kept quiet about the three of us grinding on the dance floor with boys who didn't look like they had descended from St. Olaf.

Whatever happened in Uncle Sam's stayed in Uncle Sam's.

It was the beginning of a lifetime of gay bondage. Um, well, you know what I mean.

My first night at the club, I was overwhelmed by feeling so New Yorky. The New York of my mind.

The club exceeded my expectations.

It had a Plexiglas dance floor that changed color while the DJ booth blasted Blondie and Sylvester. And just like New York, Uncle Sam's charged three bucks for a 7UP. I could only afford one, so I sipped it slowly.

After a while, I wandered away from the corner my girlfriends and I hovered in and stood by myself on the side of the dance floor.

I wanted to take in the place on my own, every inch of it, without interruption.

I leaned against the railing at the perimeter of the dance floor. I was convinced I looked super hot in my striped tube top dress and heels, as I "got down" to the Ohio Players. Brooke Shields had nothing on me.

I wondered why every guy in the place hadn't lined up to dance with me.

All of a sudden, a guy came up to me. A hot guy. A guy I didn't know. He was not from our school.

I didn't know what school he was from, because he was black *and* punk. My guess was West High. It was the hip school, the Williamsburg, Brooklyn, of high schools, located in the neighborhood with the best thrift stores.

He wore a white tank top, black jeans, and had a 'frohawk.

Everything about him seemed effortless.

I greeted him with awkfidence.

awkfidence: /'awk-fə-dens/ n. *A posturing developed in the bedroom mirrors of teenage girls that combines awkwardness and confidence, which they believe to be alluring, but when executed in public has the unintended effect of cringeworthiness.*

"First time here?" he asked, looking at me with a once-over that I was sure the cool the world over possessed naturally.

"You kidding? I come here all the time. I even come on the weekends. I have a fake ID."

It was a total lie, but I thought it made me sound impossibly "with it."

My girlfriends had now approached behind him, flailing at me to move back.

God, why are they being so racist? I thought to myself. *He seems so into me.*

"*Reeaallly,*" he said, all smooth. And then he effortlessly walked away. My friends raced up to me, horrified.

"Lizz, you needed to step away from him."

"Why? Because he's black?" I demanded in a tone of wounded outrage at the complete unhipness of my friends.

"What? No! Because the black light from the dance floor is making your zit cream glow in the dark!"

I was paralyzed with sheer disbelief. This was a joke, right? But they were dead serious. I wanted to pull that tube top right over my head. I turned and watched the guy walk away; he never looked back. No wonder he seemed to do everything effortlessly. Why make an effort with a rank amateur?

I pulled a small mirror from my purse. It was worse than I could have imagined. Every zit I had tried to cover up was a neon spot on my face. I looked like a teen runaway pinball machine. How was I to know Clearasil was a glowing agent, and that the second I neared the dance floor, trying to impress guys from other schools, I turned into a Lite-Brite board?

Then I really freaked out.

How many times had this also happened to me at Spencer Gifts?

This was worse than walking the halls of school with your sweater tied around your waist, which was the universal sign that you had your period, or worse, that it had you.

I was a zit cream pariah.

I looked desperately for the guy with the 'frohawk, expecting to see him and his friends pointing and laughing.

But as I scoured for him in the sea of teens on the dance floor, I noticed something else. There were dozens of first-timers who had also not been told. I watched as some version of my conversation with Greta and Joan happened in pockets all over the dance floor. First the stunned face, then the bowed head, then a race for the bathroom. And I'll give you one guess who one of them was.

"My dad knows the owner."

I made sure she didn't see me. Knowing that she was a first-timer saved me, and the evening. So I joined the other first-timers in the ladies room, wiped down my face, reapplied my blusher, and then Greta, Joan, and I danced all night with one another in a sea of kids who were supposed to be at the movies or bowling.

The shame of the Clearasil glow faded as the DJ played "Soft and Wet" by a local guy called Prince.

It was so New Yorky.

Thus began a thirty-year love affair with Uncle Sam's, Prince, and boys from other schools.

WETUBE

Our cousins, the Graysons, owned a lake house about three hours north of Minneapolis. Each summer they would invite our family to vacation for a week. The place was a white Cape Cod on a beautiful lake with a dock and a sandy beach, nestled in a forest of tall pines.

The Graysons had seven kids, and when you added the five Winstead children, along with both sets of parents, there were sixteen people running amok. It was a week of controlled chaos.

Very controlled. We are Scandinavian.

The grill was always fired up, ready to char any kind of meat at a moment's notice, and Dad and the rest of the men used cooking outdoors as an excuse to drink Hamm's beer during the day. The teenage boys played something on the lawn that involved tackling one another, and when they bored of that, they switched to a game of one-sided enjoyment that involved throwing the teenage girls off the dock into the lake.

Those of us under the age of ten rode the tire swing and had gunnysack races on the lawn. Every day at lunchtime we had a hot dog picnic on a scratchy plaid blanket near the lake. It was heaven—mostly because the Graysons were rich and always had brand-name potato chips like Old Dutch and endless supplies of Grape Crush.

It was the 1960s, so naturally as our moms prepared our lunch they simultaneously coated us with some toxic mosquito repellent now banned all over the world, even in China. And just as naturally, the adults always chased us down and barked vacation orders: "Make sure there are enough life jackets in the boat!" or "No Popsicle-eating on the porch swing!"

Everyone seemed frantic to cram in as much fun as possible, like it was in limited supply. Except our moms.

From what I could tell, it was their job to facilitate the fun, watch the fun, and clean up after the fun. They spent all morning making food, washing beach towels, setting tables, and making sure the menfolk always had a cold beer and remembered to flip the meat on that grill.

Moms always ate in motion.

But every afternoon around three, the flurry died down. That was when my mom grabbed me and one of the old inner tubes that had been baking in the sun against the house, and the two of us headed down to the lake. She waded waist-deep into the water, dunked the tube on both sides to cool it down, and placed it over her so she looked like she was wearing a rubber tutu. She lifted me up facing her and I wrapped my legs and arms around her tight as she lifted herself onto the tube, her butt sinking into the water, elbows and legs resting on the tube. When she settled in, she patted me on the fanny, which cued me to release my arms and legs, and, like a flower blooming, I opened up onto her lap, ready to float. I fit perfectly. My little bird legs straddled her torso and were just long enough to hook my heels on the outer sides of the tube, my back resting on the inner. Then she paddled us away from shore, away from the Wiffle ball game, away from the men in their plaid shorts and their Munsingwear shirts and their Hamm's, away from the older kids and their loud carryings-on.

It was just the two of us off on an adventure to the middle of the lake. It may have been the middle of the lake; it may have only been thirty feet out. But to me, sitting with my mother on that inner tube, it felt a world away.

I must have been five or six at the time. As I wrote about it, I wondered how much I Lizzmember the truth. Had I actually forgotten vital information about this time, or any story I told here? I'll never know for sure, but I think the reason the "WeTube" memories are so vivid is that it was a bliss that was destined to be short-lived. Those were the years before I was old enough to know about life: about conflict and politics and sex. And I never dreamed that I would grow up to fight with my mother over issues like abortion and our black president.

No, then my world was an ideal place. And Mom was the perfect inner tube captain. With each long stroke of her arms I watched the cabin get smaller and smaller, the voices duller and duller, until the loons were the only conversation we heard. We tickled each other's feet, sang "Boogie Woogie Bugle Boy," and then lay back silently and listened to the lake lap gently against the sides of the tube. The sun beat down on the old black rubber, but Mom always knew the exact moment to cup her hands in the water and cool it down just before it got so hot it burned.

I closed my eyes and dreamed that we floated to the other side of the lake, where the trees were lollipops and the cabins were made of gingerbread, just like in the Candy Land game.

I had not yet learned to swim, but I had no concept that this was a problem. Mom never mentioned that if something bad happened to the old rubber tube, I would need to swim. I had no concept that anything bad *could* happen. Mom's lap felt like the safest place on earth, and that feeling of safety became the foundation of my fearlessness. Unbeknownst to her, because she never mentioned drowning, tube malfunction, or motorboat decapitation, I didn't know I was supposed to be scared.

And in a nutshell, that is why I dove into everything headfirst. By some fluke, my folks forgot to ask me the question most crucial to ensuring a lifetime of self doubt: "What if you fail?" Then as now, I looked at life's challenges as dares rather than uphill battles, and consequently the results of this glaring parental oversights led to a liftime of me torturing them with my chronic pluckiness.

Mine was not a noble courage; it was more like courage by omission. This turned me into a Wile E. Coyote of sorts, my roadrunner being the dreams I had. I was like the coyote in that when I wanted something, I just went for it. I chased it as fast as I could without thinking of ramifications. The difference between me and ol' Wile E. is that when I'm in hot pursuit of my roadrunner and end up off a cliff, as I hover over the chasm, I simply never think to look down, because my parents forgot to tell me to. So instead of plunging into pain and failure, I just run to the other side of the canyon and figure out a new route to reach my goals.

Look, I don't want to give you the impression Mom was remiss in her required duties of self-esteem shrinkage. Sometimes Mom picked me apart, like she was a finalist in a chicken wing–eating contest. It just came later in life. But when I was young, she seemed a bit shell-shocked that she had created such a determined dervish, and so our relationship was a peaceful but bizarre coexistence. She didn't know how to control me, so she just kept reacting with those same two words I have come to associate with her: *confused* or *exhausted*. Those two words were interchangeable.

I can't stress enough that confusion or exhaustion were her reactions to almost everything. I was just one item in a laundry list of things that got her panties in a confused, exhausted wad, so I always looked at it as *her* problem.

But focusing seemed to be the most exhausting thing of all for Mom. It was routine that over breakfast she would ask me about my daily schedule. I rattled off the usual "I have gymnastics, then Girl Scouts and a science project . . . ," and then I would notice she was half listening as she became fixated on a smudge she spotted on the window in the dining room. A smudge that was far more engaging than whatever I was talking about. A smudge that must be removed at once, and so I continued for my own amusement, ". . . and then I am gonna set the curtains on fire and strangle Grandma in her sleep."

By then Mom had cleaned the window and had stepped back to survey her work, only to find another smudge that needed her attention. As this process continued for the duration of breakfast, she at some point found my voice a distraction and invariably announced, "Lizzy, your life totally confuses me." Then she would turn on the TV and after five minutes would say, "These Vietnam War protestors exhaust me."

My dad joked she would have to be hospitalized for exhaustive confusion when they implemented Vatican II.

Mom was easily confused and easily exhausted. Or maybe it was just her way of saying *Fuck it, you're gonna do what you want to, anyway, and I can't stop you, so I'm gonna just tune out.*

But her chronic bemoaning of confusion or exhaustion didn't mean she wasn't my champion. She may have been exhausted and confused by me, but she'd be damned if someone else tried to steal my thunder.

In short, she was five feet tall and one hundred and ten pounds of no bullshit. When she took action, she took no prisoners. For instance, when I played Marian in the Minneapolis Southwest High School production of *The Music Man*, I received a scathing review in the school newspaper. The reviewer happened to be a girl who auditioned for the part, too, and she was out for blood. I was devastated, not only because of the slam she threw my way but because it came from a girl with an ax to grind. (Maybe my lifelong mistrust of the press started then.)

The day the review came out, I read it to Mom through my tears, wanting nothing more than for her to comfort me. She hugged me for a few minutes, then mumbled something to herself about how hard I had worked and that this was garbage.

Never mind comfort. Mom took covert action.

Unbeknownst to me, she called the high school principal and demanded a retraction, and noted the obvious conflict of interest that allowed the girl who did not get the part to review the girl who did.

Right before graduation, I opened the school newspaper's last issue of the year, and there it was: a personal note from the principal apologizing for the review. It did not mention that the girl who wrote it had lost the part to me, but it did include some crappity crap that the play was a smash and that all the performers were very talented and dedicated. That crappity crap made me feel better.

I'm glad I never knew Mom did this until years later. I probably would have discouraged her. But I am sorry to report that Mom's advocacy for transparency in journalism evaporated as we both got older and she became a Foxogenarian.

Foxogenarian: /fäks-ə-jə-'ner-ē-ən/ improper n. *Elderly person with hearing loss who gets all information from Fox News, consequently forming opinions based on getting half of half of the truth.*

Mom's half listening, half hearing was half charming, half maddening. The charming half were her malapropisms: "I am losing my eyesight because I have Immaculate Degeneration" or "Can white people get Citrucel anemia?" The maddening half came when she formed her worldview based on it: "I don't think the taxpayers should bail out those banks, I think the government should!"

She also took what she half heard me say about myself and created her own version of me.

And it wasn't all terrible.

Over the years I often ran into people she had chatted me up to and heard about a woman I hardly knew. Once I was at her local grocery store and a checkout clerk looked at my credit card, looked at me, and made the connection. "Oh, say. Your mom told me you are starring in a Broadway show!" Actually I was doing shows at a club in Lexington, Kentucky, called Comedy Off Broadway. But I didn't correct the clerk. I liked her version of me better.

Mom often cheerleaded about me to everyone but me. She even had a boxful of me, never missing a moment to clip my name out of the newspaper, even ads for shows where I was billed as "And others." And even when I was an "other," she cut it out of the paper and showed it to anyone within spitting distance. She was diligent about those clippings, and in the early days of my career, as I wasn't married and had no plans to have children, the articles and ads were as close to baby pictures from me she could produce to her friends. As I was giving birth to a career, she crammed that square peg into the round grandchild hole any way she could.

She upped the ante when I started appearing on local TV. My folks didn't own a VCR, so whenever I appeared, Mom took pictures of me on the TV screen. Actually, the pictures were probably better than video, as she enjoyed the idea that I was on TV but had no interest in even half hearing what I had to say.

I found out just how little interest during one of our unfair and unbalanced fights a few years ago. I respectfully challenged one of her talking points, saying something like, "Jesus, Mother, do you ever watch any other network besides this Fox shitshow to get a different side of the issue?!"

"Of course," she answered. "I watch Lou Dobbs on CNN."

I believe in full disclosure, so I am forced to admit that my response amounted to a blank stare.

At which point she added, "I also watch you on MSNBC. But with the sound down, just to see what your hair looks like."

There it is. Sometimes Mom's humor stung with a brutal honesty that only she could produce. Once I got my self-esteem out of traction, I always remembered where I got my humor, and the inner tube strength that made it possible for me to see the genius in it.

And then I put it in my act.

ALL
KNOCKED UP

I got pregnant the first time I ever had sex. Call it luck of the
draw. Actually, call it luck of the withdraw, because that's what
it was. Or rather, wasn't.

Let me explain.

I was seventeen and had it all figured out. I thought of myself as
being very well-rounded. Because I was told I was. I was an effortless B student, meaning I got a B without having to do much, so why
make an effort for an A? I had no interest in going to Harvard, and
all that extra studying would have cut into my student council

activities, my rehearsals for *The Music Man*, and my campaign to become captain of the dance line. (Yes, I won.) I was involved in everything, hence, I was popular. So obviously, I couldn't get pregnant. I had the lead in the school play! I was in student government! And I had pom-poms in my room! Girls like me were too busy to get pregnant. An egg couldn't survive in a body this active!

I know, my lack of attention in sex-ed class is showing. But I didn't have to listen in sex ed. I was seventeen. I had it all figured out.

It was only the burnout girls who got pregnant. You know who I mean: those bleached blondes with crispy feathered hair; Britannia Jeans–wearing girls whose boyfriends swam at the public beach in their long pants and rolled up their Marlboros in their T-shirt sleeves. My boyfriend was a hockey player who wore his letter jacket to the beach.

Plus I had Catholic sex education on my side. And since basically that consisted of one movie about why we bleed, the only detail I really learned about premarital sex and birth control was during sermons, and that was that they were sins. The lack of explanation of what they actually *were* led me to believe they were sins that only plagued those unfortunate Lutheran girls.

But then I was sent to public high school. I fell prey to the influence of those slutty Lutherans (and, okay, perhaps my own hormones), and I gave in.

But I was seventeen, and I had it all figured out.

If I used birth control *and* had sex, I would be committing two sins. So I did what anyone with a shred of insight would do: minimized my sinning. I opted to commit one sin. The one that was more fun.

When I missed my period, I thought it was due to the stress from the many activities we popular girls involved ourselves in. I just figured God was smiling down upon me and held up the monthly bloodbath because I was just so busy.

And then the second month rolled around. Again, no period. But because I had it all figured out, I wasn't scared, just puzzled. I began to think, *I really should find out that I am not pregnant.* But how? There was no one to talk to. Mom would have sent me somewhere "wayward girls" go to be branded as "wayward girls" for all of eternity. And my friends? We never talked about sex with one another. We were all "good girls" and lived the lie that we didn't "put out" and thought people really believed that shit. And in requisite high school form, I had seen girls banished to social Siberia for wearing painters pants after Labor Day. So even a hint of gossip this good would have spread faster than all of our legs on prom night.

So much has changed since then. Today MTV has a show called *16 and Pregnant*, which responsibly makes reality stars out of knocked-up teens. And home pregnancy tests? They are so last century. Nowadays, I think there's an app that calls your iPhone to warn you that if you finish that third cosmo, you may wind up with a wombmate.

But back in 1978, there was no MTV, and home pregnancy tests weren't just pee on a stick and panic. It was a two-hour chem lab that was not conducive to either my very busy schedule or hiding it from my mom. Plus, the ten-dollar price tag was pretty steep, and every penny I earned waitressing at Woolworth was going to those satin track shorts I had on layaway at Foxmoor Casuals.

"But Lizz," you ask, "you were captain of the dance line. Why didn't you just raid the car-wash fund you had going for those new costumes?" Because that was for *costumes*. Why are you so dishonest?

Luckily for me, I had an expert source for all things sex related: my devoted hockey player boyfriend. He would have the answer. He always did.

"What the fuck? You weren't on something?" he asked with all the loving concern that so many guys with a mullet have.

"I was on you. I thought gravity would prevent something like this."

"Well, you dumb bitch, you are on your own here. And I'm not driving you home."

Hockey players are known for their brevity.

It was not the brevity I had hoped for.

As I rode on the number 6 bus home from my now ex-boyfriend's house, I was overcome with one of my emptiness headaches. Without him, there was no one to talk to, no one who knew, and no one left to tell me I was not pregnant. I had nowhere to turn. My head was now so heavy with the weight of my fear, I could barely hold it up. God, the pounding. Each thump reminding me I was all on my own. The sound seemed to say *dumb bitch, dumb bitch,* banging against my skull on the *bitch.*

I slunk into my seat and leaned my head against the window of the bus, trying to find some relief. And then I looked up.

Between an ad for some kind of "We Treat Feet" place and a continuing education banner I saw:

THE SOUTHWEST KARE KLINIC. FREE PREGNANCY TESTING. CHOICES. OPTIONS.

I thought I was dreaming. Could it be I had a guardian angel?

Free—*and* it was only six blocks from my house! No raiding the satin shorts fund to find out I was *not* pregnant. God was smiling on me again. No one needed to know I had sex. I could still live the good-girl lie—er, life.

My head immediately began deflating. The *dumb bitch* mantra went from a roar to a whisper. The sign was a sign. Clearly a dumb bitch would not have recognized this.

I would go to the Kare Klinic right now and get the answer I was looking for.

Ten minutes later, I arrived. I walked in and found I was the only patient. No lines, no waiting. Another sign. There wasn't a reception area, per se, and I wasn't greeted by anyone, but I found comfort in the homey décor; it looked more like a basement den than a Klinic. There were plaid couches, dark wood paneling, and a glass coffee table strewn with some magazines about Christianity. Bonus: They are Christians, which are sort of like Catholics, so clearly they would understand this was never to be talked about.

A small placard sat on the coffee table and read something like THE RESTROOM IS THE FIRST DOOR ON THE LEFT. CUPS ARE PROVIDED FOR YOUR URINE SAMPLE. WHEN YOU ARE FINISHED, LEAVE IT ON THE BACK OF THE TANK AND CLEAN UP ANY RESIDUAL URINE. SOMEONE WILL BE OUT TO SEE YOU SHORTLY. I followed the instructions, left no residual anything, and sat down on the scratchy plaid couch. As I looked around the room, I noticed no medical brochures, no posters of the human body, no big plastic heart—nothing that you'd normally see in a doctor's office. I suddenly didn't like the feeling of being in someone's den. I wanted to feel like I was in a doctor's office.

As I looked around the waiting room my fear headache started to intensify, because some of the same artwork we had at home hung on these walls. There was a pair of those uninviting creepy bronze mounted hands that are cut off at the wrists that seemed to say *Like to help ya but can't*. And the only heart I saw displayed anywhere was thorn-covered like the one in our house, and even scarier because it had a cord that made it light up. I was pretty sure that eventually, if I stared at this one long enough, it might start throbbing, then shoot blood at me.

The thumping in my head got louder, this time chanting *dumb whore*, and the word *whore* hit more intensely than *bitch* and crashed against my cranium like waves breaking on a Scottish cliffside.

Why don't I feel safe? I wondered, but I could barely register any thought over the whore storm in my brain. It briefly subsided when from behind the door plastered with the "Footprints" poem (the classic Christian story of Jesus strolling, then carrying someone on Malibu Beach), a woman who wore a white lab coat emerged carrying a clipboard and a huge book. I felt a bit of relief. A doctor was here to make everything okay. (It wasn't until *much* later that I realized everyone who sells Clinique at Macy's also wears a lab coat and that she wasn't a doctor.)

The woman sat next to me and said, "We have your test results, and they're positive."

Gone was the pounding in my head. "Finally something positive!" I rejoiced, thinking, *Positive for me.*

"Well, good, you are going to have a baby," she said.

"What?!" I thought, *That's not positive, that's negative. She should have said it's negative. Negative should be positive in this situation.*

Whore. Bang. Whore. Bang. Starts up again.

Now she continued the "positive" news as she opened the atlas-size book she carried. "I want to show you some pictures of your baby," she said—as if we were about to peruse a collection of fabric swatches.

Pictures? I said to myself. *From my pee?*

She went on: "This is the size of your baby now . . ."

I looked at the picture. It *was* a baby. But it was a huge, mutilated, bloody baby.

And before I could spit anything out like *Where am I storing* that? she turned the page and said, "And this is your baby in five months."

I swear to God, it was a picture of a six-year-old kid on a bike.

The pounding in my head was relentless as I thought to myself, *None of this makes sense. I have a twenty-two-inch waist!* and *How's the bike gonna get in there?* My confusion was unbearable, and her detachment was bone-chilling as she closed the book and calmly said, "So you have a life to think about now."

That's what I'm thinking about now, I thought. *My life. What about what I want? What about my life?*

CRASH, BITCH, BANG, WHORE, STUPID, WHAT, HELP, POPULAR, DUMB, DUMB, HEEEEEEEELP!

"What are my choices?" I blurted out through the cacophony in my brain.

"You already made choices," the "doctor" said.

I didn't know what to say. Do I tell her I chose to commit only one sin? I thought I had it all figured out. I babbled to her what I believed to be very compelling reasons I couldn't be a mom. "I have choir practice, student council, I have pom-poms in my room. My boyfriend is a . . ." Each straw I grabbed at seemed to weigh a thousand pounds. So like a fish out of water that finally gave up the fight, I spit out my truth. "But I don't want a baby. I never want a baby. I shouldn't be a mom. I would be a terrible mom. I want something else for my life. I need your help."

"That's why I am here. We offer lots of options," she said, as though I had finally gotten through to her. Those ten words turned off all the voices in my head like a light switch.

"Whew," I exhaled. *Now we are getting somewhere,* I thought to myself.

"You can carry the baby to term and keep it, *or* you can carry the baby to term and give it up for adoption."

And then silence as I waited for some more options. Nothing. I was stunned.

Lots? Two is lots? This woman can't count. I can't count on this woman!

"But what about abortion?" I blurted out.

ABORTION. I just asked about abortion! WHY DID I JUST SAY THAT? OUT LOUD?

Wait. Now I started rationalizing to myself. *I know it's a sin, but since I didn't use birth control when I had sex, if I have an abortion I would only be committing two sins, which is better than three sins, so God would see I was, was, was trying to be good, and from now on, God, I promise NO MORE SEX, and, and I will only give blow jobs, and, and. . . .*

"We are pro-life. Abortion is against our law," she said.

Wait a minute. *Our* law? Whose law was she talking about? I had no idea that abortion was against our law. I knew abortion was a sin, but I thought it was a legal sin, like eating meat on Friday. I didn't want to break our law. Oh my God. I was a criminal. I asked her to break the law with me. I was a lawbreaking whore. And this doctor now knew it. I wondered if she would report me.

I was having a hard time hearing her and was scared of who she was, and of who I was. I was scared she would send me to jail. I just wanted to get out of there fast. I didn't care where I went, but I needed to go somewhere. Anywhere.

I had nothing figured out.

I got up to leave, and as I walked to the door I said in her general direction, "I just need some time to think about my choices."

"Good idea. You take all the time you need." And then came the clincher: "Remember"—she looked down at her clipboard to recall my name—"Lizz: Your choices are mommy or murder."

I walked out. She had just reaffirmed everything I now feared. *I am a dumb bitch. I am a dumb whore. And a criminal.*

She defined me. This woman, with her lab coat and her laws, who spent her days impersonating the two types of people outside of their parents whom most teenagers trust the most—a physician and a person of God—and on this gray winter day in 1979, she looked at me, a completely clueless seventeen-year-old girl, right in the face and confirmed, "Your life is insignificant."

How could she say she was pro-life when she wasn't pro *my* life?

How indeed.

I was so desperate for guidance, for someone to whom I could say "Help me figure this out. Help me grow. Help me experience and learn. Help me weed out things that hold me back and help me nurture the things that make me flourish so I can give back."

This woman saw no worth in my growth. She was invested only in keeping me inexperienced, vulnerable, and insecure. And the hailstorm of fear she rained down upon me was to ensure I remained "manageable." Manageable. Because in order to keep the world going the way she and her ilk liked it, I needed to become not what I wanted, but what they needed me to be.

I turned my back on her that day. Her tactics preyed upon my fear. But my fear was that her purpose was going to kill my potential. I could not let that stand.

I didn't know much about what was happening to me. But even I knew that was not pro-life. *That* was profane.

STAGE TIME

After I graduated from high school, I worked for a year as a clerk at a clothing store to save money for college. Anything left over from buying new clothes with my 20 percent discount went into the special kitty: my vintage clothes kitty. So when I enrolled the following year, it was without any real direction and without a whole lot of money. "Live somewhere in Manhattan" wasn't a degree offered at the University of Minnesota, so as a freshman I meandered through my prerequisite courses with all of the focus I showed when I cleaned my room as a kid so I could go out and play. In other words, with minimal effort and a profound lack of enthusiasm. That whole "Why try for an A when a B comes naturally?" philosophy was still in play.

But as for the going out to play part, I was very committed. The first activity I committed to was joining a sorority.

I know, right?

It wasn't because I had some need for a creepy social status or an "MRS" degree. (Remember, my yearbook entry didn't say my future plans included "Live somewhere in Greenwich, Connecticut.") Nope. My intention was to live the girl version of *Animal House*, full of theme parties, beer drinking, and spontaneous road trips to see new bands. I wanted to bond with rebellious girls and torture the ones whose rituals involved golden keys, pearls, and closets full of skirts and tops in various shades of fuck-proof pinks and greens.

The first day of the weeklong sorority ritual known as rush, I decided to work a Laura Petrie look: heather mohair cowl-neck sweater, hunter green capri pants, and a pair of black ballet flats. All from my favorite boutique, Salvation Armani. Total cost: about six bucks. I wanted *Animal House*, so I dressed like the girls in *Animal House*.

Most of the other rushees in my group wore some version of an outfit that screamed "lawn activity." But there was one girl in my group who stood out after a closer look.

She had perfect Swedish skin, big brown eyes, and one of those sweet turned-up noses that was adorable rather than fire-breathing. Her hair was shoulder length and grazed the floral yoke of her navy blue Fair Isle sweater. Those sweaters were a statement, like a gang bandana—just not the gang I wanted to join.

Normally I would have dismissed her as a suburbot, but then I saw it.

Affixed to her backpack was a badge of cool that overshadowed all of that *and* trumped my entire collection of vintage cashmere: an Elvis Costello pin.

That pin had a gravitational pull on me. I had to go introduce myself.

"Hey, I'm Lizz. I love your pin." I sang-ish my favorite Elvis lyric to her: *"Sometimes I think of love as just a tumor . . ."*

She joined in to finish, *"you've got to cut it out."*

We laughed.

"Thanks!" She was excited. "I've had ten girls wearing my exact sweater come up and tell me they like my sweater."

Then she got her first taste of Lizz: "I like your pin more than I like your sweater," I blurted out.

She smiled even bigger. "No one has said anything to me about my pin! *This Year's Model* is the best record." (Yes, it was still the era of vinyl. *Record*: Google it.)

"That's what I thought, too!"

She added, "But I do like *your* sweater."

"Oddly enough," I replied, my voice dripping with Lizzicism, "I have had no one in the same one come up to tell me!"

We both laughed. God, we were hilarious.

"I'm Christine."

As we wandered from house to house in this speed-dating sorority judgeathon, we swapped stories about our favorite thrift stores and music. It turned out she was from Minnesota, too, and that we both loved an independent record store called Oar Folkjokeopus. At the time, it was the Minneapolis version of Championship Vinyl in *High Fidelity*.

"Where are you from?" she asked.

"Minneapolis. I went to Southwest High School. You?"

"I'm from Edina."

Wow. Edina was the country cluburb of Minneapolis. It bordered the neighborhood I grew up in. It was the madras plaid headquarters of the Upper Midwest.

My parents bought their first home in Edina in the 1950s before it grew into *Edina*. It was a tiny two-bedroom rambler on a street defined by tiny two-bedroom ramblers. As the mansions and money started pouring into town, Mom and Dad saw that it would be hard for them to ever keep up with the Svensons, so they moved just over the border into the city. They made sure we didn't grow up the poor kids on the block. That was important to them.

We knew we weren't rich. But we never knew we were poor.

I knew some Edina kids from grade school at Christ the King. Their families went on fancy vacations to Disneyland and ski trips in the winter. It was a status symbol to have the most lift tickets on the zipper of your ski jacket.

And these kids always had the coolest shoes. Shoes were *everything* when we had to wear a uniform to school.

"If you are from Edina, why do you hang out in Minneapolis?" I asked, assuming Edina had endless pockets of rich-people fun that I wasn't privy to.

"There's nothing I like to do there." She sighed. "Edina is booooring."

Wait. You can't buy your way out of boredom? Scratch *Get rich* off my to-do list.

So as we walked up the sidewalk to one of the ivy-covered sorority houses, Christine turned to me and asked, "Why are *you* doing this whole sorority thing?"

"Well . . ." I decided to be honest. "Partially because I love the movie *Animal House* and want to find the chick version of that." Then came my real reason: "And part of me just wants to be contrarian. I am not this type, so I want to see what happens to girls like me who come to join. I mean, there must be *some* girls like us in sororities, right? How about you?"

She leaned in and whispered, as though if someone were to hear her she would be hauled off to testify before the House Un-American Activities Committee. "I'm an art history major. I look like 'this type,' but I'm kind of this type's worst nightmare."

I liked Christine more and more.

The sorority selection process was as shuddersome as you might think. After each day of rush, we received return invitations back from the houses that saw something in the rushees who seemed like-minded. In turn, we dropped houses that we felt were not the right fit.

Some were easy. On day two, the highfalutin sorority was a mutual drop. After conversation number three with women who uttered something like, "Daddy says [*fill in phrase from spoiled girl whose goal was to replace daddy with a rich husband who would continue to keep her in a prison of stuff upon which she heaped misguided value*]," I couldn't mask my disdrain.

disdrain: /dis-'drān/ n. *The involuntary expression one makes when a vacuous conversation drains the face of boredom and fills it back up with utter disdain.*

Many of the sororities felt like the stereotype, but Christine and I found one we connected with: the sisters of Delta Gamma, the DGs—or ΔΓ if you feel you must use letters from the Greek alphabet. It was one of the few sororities that didn't feel like it had a defined type.

Sure, it had its fair share of young women who needed plaiditude adjustments. But in my opinion it was the *House* that had the most *Animal* potential. The women we met there listened to us rather than talked about themselves. And they laughed louder than the other girls. Some of them even went to public high schools. And *some* of them even liked my sweater.

But of all the women I met at Delta Gamma, the woman who sealed the deal for me was a junior named Sandy. Sandy reminded me of a young Suzanne Pleshette: stylish, not preppy, wearing gauchos and boots instead of pants littered with embroidered whales and tasseled Weejuns. She had short raven hair, eyes that squinted when she smiled, and even in her early twenties, a smoker's laugh. She seemed naughty and filled me in on the DG stuff I really needed to know: It had a "tolerant" alcohol policy and allowed boys on every floor.

Very *Animal House*.

Sandy asked me about my interests.

"I love acting, history, and music. I love to dance and I'll try anything once."

She didn't ask about my major, what my long-term goals were, or all the other questions I was stunningly unimpressive at answering.

"Me, too," was Sandy's response. "In fact, my boyfriend runs First Avenue."

For a second, I stopped breathing.

First Avenue was the new name of Uncle Sam's.

Over the past few years, it had gone from being mostly a dance club to a club that brought to Minneapolis all those acts I dreamed about seeing at CBGB in New York. Sandy was now royalty to me.

"We can get in for free anytime," she said.

Now she was the Pope.

So with Christine, Sandy, and a few other rogue DGs, I found my pack. It may not have been full-on *Animal House*, but it had a full-on subculture that filled the bill for me.

I dove in headfirst as a pledge, and with classic Lizz enthusiasm. I took the reins and helped plan a pledge outing with the Delta Gamma charity, working with the blind.

We decided that year to focus on children. People tossed out ideas, such as take them to a concert or out for Japanese food as a cultural experience. I shut that one down because I couldn't imagine kids eating raw fish, especially if they couldn't see it. It sounded more like a trick than an outing. These were kids, I thought. Let's have some fun.

That was when I pitched my stroke of genius.

"Why don't we take them cross-country skiing?"

Christine looked at me in horror, as if I had just said *Let's round them up and drown them in a wading pool*. Which, knowing how much I loved kids, would not be an implausible suggestion.

"What?!" I said with totally misguided righteous indignation. "They probably *always* just go out to eat and go out to hear things. Why not get some exercise, feel the crisp wind on our faces? It'll be fun!"

The other women looked at me with varying degrees of skepticism, but not out-and-out rejection, so I pressed on. "Guys! I am not an asshole; I'm not suggesting *downhill*. It's *cross-country* skiing. How hard can it be?"

Christine chimed in calmly but sternly, "Lizz, it's hard." Then she polled the group: "How many people here even know *how* to cross-country ski?"

Out of about fifteen girls, only three raised their hands. Christine thought this fact alone would shut down the idea. Oh, no. I saw this as a selling point.

"Okay, we will get some guides to come with us." And then came my clincher: "What would be more empowering than all of us together learning a skill?"

That seemed to be the line that sealed the deal. So thanks to my impressive powers of persuasion, I convinced everyone but Christine that fifteen girls, twelve of whom had never cross-country skied in their lives, should take blind children cross-country skiing.

At the zoo.

The scarier part is that six sets of parents actually agreed to let us take their kids to do it.

Thank heaven an act of God saved all of us. On the day of the outing, Minneapolis had a major snowstorm and we had to cancel. We never rescheduled. I don't remember what we ended up doing with the kids. It probably involved eating or hearing.

One aspect of sorority life I had not counted on was the mandatory obligations required to be a member of the Delta Gamma sisterhood.

Monday was the most important night. It was compulsory to be at the sorority house. We had a formal dinner, followed by the weekly meeting.

A meeting full of tedium.

We voted on officers, when the cook should get a raise, and what our party themes would be for the semester.

I don't remember what else happened at those meetings, because Christine and I usually sat in the back with our Sony Walkmans, listening to music.

We were quite stealthy about it. We used thick plaid headbands to hide the wire that connected the headphones and pulled our hair forward to cover the actual earpieces. We kept the music on low so we could still partially hear what we *needed* to hear, the important stuff, such as when to raise our hands to vote for either a luau or Wild West theme for the mixer with SAE.

The second those meetings were over, we bolted.

Monday was also dance night at First Avenue. And now, thanks to Sandy, we were perpetually on the guest list.

Just being there every Monday night, dancing to Gang of Four and Clash imports, felt epic. And after a year, those Monday nights went from epic to historic. Prince started showing up at the club. He always wore some fabulous combination of ruffles and jewel-tone velvet and always looked exactly like what he was: a superstar. By his side was his bodyguard named Chick, an imposing man who would have made an awesome department store Santa. Together they stood in the DJ booth and watched the dance floor below.

Prince seemed mesmerized by the energy and the music and how each person moved. I wondered what each mental snapshot he captured told him. I wanted to be one of those snapshots, so when he was there I danced extra dancey. Even bigger sidearm swoops and even jerkier head jerks. They were the requisite moves for anyone flailing about to new wave music in the '80s. I was masterful.

I was just sure of it.

Prince's albums *Dirty Mind* and *Controversy* were big hits at the time, but he was still performing "secret" shows at First Avenue that often began at midnight and went till way after closing. Sandy knew when they were going to happen, so Christine and I never missed one.

Prince jumped on stage around midnight. At one A.M. the bartenders stopped serving booze, locked the doors, and Prince continued to play on and on. He performed with an unbridled fury that seemed to say *I may erupt if I don't get this out, so step back if you don't want to get any on you.*

I hoped he would cover me in it.

His music made me move in ways that have served me well. And his lyrics made me jealous I didn't write them. *"Half of the staff of their brain is on vacation."* That one line turned me into a green-eyed fanster.

Listening with a jaundiced ear was how I determined my musical tastes. I especially loved the dark lyrics that stung with a comedic edge. When Christine and I heard a song that we loved, she'd sigh and say, "Amazing. I wish someone would write that about me."

But I always sighed and said, "Amazing. I wish I *wrote* that." I wanted to turn a phrase that made people sigh.

Sure, I used to pluck out some songs on the guitar for church, but I was no musician. And I was certainly no lyricist. I was barely a college student.

B y the time my junior year rolled around, I needed more *Animal* and less *House*, and the sorority offered me only so much. Let's be honest: Any way you slice it, even though the sorority did allow boys on the third floor, there still were pin ceremonies and paddles. It was a PG-rated *Animal House*. (I didn't call having sex with my boyfriend in my room rebellious. I called it Tuesday and Saturday.)

I wanted unbridled everything at this point, so I moved into an old prairie style house off campus with a few of the rebel Delta Gammas in a neighborhood transitioning from being an enclave lousy with junkies to an enclave lousy with junkies in bands, affectionately known as the Punk Rock Ghetto. It was an area of indie record stores, cheap bars, cheap restaurants, and even cheaper apartments. And lots of music.

In the 1980s, Minneapolis was not just Prince. The Punk Rock Ghetto cranked out musicians faster than you can slap up a Starbucks today. It was a time when I no longer waited for my favorite bands to come through town. Many of them were actually *from* here.

Once that started happening, not only did I *listen* to music that sent me into a creative longing, the torture got worse because I'd see the actual musicians stumbling around my neighborhood and instantly one of their lyrics nagged at me. If I walked into the ratty old bar called the C C Club, there sat Paul Westerberg drinking at a booth, and I thought, *"The only exercise you ever get is the shakes." If you do nothing else with your life, you wrote that. Genius.* Or I saw Bob Mould at Oar Folk: *"Is that a head on your shoulders or something you use for ornamentation?"* I wanted to ask ten people a day that question.

There were so many lyrics; each was like a piece of kindling fueling a pyre of envy I wanted to throw myself on.

I wanted to say things like that. I needed to say things like that.

Christine had started dating a guy named Danny, a songwriter and musician she met at one of the Prince shows. He was in a band called Loud, Fast Rules and needed an apartment. The rogue DGs had an opening at the house, so he moved in. Danny was a cute skinny blond guy. He was slogging through life like the rest of us. He was in school full-time, bussed tables at a Japanese restaurant downtown, and played gigs at night. I hadn't seen his band yet when I met him; I hoped I liked it. But if I did, I didn't know if I could handle living with someone whose lyrics I coveted.

We were all barely scraping by, so to earn extra money we threw rent parties. At the end of the month, we packed the house full of sorority girls, frat boys, guys in punk bands, and their girlfriends. Everyone got along great, mostly because the conversations consisted of the frat boys telling the musicians how much they loved their bands. We charged per glass to drink from the keg and we almost always raised the money we needed for rent.

It went pretty well for about a year—until that good ol' magnanimous ex–hockey player boyfriend of mine from high school showed up at one of them, extra drunk for a special one-night-only performance called "Still Rageful After All These Years."

I guess after five years he just needed to tell me again that I was a useless cunt.

He looked bloodthirsty, like he had come to finish something. "Which one of these losers are you fucking?!" was the only number he had prepared for his little spectacle. He repeated it over and over. The guys he came with were holding him back as he tried to get to me. They all still had the unmistakable glow of those people who peaked in high school. I didn't say anything to him. I just stood there, arms folded, not even looking at him. I just kept nervously repeating to his friends, "Just get him out of here, please."

I was mortified. He was wrecking the party, and everyone looked at me like I had shit on the keg tap.

Then he reprised his tune. "Which one, bitch? Huh? HUH?"

His buddies pulled him backward out the front door, down the steps, and onto the front walk as he screamed, *"SLUT, BITCH, YOU FUCKING BLAH BLAH, INARTICULATE STRING OF LIQUOR-FUELED CLICHÉS."* He was desperate to lunge at me. I was terrified he would slip out of his jacket and go for my throat.

I looked around at the guys at the party, these frat guys and punk dudes, and realized there was about as much muscle mass in the entire group as there was in this hockeytard's frontal lobe. There was not a hero in the bunch.

I had to be my own hero, as long as they kept his damn jacket on him.

So I opened my mouth and let him have it.

"YOU WANT TO KNOW WHICH ONE I FUCKED? ALL OF THEM!!! I FUCKED ALL OF THEM! But the only LOSER I fucked is you!"

Well, *that* felt fun to say.

And I had nothing to add to it.

My landlord appeared at the same time they got my ex to the lawn.

"Hey, what's going on here?" He was not pleased.

The Mulleted Wonder took a swing at him, but thank God his friends wrestled him to the ground and he didn't make contact.

"Out of this yard right now, or I am calling the cops!" my landlord screamed.

My ex's best friend, Matty, a guy I always liked, apologized. "We told him this was a bad idea, Lizz, but he insisted on coming. Sorry."

"Don't be. I needed to get that off my chest."

Hockey's henchmen pulled him away as he continued his prose-filled rant.

My landlord kicked everybody out and told us we had to be out when our lease was up.

Animal House didn't end this way, dammit.

So I needed a new place to live, and some serious focus.

Christine and I were each other's right arms. Even when there were boyfriends, they came second. They just weren't as much fun.

One evening, we spent a rare night in for a two-woman slumber party. We turned on *The Tonight Show* and howled at George Carlin.

Christine turned to me. "Why don't you try doing that?"

"Try what?"

"Stand-up comedy. You are always making comments about TV commercials and how shallow everything is; maybe you could do a routine about it."

I had never thought of that. I was always more of the class cynic than the class clown. Sure, people laughed at what I said, but I never thought I could do that intentionally. My jokes were always more of a spur-of-the-moment thing.

I had watched a lot of guys in suits and ties telling jokes on *The Tonight Show*, and I loved George Carlin's album *FM & AM*, in particular his material about Catholicism. But I never thought when I watched or listened, *Hey, what if I tried to get up and tell jokes about how I see the world?* I never saw someone like me doing it.

Maybe I never thought of it because when I say *me*, I mean a young woman. If I did see a woman, it was Joan Rivers complaining about her husband, and since I didn't have one of those, it never crossed my mind that I could talk about *my* life on stage for a career. Maybe my subconscious told me it was like the priesthood, where young women weren't allowed because of some infuriating gender excuse, and I would be forced back into the financial shackles of babysitting kids I still couldn't stand as an adult.

I pondered this a bit more. I did get a rush from people laughing at what I said. I loved holding court, and I could get people to listen. I felt important when people listened.

So I secretly started making up a routine.

I scribbled some thoughts on paper, but made up excuses to myself as to why I didn't go try it: *I had to help decorate for Campus Carnival* or *Tonight I really, truly, actually have to study.*

But I kept scribbling thoughts down in a notebook. I called it "preparation."

I scribbled for about six months, here and there, watched more episodes of Letterman and *The Tonight Show* to see the comics.

Then it dawned on me: I should probably go see a stand-up comedy show live if I was thinking about doing stand-up. I am a real detail person, as you can see.

There was a review at a comedy theater near campus called Dudley Riggs' E.T.C. starring Jeff Cesario, Joel Madison, Alex Cole, Sid

Youngers, and a woman named Susan Vass. I went by myself to the theater. The line was around the block. People were being turned away. Somehow I managed to score a last-minute cheap rush ticket, probably because it was a single seat with a slightly obstructed view in a corner near the back of the room.

The theater was dark and mysterious, a candle-lit cabaret with rickety chairs and tables. A spotlight flooded the only prop onstage: a single microphone. The audience members were crammed in tighter than Christmas mass. Everyone drank and smoked, full of anticipation.

It felt clandestine, like anything could happen in this room; if you were not here tonight, you were missing something historic. My heart raced at the thought of all of the potential that surrounded me.

The comics took the stage and effortlessly talked about life, dating, sex, family, religion—whatever excited or enraged them. The audience simply hung on their every word, and wildly laughed and applauded. So did I.

Before this night, my jealous admiration had been relegated to a simple phrase in a song. Now every word each of these people uttered hooked me into their world.

I needed to do this. I wanted whatever this thing was. Putting it off was no longer an option.

So after six months of hemming and hawing, I finally got the courage to give it a try. And on December 18th, 1983, I hit the open mike at Dudley Riggs'.

Christine was the only person I told I was finally doing this, and she came with me. We held hands walking up to the door. I tried to be brave. It must have been obvious I was terrified, because Christine kept saying over and over, "I am so proud you are doing this," like I was going to donate one of my kidneys to a dying orphan. I actually felt like I might lose an organ of some kind.

We walked in the door, and this time the vibe was different.

There were no lines out the door on open mike night. The room was a quarter full, mostly friends of newbies like me.

Jeff Cesario was the host. He was the handsome Italian from the review. He was so relaxed: jean jacket, Twins cap, no notes. The only paper he had was the run of show. He put us on in order of our experience. We each got five minutes.

I was second to last.

I left Christine in the audience and went backstage to watch the show from the wings. The comics went on, one by one. Each had a varying degree of polish.

There *was* energy in the room, but it was more fearful and excited, the kind you feel when you watch a one-year-old totter through its first steps. The people in the audience held their breaths and hoped each joke would work. When it did, they exhaled in relief and applause, and inhaled again waiting for the next line.

It felt like giving a kidney would have been a more prudent—and less traumatic—thing to do tonight.

Finally it was my turn to go on.

Jeff Cesario started my introduction: "This is her first time onstage . . ."

I said to myself, *If nothing else, I am being introduced by Jeff Cesario, and that is something I can brag about.*

". . . so make her feel welcome. Lizz Winstead."

The audience clapped; I walked out and stood at the microphone.

I couldn't see them. They had disappeared into the darkness. I felt utterly alone. The only way I knew they existed was to make them feel something so that they'd react.

I started with my jokes. I had no order or through line; I just started telling them.

"Nebraska is proof that hell is full and the dead are walking the earth."

The exhale of laughter blew back at me.

I fired off the next one I remembered.

"You people look good, in shape. I myself am a runner. I run to the store for cigarettes."

They laughed.

"I don't want to say I smoke a lot, but I have an ashtray in the shower."

They laughed again.

I am funny, I think.

But that was it for my *A* material. My brain flittered onto whatever else it retained. I started to talk about anything. I was running on pure adrenaline.

"The only thing scarier than a biker? The biker's girlfriend."

"Have you seen these ads on TV for disposable douche? Who's saving it?"

I can't remember what the *C* material was, but I am sure it was as cringeworthy as the *B* and most of the *A* material.

After my five minutes I got offstage, and Jeff Cesario said, "You have some funny stuff. I hope we see you back here."

Holy shit. Strangers laughed at my act, and so did Jeff Cesario.

I ran up to Christine. She was beaming!

"So was I good?"

Always the pragmatist, she replied, "Good enough to do it again, that's for sure!"

That night I figured out what I would do when I "moved out to live somewhere in Manhattan." I finally had a long-term goal.

But there was one problem: Stand-up comedy was not a major offered by the good people at the University of Minnesota.

Mondays at First Avenue became Sunday, Monday, Tuesday, and often Wednesday. There was a band every night. Guys from the neighborhood. The Suburbs, the Replacements, Hüsker Dü, either opened for big acts in the main room or played in the smaller adjacent bar, that glorious haven of man stink called the 7th Street Entry. There wasn't a night I wanted to miss.

And that got to be a problem.

I was now onstage myself four nights a week, and afterward fed my full-blown music addiction. I also worked two jobs: I alternated my days from cash register clerk on the fashionable third floor of Dayton's, that upscale department store downtown, to food runner at a not-so-upscale burger/rib joint called Grandma's. Add to that trying to keep up with school and sorority. Something had to give.

I made very little money at either job—minimum wage in the retail, and being one step above bussing tables might qualify as deficit spending in some cases. Marie, one of the waitresses at Grandma's, moved to a new restaurant called Faegre's. She said that the new place was hiring full-time lunch staff, and she told me to use her name if I wanted to apply.

I took my usual ten minutes of introspection when making huge life choices. If I worked full-time days at Faegre's, I could go home, write material in the afternoon, hit the comedy clubs, and still make it to First Avenue by eleven to hear music. I could perform what I loved and then watch other people perform something else I loved, all on the same night.

It was perfect.

Wait. I forgot to schedule in sorority *and* school.

There were open mikes Sunday, Monday, and Tuesday nights, and I was getting stage time opening for headliners at the comedy clubs around town on the weekends. The sorority became a place that distracted me from comedy, a place where Casino Night parties at the fraternities seemed less and less relevant to my life.

And my course load reflected my rudderless direction: full of disparate interests like feminist theory and the history of anything, which helped me shape my worldview but didn't help me shape my burgeoning career. The audiences weren't really begging for a lot of jokes about Andrea Dworkin or the Weimar Republic. I figured I could read about those things in my free time. When I managed to get some.

Christine also divested from the sorority. She made art history classes, her work, and music her focuses, while my real school was now the stage. I attended "class" (read: performed) regularly at places like the Comedy Gallery and Dudley Riggs'. But the most important change was, for the first time in my life, I no longer wanted to skate through something and get a B. I wanted to work as hard as I could in comedy to get an A.

So I dropped out of college to pursue my education.

Faegre's was a chichi restaurant located in the heart of the warehouse district of downtown Minneapolis. It sat on a corner, and the floor-to-ceiling windows made it a fishbowl of the who's who of Minneapolis that made up its clientele. Local artists, ad execs, newspaper editors—I spilled on them all. Yes, I was that kind of waitress.

I was horrible at it. My saving grace was that for a lot of people, I provided a laugh in the middle of the day. I knew nothing about sauvignon blanc or arugula or monkfish. Until I worked at Faegre's, I thought garlic was a salt.

I was hired because Marie put in a word for me and exaggerated my role at Grandma's. I guess I interviewed well.

It was all trial by fire.

If I overheard a table grumbling "The service here is awful" because I had not been over to them, I would breeze by and say, "How would you know, you haven't had any yet. Cocktail?"

They laughed. I got them a round of drinks on the house and they asked to sit in my section the next time they came in. No one complained as long as I made them laugh and plied them with free drinks.

My bartenders understood. One of them was a playwright, and the other, coincidentally, was the drummer in my roommate Danny's band, Loud, Fast Rules, which had changed their name to Soul Asylum. We had to help one another out, because this was all of our means to an end.

The good news was that most of the waitstaff at Faegre's knew what they were doing. You could not get a more fluid dining experience from a more graceful Faegre's waitress than a young journalism student named Michele Norris. Michele was a statuesque African-American woman with a chic boxy Afro that gave her another three inches of power. Her calm seemed to quell the riptide I caused in that dining room on any given weekday.

Michele and I bonded over the difficulties in the chosen careers we were trying to break in to. We both wanted to have a voice in the world and we shared a burning desire to be heard. And we were both entering professions dominated by men, she as a journalist, and me as a comedian.

We spent many post-lunch-rush afternoons sipping merlot and sharing our fears about the lack of females in power and how we were often pitted against other women for those few coveted opportunities offered to us. We indulged each other in our hopes that the quality of our work would trump any gender bias and that our gender would enhance our insights. We were vulnerable with each other and bolstered each other so that we could each face the challenges that presented themselves to us on our respective journeys. We both had chosen fields where the sharks could smell weakness. We were not going to allow the other to get eaten.

And the smattering of female voices in that comedy scene was a microcosm of the national landscape. There were some hilarious ones; Phyllis Wright, Susan Vass, and Pricilla Nelson were my faves. But we were rarely booked together, as there was a perception that we were all the same, just one long interchangeable man-bashing menstruation monologue. And if we had the occasion to work together, it was billed as a novelty show, often with a hook like "Five Funny Females!" or "Ladies' Night." Sometimes when this happened, it felt like the message was "Think of them as hookers. They're all the same. Just pick one, pay your five bucks, and you'll get a blow job." Ironically, years later I appeared in an HBO special called *Women of the Night*. Equality was a slow process.

Even when we proved the agents and the bookers wrong by sharing our unique viewpoints on the same night, the stereotype lived on, because often the club bookers didn't bother to sit through an entire show, which would have shattered their preconceived notions. It was maddening.

During this period I was lucky to have Christine and Michele. And I knew it. I needed women in my life as I embarked on a career dominated by men, many who had the self-esteem of an abandoned pit bull and who weren't shy about expressing their opinions of me, my humor, and women in comedy in general.

The reigning king of comedy in town at the time I started out was a stand-up named Scott Hansen. He was one of the exceptions to the sexism rule. He saw me as I had hoped: a comic first, a woman second, and a pain in the ass third. I saw him as a comic first, a pain in the ass second, and a pain in the ass third. He was a comedy booker. *Pain in the ass* is in the job description.

It should not be confused with *asshole*.

Scott was a big guy—maybe the biggest guy I have ever seen. He had the face of a sixteen-year-old boy on the body of four sixteen-year-old boys. He had a club called the Comedy Gallery that had become the First Avenue of stand-up. It was a cool small room with a classic brick wall backdrop that sat about a hundred and fifty people above a throwback steak joint right in downtown Minneapolis. He brought in national acts like Jerry Seinfeld, Jay Leno, and Richard Lewis. The place was packed every night.

Roseanne Barr was my favorite headliner. At the time, she was a Denver comic that came through town quite a bit, and we became friends.

It was always a joy to see a woman owning her truth. She always requested me to open for her because she wanted to help out women in comedy. She was the first female headliner I had ever seen live, and she remains one of the best comedians I have ever seen.

She was an inspiration, not only because she could command the stage but also because she made it a priority to support the thimbleful of women trying to make it in the testosterone factory we were all working in. "We gotta help each other, kid, because there is power in numbers," she once said to me. I wished I saw more numbers.

Scott saw my dedication and, more importantly, my potential, and he started to give me guest spots on shows with big guns to help me get more exposure. I focused on working out who I was and what I wanted to say onstage. It was tricky because I had to develop material and confidence at the same time.

The material I wrote often started out falling flat onstage. The confidence came when I got back up onstage with that same material, revised, and revised again until people laughed. When I finally worked out the kinks, I added a notch of confidence to my belt.

Most comics from other cities moved to New York or Los Angeles because there wasn't enough stage time in their hometowns. The problem with trying to hone your act in a town where the industry lived was that these young comics competed with the best comedians in the country to get ten minutes on a stage. And if they were lucky enough to score a spot, they ran the risk of being seen by talent executives before they were ready. That can set you back years and sometimes kill a career completely.

I was lucky. By 1984 there were half a dozen clubs in the Twin Cities, so night after night I fell on my face and was able to get up and do it over again until I got it right, sometimes on the same night, unencumbered by the judgment of the kingmakers.

And the word about this booming scene soon got out. Comics started to move to the Twin Cities so that they could develop before they went to one of the coasts. A crazy guy came up from Iowa with a bizarre act called "Tom Arnold and His Fabulous Goldfish Review." He brought a goldfish bowl onstage and, to the tune of Herb Alpert's "Mexican Shuffle," did tricks with goldfish, like putting one in a condom, tying it to a toy motorcycle, and sending it through a flaming tennis racket.

No one else was doing that in Minneapolis.

By this time I had moved up to be one of the hosts of the open mike at the Comedy Gallery. One night I got a call at the club from a comedian named Frank Conniff who had arrived in the city from Manhattan. He didn't initially come to Minneapolis to do stand-up. Let's just say he came to get a quickie divorce from his old ball and chain called booze.

(Sidebar: Along with the amazing music and comedy, the Twin Cities boasts one of the best drug and alcohol recovery centers in the country. Sometimes I randomly saw big celebrities walking downtown and always thought, *You are either here fucking Prince or for rehab.* Sometimes they ate at Faegre's. They were never seated in my section.)

I didn't care why Frank was there; it was beyond cool that someone from New York was coming to do open mike. I couldn't wait to grill him about where I should live in Manhattan when I got there. He read a small article about me in the local paper and tracked me down to ask if he could do a set. I told him to come

down and we would put him on. He had five minutes at the end of
the show.

Frank walked onstage wearing a red T-shirt, a tan sport coat, and
tan slacks. He had a head of thick wavy blond hair that had a mind
of its own. It was how I imagined a lesser-known writer from the
Algonquin Round Table might look. He was hilariously dark, as he
talked about alcoholism, masturbation, and self-loathing. During
his set, a patron got up to use the restroom and Frank bellowed,
"You can't walk out on me, I'm Charles Foster Kane!"

He won my heart—and eventually the heart of Joel Hodgson,
who hired him to be TV's Frank on the cult classic *Mystery Science
Theater 3000*. I hoped I could hire him one day, too.

Minneapolis had now become a nationally known hot spot for
comedy, and I was swept up in it. Local comedians started to get
their breaks. Louie Anderson was on *The Tonight Show*. Joel Hodgson was on Letterman.

Meanwhile, I was developing an act and a tiny local following.
Now my customers at Faegre's would say, "I saw your show last
night. You were pretty funny." Not a rave, but I took it.

One weekend when Roseanne Barr came to town, Tom Arnold
popped down to the club. I introduced them after the show. They
seemed to hit it off.

Christine came to meet me as she often did to head over to First
Avenue, so they asked to borrow my car to go get something to eat.

Then they disappeared for two days.

I finally tracked them to a hotel and retrieved my vehicle. I never
asked what happened in the hotel or in the impressive Ford Escort
I drove, so the rest of the story is theirs to tell. (Rosie and I still
laugh about it.)

B y 1985, the Punk Rock Ghetto was full of both misanthropic musicians and comedians, and the two scenes had melded. We joined one another at the C C Club for drinks, went to one another's shows, swapped war stories, and took turns buying rounds. I'm sure the same twenty-dollar bill stayed in circulation in that neighborhood for years.

Michele and I became close friends and decided to be roommates. It was the worst idea a journalism school student ever had. She clearly didn't do enough research about me.

It had been just under a year since the house parties for rent money stopped. Danny and Christine moved in together, and Michele and I found another little place in the neighborhood. And even though I say those parties stopped, the truth is they really just morphed into late-night comedy writing sessions. A few times a week, Frank, Tom, and some other locals gathered at our place. Laughing, talking, drinking, and scrawling things down in notebooks, trying to punch up one another's bits around the dining room table of our sweet little country-style house. By day the sun really highlighted the frosted glass sconces against the floral wallpaper. The barnwood table had a vase of white tulips. By eleven P.M., the flowers were replaced with bottles of Bud and pizza boxes. A cloud of smoke obscured the sconces.

Michele was desperate to study—she was still in school, after all, unlike me—but she often got sucked into the fun, tossed in ideas, and laughed at things in spite of her better judgment. My guess is that a lot of those jokes seemed tame once she got into the belly of a real newsroom.

We both survived on very little sleep, but we still managed to get to work at ten A.M., get those breadbaskets filled and those napkins rolled for a day of slinging sea bass to the downtown trendsetters. If my late nights and filthy friends ever made her angry, Michele never let on. She saw that, even though what I was doing seemed ten times more fun than sitting with a pile of textbooks and a typewriter in her bedroom, it was as difficult as the career she was embarking on.

We were both very serious about what we were doing. My process was just a lot louder.

We were all just oddballs trying to make it, and had built a community based on taking a shot at our dreams. And now I was not just a dreamer, but also a participant. As I found my voice, both as a writer and as a performer, and as it grew stronger, my jealous appreciation at the lyricists' talents turned simply to appreciation.

I no longer wanted to write like them. I wanted to write like me.

THE RED V
OF COURAGE

L
I
Z
Z

W
I
N
S
T
E
A
D

Comedienne

S ome of the questions I get asked the most about doing stand-
up comedy are: How can you stand in front of people and tell
jokes? What if you bomb? What if people hate you? Do you
ever get afraid?

Fear of performance failure comes from the false premise that
there is some way of writing or telling a joke that everyone will love
and that somehow you should try to figure out that technique before
you start. I can't control what people like; I can only control what I
want to say and how I want to say it.

Think about it: There are people who hate chocolate and puppies and sex. And you know how I feel about babies.

I care about every idea I put out into the world. I think about every thought and every joke, I ponder it and refine it. And I can defend it. Even my most frivolous of thoughts I consider before spewing.

But just because I care about them doesn't mean others will. I can only promise that with every essay and every joke I write, I have put thought into them. You don't like it, well, that's not my problem. I tried.

Also, I was lucky to have learned very early on in my career that humans will forget even the most amazingly awful things that happen onstage if you give them a reason to.

M y first paid gig at comedy came about six months after I started doing stand-up. It wasn't at the Comedy Gallery or Dudley Riggs'. It was at First Avenue.

First Avenue; my Carnegie Hall, my Royal Albert Hall, My [Name Your Own Dream then multiply it by a thousand] Hall. That's how big of a deal this was for me.

It was 1984, and for years, every Thursday night the club had an air guitar contest called "The Great Pretenders," and the contest needed a new MC. It had been a regular gig for comedians Jeff Cesario and Joel Madison, but they were both moving to LA so they passed the gig down to me. I was excited because way before my foray into comedy, Christine and I and many of our friends made these contest nights must-see clubbing.

There were always one or two performers who were really creative and did full-on "Thriller" zombie numbers or interpreted Duran Duran's "Girls on Film" video, complete with pith helmet hairdos and sumo wrestlers. But most of these pretenders couldn't even pretend they were good. They were the lip-synching equivalent of drunkenly walking out of a public restroom with barf in your hair and your skirt tucked in your tights.

And that's what lured us down each week: the promise that there would always be some dreadful rendition of *"Oh Mickey you're so fine, blah blah blah blah blah blah blah hey Mickey!"* a few fabulous queens doing "It's Raining Men" and week after week the same chubby black woman dragging her Jack Sprat boyfriend down to the club and mouthing to him the lyrics of "And I Am Telling You" from *Dreamgirls*.

It was like the *American Idol* auditions every week, and I could always be counted on to provide brutal running commentary to everyone within a twenty-foot radius of us in the audience. So when some poor woman finished doing a Romeo Void song, I might have said something like, "Honey, after seeing that, no one would like you better if you slept together."

Everyone laughed, and I got so carried away with my show-within-a-show act that when I saw Jeff and Joel at Dudley Riggs' that first night I went to check it out, I didn't even make the connection that they were the same guys from First Avenue. I was busy clowning on the floor for the people around me. The actual MC's presence didn't even register.

I guess it's fair to say that unbeknownst to me, but apparently not to Christine, I was honing my craft. Now that I knew Jeff and Joel, I was extra honored they thought I was the comic most appropriate (or inappropriate) to take over their gig and, truth be told, I was. For the previous three years I'd been spending more nights than I should at this club. I was the "alternative" comic and was sporting a serious swoop hairdo worthy of a Patrick Nagel lithograph to prove it. The "alternative" to what remained a mystery.

The gig paid fifty bucks and came with free drinks and my own coveted spot on the permanent guest list. But there was no bigger reward than being able to work the same stage as the Replacements and Prince.

I never thought any "performance" I would give on that stage would make the impact that my local heroes did, but I didn't care. To be honest, it turned out to be more of a job than a performance. My role was to keep the acts coming on and off stage and to kill time between each pretender with my Simon Cowellish barbs, slam the people in the audience, or dis the new Culture Club video. In other words, stick to jokes about anything that was in the zeitgeist of the lives of these club rats.

When I started MCing, the audiences continued to laugh, just as they had when I was doing it for fun. But to my surprise, now that I was doing onstage in front of the whole club what I used to do in relative obscurity, some of the acts got pissed.

I didn't blame them. But I realized I was there for the audience, not them.

These "acts" were people who would be singing if they could sing, but they couldn't. And now they proved they sucked at pretending to sing. When they sucked at pretending, how bad could I really feel for them? Nowadays on the television programs that reward the cream of the creative crap, the hosts are twice as scathing as I was, and they make millions.

If only I had stayed shallow and mean. Well, I evolved from shallow, anyway.

The purpose of these Thursday night contests was that they served as elimination rounds for the big event. Each winner over a twelve-week period would move on to the finals for a chance to win $1,500 and the title The Great Pretender, an honor that to this day is ranked one notch above becoming Miss Wasilla. Because the contestants were a Superfund site full of talent, attendance to these prelims was always sparse. Maybe a hundred people showed up, and of that number, 80 percent were contestants and their pals, and the rest were people who came to see Kabuki karaoke. But the finals were a whole different story.

All of the acts were great. Their costumes were elaborate, and they definitely had rehearsed to be (dare I say it) pitch-perfect. It was sold out weeks in advance. Vanity of Vanity 6 was a judge.

Yes *way*.

So when I was asked to host the finals, it felt like the Oscars. There was a special stage for me, dead center, with my own steps, right in front of a huge video screen. We even had a rehearsal. When I spoke, a spotlight shone only on me, Lizz Winstead, host of the finals of the Great Pretenders. I mean, there was French onion dip and carrots in the dressing room and ads with *my name in them* in the local Twin Cities alternative weekly. (Okay, maybe not the Oscars, but definitely the Oscar Meyers.)

But what would I wear?

The finals were held on a hot Minnesota August night, when the average temperature is ninety degrees with 90 percent humidity. It's the kind of weather so sweat-inducing that within a minute, you look like Robert Motherwell did your make-up. So wardrobe was tricky. I wanted to wear something provocative, punk rock, sexy, feminine, glamorous, and lightweight. Naturally I chose a ragged old 1950s wedding dress I found at the local thrift store called Ragstock where you bought clothes by the bag.

This was three months before "Like a Virgin." I know you were wondering. Ahem. Again, ahead of my time.

This dress was perfect. The top was strapless (glamorous and feminine) with a plunging sweetheart neckline (sexy) and had only minimal yellowing in the pits (punk rock). It was obvious that one of the previous owners had an "If I cut this off I can wear it again" delusion and had snipped in a precision- free way so it came waaaay above my left knee and then just below my right (provocative *and* punk rock). The rest of the hemline was made of varying kneeish lengths and had layer upon layer of netting, which made a perfect bell shape from waist to knee. (Fuck the lightweight part; how hot could an oversold nightclub get in the dog days of a Minnesota summer?)

Finally the big day arrived.

The air-conditioning at First Avenue had been out for twenty-four hours. In the club it felt like the eye of Sauron. And it was only three P.M. The performers were panicking during rehearsal, sweating through their Adam Ant war paint and full leather. Imagine how hot it would be when the club was full. I was very glad I had my own platform because I feared I would slip and fall on the river of eyeliner that I knew would flood the stage.

An hour before showtime, with still no air-conditioning, I put on my gown. I accessorized with a pair of black tights, combat boots, and a black velvet 1940s hat with netting that covered the swooping bang that curved over my right eye, like Veronica Lake as interpreted by Ricki Lake. My last and most brilliant touch: bloodred lipstick. I had never felt more dazzling in my entire life.

But within five minutes, even before getting onstage, I was slopping sweat, enhancing the yellowing of the pits and feeling my belly button fill up drip by drip, the overflow running down my stomach into various portions of my underpinnings.

There was only one way to get partial relief, and that was to get rid of my underwear and my black tights. We were five minutes to curtain and I unstuck myself out of them.

The relief was instant.

I spotted Christine in the crowd and waved her over. I handed her the tights as the lights started to go down. Just as they were about to introduce me, Christine looked at me like I was about to jump out of an airplane and hadn't checked my parachute. "What if you can see through the dress?!" she said in a panic.

"Fuuuuuuuuuck." All I had been worried about was whether I had lipstick on my teeth.

"Stand right here, look very closely, and give me thumbs-up or thumbs-down. I only have to talk for a minute at the beginning and introduce the judges—"

"Please welcome your host . . ."

"If it's bad, I can put them back on before the second act."

". . . comedian Lizz Winstead!"

I walked up onstage ready for utter humiliation. I forgot to ask Christine if I had lipstick on my teeth, so that added to the dearth of dignity that I was sure was about to befall me. *Please God, please God, do not have this dress act as a peep show window,* I prayed.

As I came out onstage and climbed my stairway to what was sure to be instant ignominy, I was dying inside, frantically licking and sucking my teeth. I hit my platform, the spot came up, and there I stood as fifteen hundred people all stared at me. *Keep talking, have energy, you have never looked hotter,* I told myself.

"Good evening, and welcome to the finals of the Great Pretenders! We have twelve acts tonight, and one of them will walk away with fifteen hundred bucks and the title the Great Pretender!"

The audience burst into thunderous applause! They were psyched! And it seemed they weren't looking at me as if I had been sent from the circus. I looked over to Christine and she gave me a hearty thumbs-up. They couldn't see my lady slice, either.

Crisis averted. God is good.

I breathed a huge sigh of relief and got the housekeeping out of the way. I ran through how the night was going to go, plugged some upcoming shows, and introduced the judges. They sat at a table on risers behind the dance floor. There was Chrissie, the woman who was the booker of the club and the one I needed to impress the most, two journalists I should want to impress the most, and Vanity, the one I really wanted to impress the most.

Vanity. Wow, I just introduced Vanity.

I noticed the flashlight from the DJ booth, which was my cue to introduce the first act. The night was off and running.

"Are you ready for your first contestants?" I asked as the screen behind me slowly started to roll up. The audience screamed with delight.

"Your first act . . ."

The crowd was going crazy. I was really psyched. But unbeknownst to me, they weren't screaming because they were excited. They were screaming because the back of my dress was rolling up right along with the screen. And now so much fabric had been pulled that the front of the dress split.

That was when I noticed.

It was hard not to. My feet were three inches off the ground.

And then a lurch, and the screen suddenly stopped. Broken by the weight of my layers of fabric gumming up the mechanism that made it roll up. And then I felt the breezy air blowing against my . . .

THIS. WAS. NOT. HAPPENING.

I was hanging from the screen, trapped with my vajesus exposed to God and Vanity and everyone in the club.

And to think five minutes before I had been worried about lipstick on my teeth.

I now realized why people were screaming. Then they started to laugh. The laughter started slowly. Then it built, distorted and ominous. Hanging there, I looked into the crowd and saw groups of people cackling, couples pointing, doubling over. I saw strangers, random people I knew, Christine, Chrissie, and Vanity. Oh my God, Vanity was laughing at my vaganity.

I began to feel like Carrie at the prom.

I was in panic mode. I knew I only had a split second to do something to turn this around. So I went with my instinct.

I kept talking.

But with my big '80s vagina the club's immediate focal point, I had to get people to listen to what I was saying, so it had better be fucking funny—funny like I had never been funny before and maybe never would be again. This was about survival.

I decided to run with the *Carrie* visuals that kept coming up.

"The only way this could be worse is if a bucket of pig's blood fell on my head," I said to the crowd.

They continued to laugh, but the tone changed. They were laughing at the joke. They had gone from laughing at me to laughing with me.

I can turn this around, I thought. *Keep talking, just keep talking.* I tried not to move too much in an attempt not to trigger a bigger malfunction. I continued with the *Carrie* theme. "Mama told me you would laugh at me," I said in that Sissy Spacek alto twang.

The crowd laughed again, and now they were clapping. Then it subsided and they were waiting for my next line. Now they were listening to me. The fact that I hung there with my she-joy center stage didn't seem to matter.

"Well, maybe you all have seen my vagina, but at least I'm not showing my dirty pillows."

That one got full-on applause. I heard some guy say, "She must have planned this."

If you want to think that, dude, go ahead. Spread the word: Lizz Winstead goes to any lengths for her audience.

I had one *Carrie* reference left. Plus it was 1984, so I combined it with a topical reference.

"Let's call this *Carrie 2: Electric Boogaloo*." They roared at that one. I was vag-out killing.

Now I was out of material, and just as I started to soak back into the reality that I was both hanging out and hanging by a mechanism that could crash down on me at any moment, leading to an obituary that would read COMEDIAN DIES DOING PORN ACT ONSTAGE, I saw the adorable stage manager, Joey Grimes, climb onstage with a pair of scissors.

Fuck. I had forgotten how cute he was. He looked like Spicoli in *Fast Times at Ridgemont High*. We often talked about music and comedy. He knew everything about all those power pop bands of the '80s, like the dB's and the Bongos, and he loved Joel Hodgson. And he had the coolest collection of vintage cowboy shirts I had ever seen. I always thought he was dreamy but way out of my league. He was older, lived alone, and was a stage manager at this club I had immortalized in my mind since I was a kid. He looked like a movie star. I was twenty-three, a struggling comedian with two jobs, and now, he and the entire city of Minneapolis knew, had an ill-tended girly garden.

I forgot he was here.

Joey hopped onto the riser with me, all business, and without even looking at me said into his walkie-talkie, "Cut her mike." *Boom!* The lights dim, music starts, and like nothing had happened, people started dancing.

"Oh shit!" Did I just bomb? Is the show canceled? Have I messed up the whole night? Did he think I was a total loser for those jokes? I know *Carrie* came out, like, five years ago, but it seemed fitting.

They laughed; I did not make that up in my head.

Joey took off his cowboy shirt, tossed it over his shoulder, and whispered very close, "I have to cut you out of this dress. I'm gonna stand in front of you when it falls off. Put on this shirt quickly. You are hilarious. Can I take you out for dinner this week?"

I never realized how big my crush on Joey Grimes was until that very moment.

My heart squealed. Dinner with Joey Grimes? Joey Grimes wanted to have dinner with me? Wait. Did he like my vagina or my jokes? I couldn't even think about that right now. I still had to host this whole show.

"Can I wear your shirt the rest of the night?" I asked.

"You're already trying to steal my stuff? We haven't even had dinner yet!"

"I know, and I've already shown you the goods."

"I was laughing so hard, I hardly noticed."

"Liar."

Joey Grimes liked me.

He kissed my cheek, pulled the mounds of netting out of the screen, and voila, it continued to roll up. He signaled to the booth and said, "Your mike's back on; wanna start this show?"

I had just finished buttoning up my cowboy shirt-dress, and Joey headed down the stairs. The music faded and the spotlight came back on me. I had a show to host. My show. "Welcome back, people. I just realized, I hope you can't see through my shirt."

That audience was mine.

"Please welcome your first act . . ." (No one I have asked can remember who it was. I know whoever it was didn't win. The winner was a group of students from Macalester College doing a big and hilarious production of "Convoy," led by a young theater major named Peter Berg. Google him; it'll be worth it.)

That night, so very early in my career, I developed a sense of confidence that an entire lifetime may not have taught me. I took a horrible moment and defined it in my terms. And I defined it as funny.

The audience members didn't forget about the vagathon, I'm sure. They just looked at it as part of the night. They had moved on the second I gave them a reason to. The attention span of the human mind is very short. People forget the lessons of 9/11 or Hurricane Katrina, so they're not going to remember my vagina, never mind a shitty joke I tell, unless I allow it to be the last word. That choice is mine.

LONG DAZED
JOURNEY
INTO LATE
NIGHT

For years I had made a decent living doing observational humor. My act had jokes like, "Ever notice when you play Monopoly with bald guys, they always pick the hat?" and "Maybe there should be a law that male Great Danes should wear underwear in public." Good, solid jokes. Jokes that got me booked at some club in a midmarket town in Ohio and put a commission into a lazy agent's pocket.

But I began to notice that even these surefire jokes started to fall flat. And I wasn't connecting with my audience. I started to feel alienated from them, as if I were performing a different show than the one they came to see.

At first I couldn't figure out why. So I taped my shows to see if my timing was off, or if I had forgotten to say something that was integral to the joke. When I listened to the tapes of my show, I noticed that I had subconsciously started reframing my setups. I had moved away from saying "Ever notice . . ." to "I'm telling you, when you play Monopoly with bald guys, they always pick the hat." And "Maybe there should be . . ." became "I think there should be a law that male Great Danes should have to wear underwear in public." As I started to use more declarative language, the audiences backed away.

The punch line was the same, but by telling people "I think," I became off-putting.

Being a woman with a formed opinion was still threatening. Even if that opinion *only* involved Monopoly pieces or dog balls. And the fact that I was amplified just added to the alienation stew.

So imagine the response when I opened my set to a pack of nacho-eating, slurring bachelor party asswits at some dump with a clever name like Laff Loins with the joke "I went to college for four years and studied philosophy. I think, therefore I'm single." That got a response akin to "Fucking right you are," which led to the room filling up with hostility, like how a car with open windows fills with water as it slowly sinks to the bottom of a lake.

People in the late '80s and early '90s were *still* most comfortable with a comedienne onstage being self-deprecating. I felt the unspoken rule was "I'm fine with a woman onstage as long as her act reiterates how shitty she feels about herself."

It was mostly a guy thing.

When the women laughed at anything empowering, sometimes their dates glared at them. I watched as the women reacted to their boyfriends with either "Fuck you, it's funny," or "Fuck me, I better tone it down."

These were the obstacles *before* I started sharing my political opinions onstage. Maybe that's why I hadn't thus far. So why did I even start?

Because of a blind date.

It was January 1991. I had moved to New York City from Los Angeles six months earlier. I was also single, and most of my friends in the city were either women, gay, or comedians—three qualities I have found don't work for me in a romantic relationship.

A girlfriend had convinced me she knew "the perfect guy" (Sidebar: There is no "perfect guy"; just know this and your life will be much easier) and wanted to set me up on a blind date.

Remember those? For you youngsters, before the Internet and speed dating, blind dates were the gold standard of unrealistic attempts at forced intimacy.

I don't know what compelled me to go. Maybe the chance to have a nice meal or to get laid. I can't even remember which friend set me up. And I don't remember my date's name. I will call him Bob. Bob showed me something that night that changed my life forever. No, you can't measure it in inches. Wait, yes, you can, and it was thirty-six inches. You will understand that later.

When we spoke on the phone, I suggested to Bob we go see the Fellini film *La Dolce Vita*. It was playing at the Film Forum on a big screen. I had never seen it in a theater and I was really excited. Bob was a tad less enthusiastic, but he agreed in a tone best described as "I'm open to whatever."

We met at the theater. He was cute, in a Jimmy Kimmel sort of way, but he wore a Yankees cap *and* jacket. Waaay too much fanwear for my comfort level. (I have a theory about men: Any guy wearing more than one team insignia at the same time is a guy who won't go down on me. Discuss.) So for me, this was Red Flag No. 1. By the end of the night, there were more red flags flying over our date than in China on Mao's birthday.

We exchanged hellos. "I hear this movie is a classic," Bob said with all the insight of a Wikipedia entry. Oh, Lord, hoist up flag number two.

I bought popcorn and poured my Milk Duds into the tub. I had a sneaking suspicion that this was going to replace sitting through dinner.

As Bob drifted in and out of sleep throughout the movie, his satin Yankees jacket would slide up and down my arm, reminding me of my theory. During one of his nod-offs, he spilled my popcorn. It was my dinner. It had real butter on it. I was pissed.

I "accidentally" got some butter on his coat.

That move kicked in my Minnesota Nice guilt mechanism. I felt so bad after I did it that I overcompensated and after the film blurted out, "Can I buy you a drink and we can talk about the movie?"

It popped out of my mouth before I could stop myself. Why did I just extend this evening? What were we going to talk about? The parts he was awake for? And I was going to pay for the privilege?

That is the curse of Minnesota Nice. We Minnesotans like to give someone a chance. There's only one condition: Don't be mean. If you aren't *mean*, you get an infinite amount of chances. Minnesotans will suffer through stupid, irresponsible, freakish, obnoxious—you name it. As long as we don't see mean, you will always get a pass. And then we swallow our resentment about putting up with it, become passive-aggressive, eat slop troughs of fried food and drink to excess to mask our anger about it, and die of clogged arteries and unfinished business. But hey, we gave you a chance.

And what happens if you *are* mean? You only get a few passes—say a dozen or so. And then we start with the resentment swallowing, passive-aggressive, stuff fried food, dying-with-regret stuff. Regret that we didn't give the mean person *enough* of a chance.

Good times.

"Sure, I'll have a drink," Bob said in what was quickly becoming his signature "I'm open to whatever" tone. "But I won't have much to say. You know, I just didn't get it, and it was black-and-white."

Hand me another red flag, please.

One. Drink.

We settled in at a bar he normally went to because it had a big TV—thirty-six inches, people—and during baseball season showed all of the Yankees games. (Another novelty from the olden days: a bar with a single TV. This date was practically Brontësque in the amount of old-timey romancing we were experiencing.)

We sat at the bar, but instead of a sporting event, CNN was broadcasting the first night of Operation Desert Storm, or what became known as the First Gulf War. Everyone was glued to the TV. It was the first time in our nation's history that Americans watched a war kick off in the comfort of their living rooms. Or, in our case, in a sports bar.

Live from Baghdad, US bombers shelled the center of the capital of Iraq. And CNN correspondents were holed up in the Baghdad Hilton, reporting live and sending back video of bombs hitting targets across the area. As CNN and other networks were broadcasting these images, graphics flew all over the screen, a screen tinted in a dramatic green cast from the night-vision cameras.

CNN had even created a theme song for this war.

I felt like I was watching a video game.

Then I felt sick.

I remembered as a kid watching clips of the Vietnam War on the nightly news. I could sense death. It felt heavy and bleak and solemn, the way war should feel.

This new war felt different. It felt like a trailer for a movie about war. The reporting on it had replaced casualties with animation and had hot anchors who sat behind a news desk and talked to even hotter young reporters in hotel rooms or on rooftops in Iraq, telling us this war was the right thing to do and repeating buzz words like "Saddam madman, Saddam madman, Saddam madman" over and over.

The sanitized Stepford nature of the whole experience was mesmerizing. Both Bob and I watched, probably for thirty minutes, without talking. Neither one of us said a word about *La Dolce Vita*.

Taking in all of this imagery, I thought to myself, *Are they reporting on a war, or are they trying to sell me a war?* It was as if at this one moment my personal Pandora's box of media skepticism was opened.

I looked at Bob to see if he felt it, too. He looked at me and, in a very different tone than his usual "I'm open to whatever," exclaimed, "This is so fucking cool!"

Sold!

My mind raced. Maybe the people who were supposed to be

giving us the answers and digging for the truth were in cahoots with the people who planned the war. Maybe other parts of the government manipulated the stories we got. Maybe the products that advertised dictated all of the information we received.

The part that really hit me was that, in 1991, CNN was the only twenty-four-hour news network. No other cable news networks were around to present another narrative.

And CNN had found its narrative. It was the tale of good versus evil.

And so began my awakening to the full-scale scaring of America.

In the three hours I watched CNN's coverage of Desert Storm that night at the bar, nobody there questioned why we were bombing. The network just paraded out general after general after general to talk about how the attack on Baghdad was the right thing to do. And interspersed with the generals were the hot reporters in hotel rooms giving viewers up-to-the-minute impressions of what was happening in this new sexy war zone.

I turned to Bob. "They will trot out every fucking general who has ever been a general of anything. I am waiting for them to interview a plate of General Tso's chicken."

The whole bar laughed, but Bob didn't even respond. My first joke about the war killed, but it was lost on my date.

That was okay. It showed me that people were paying attention.

After that, I finished my fourth drink in silence as Bob and I watched. He was engrossed. I think he had discovered a new favorite sport. I was sure if I ever saw him again, he would be wearing a camouflage hat *and* jacket.

I never saw him again.

That Gulf War night planted in my brain the seeds of what years later became *The Daily Show*. I didn't know then they were *Daily Show* seeds, of course; back then they were simply the new seeds of material for my act. It was when I started to realize that our media outlets were as anemic as our foreign policy. The term *expert* was as overused as the word *awesome*. The networks' graphics departments seemed to have replaced their research departments.

As the weeks went by, I obsessively watched the coverage, I became engaged in writing material in a way that I hadn't been before. It was all so much, too much. I suddenly felt as if I had to pay attention to what I read and saw and what was reported in a whole new way.

It didn't feel like a choice, more like a calling.

I began replacing my anecdotes about being a lovelorn thirty-something with observations of a television mediapocalypse that, when they weren't providing musicians to beat the war drums, tabled politics for any story resembling a real-life soap opera.

This trend was omnipresent, and CNN embraced it really hard because it had twenty-four hours of programming to fill. And it had to be as compelling as the twenty-four hours of the ratings gold it scored by ratcheting up our emotions with what I think of as "Lifetime Television for Warmen" during Desert Storm. And boy, did the producers get lucky. All they had to do was roll tape.

Someone else's tape, even.

Three days after Desert Storm ended, four Los Angeles police officers were caught on tape beating Rodney King, an unarmed black man, fifty-six times. CNN ran with it, and thus began what I saw as the insanity and inanity of the twenty-four-hour cable news world in the early 1990s. I remember thinking, *If it's not caught on tape, they won't report it.*

Then came the wall-to-wall trials. The trials of the shitstorms they wished they had caught on tape. Jeffrey Dahmer. Tonya Harding. John Gotti. The Bobbitts. The Menendez brothers. Heidi Fleiss. That was news.

I became obsessed with how it seemed each crime had its own graphics department with bold titles, like DAHMER: MONSTER OR MADMAN? or FLEISS: HOLLYWOOD MADAM. And if two trials were going on at once you didn't have to miss a beat, because all of the gory details of one would crawl across the bottom of your screen above the already distracting stock ticker as you watched the gory details of the other.

The throngs of retired generals and what was left of broadcast journalists were given pink slips as the cable networks started the cattle call for hosts known as "former prosecutors." Almost overnight they seemingly created a cottage industry based on ex-lawyers making wild suppositions about cases they weren't actually working on, pretty much basing their conclusions on the same shit I was getting from my TV.

The number of guests rose to epic numbers, too. The basic format of every show was to cram six former prosecutors via satellite in little *Brady Bunch* boxes, with some unhinged, apoplectic host adding to the chaos of the speculathon.

This was when I first started noticing the trend of cable news hosts hired seemingly to simply "wonder aloud" with guests who also wondered aloud. Really loudly.

I wondered aloud, too, as I tried to figure out a way to make a living pointing out what clowns these people were. It actually felt like the only way I would get on TV was if I killed my parents or ran a brothel. Or if I wanted to ensure a second season, kill my parents *in* my brothel.

There was a wealth of material in breaking down the media breakdown. For example, I dubbed the Tonya Harding/Nancy Kerrigan fiasco as "The Skatanic Verses," and I often referred to Heidi Fleiss as "The Whorellywood Madam." I wished I had a team to build graphics for each of my comedy bits to mirror the insanity of how the media covered them.

But it was just me, eating dollar-store ramen noodles and scribbling jokes in my notebook that reflected what was going through my head, that the media's appetite for tragedy porn was turning us into mush-brained fear barnacles. Callous barnacles, at that.

The Rodney King controversy was profound. The problem was that these clowns covered it like other tabloid stories, rather than covering the systemic problems it represented. And to be fair, there were other important stories that interrupted the flow of these trials, like the 1991 Clarence Thomas hearings. But even a Supreme Court nomination was only going to be covered in detail because the story was chock-full of pubes and porn. And thank God Gennifer Flowers showed up in New Hampshire during the 1992 presidential primaries and spouted off about former Arkansas governor Bill Clinton. Otherwise, we may never have had any coverage of that presidential race.

I won my audiences over if I just talked about the obvious, prurient stuff, but that material wasn't particularly substantial. When I dug deeper, such as when I did my dead-on impression of Alabama senator Howell Heflin from the Clarence Thomas hearings, or I veered away from "Clinton is a pussy hound," opting for "Apparently George Bush's thousand points of light are a cluster bomb," I was greeted with a blank stare from 90 percent of the audience. They either hated my opinion or they didn't know what I was talking about. Either one was a loss for both of us. And my loss of a rebooking.

My newfound voice was not at all welcomed by my manager, either. "No one cares about politics or the media" became his mantra.

That became a persistent theme in my experience with showbiz types. When they said "No one cares about . . . ," they meant "*I* don't care about . . ." Or "Sure, that gets laughs at your little Monday night show in New York City, but no one else in the country cares."

My little Monday night show was what got me up in the morning. It was run by Randy Credico, a hilarious radical comedian who told jokes about the Nicaraguan Contras and the Rockefeller Drug Laws. He made Amy Goodman sound like Ryan Seacrest.

Randy was probably most famous in comedy circles as the guy who, in 1981, on his first and only performance on *The Tonight Show Starring Johnny Carson*, told the joke "Every time I see Jeane Kirkpatrick, I wonder if Eva Braun really died in that bunker."

Randy's Monday night show was in the basement of a bar then called the West End Gate, which had a capacity of sixty and started out about a quarter full. As the weeks went by and word of mouth started happening, it started to build. The rotation of performers were a handful of other comics whose material "no one cared about," among them Bill Hicks and Jon Stewart.

My manager never attended.

I went through a lot of managers.

Every time I tried to get a manager to think about how to create an audience for what I was doing, I was met with the same response: "Let's talk about that later." One time it was followed by "But I did just get a call for you to open for Frankie Valli in Jersey. Five hundred bucks cash."

The subtext: *Your plan sounds like something I might have to get off my ass and actually work on, so could you just shut up and want to be famous by any means necessary? It's five hundred bucks cash.*

Every time I heard some variation of this, I replied, "I am not driven by making money, I'm driven by making a larger point about the world. The money will come if we build an audience."

What they heard was, *Well, I'm not gonna build my beach house with this one.*

And what I heard was . . . wait. I normally didn't hear from them again.

I opened for Frankie Valli at a theater called the Garden State Arts Center in Holmdel, New Jersey. He wanted a comedienne to open for him, probably because he was a teen idol back in the day, he had a large female following. I also guessed that every other female comedian in the tristate area was booked that night. So I got the gig. Did I mention it was five hundred bucks? Cash?

The Garden State Arts Center was a big venue, and it was outdoors. I usually played for a few hundred liquored-up folks as I stood in front of a brick wall. No one really warned me about the subtle differences between that and having everything you say get sucked up into the sky. I was just handed a wireless mike by a stage manager and told to "go for twenty minutes."

So with no intro and no context, I walked out onstage and saw three thousand middle-aged women, most of them sitting with men who looked like Frankie Valli doppelgängers. They stared at me. They wanted Frankie. In every sense of the word. They had wanted Frankie since 1958. I was the impediment between them and Frankie.

They would have given anything to open for Frankie Valli. I was bitter that I had to.

It was a situation ripe for disaster. And that is exactly what I got.

I opened with "I think, therefore I'm single." A foxhole on Guadalcanal probably made more noise.

As I stood there, blathering jokes into the still night, I had no idea what these people would laugh at. It felt like one of those awful family baby showers from my childhood, but on a grand scale. I never thought I could feel stifled in an amphitheater, and yet there I was. There were no walls, but they were closing in on me, I felt it. If only I could have left to do cartwheels.

I ran through the comedy Rolodex in my head, trying to find a joke, any joke, they might like. *Kids. They know about kids. I'll talk about kids*, I thought. I launched into my "Kids are useless. They don't like scotch, never have matches" bit, which was met with glares.

We hated each other.

Those twenty minutes were never-ending. I had nothing to lose, so I decided to close out the hate with some "How about those idiotic Americans who bought all that Gulf War hype?" material.

A deafening silence, amplified by the planes as they landed at nearby Newark Airport.

I looked at my watch; nineteen minutes. Good enough. I had inflicted enough pain on them and on myself. I just wanted to get out of there.

"Thank you, good night." The smattering of applause I received was probably generated simply because I was no longer talking. It was an undeniable tank. It was what's known among comedians as a shame show: Shame on me for taking the gig, and shame on you for booking me.

I didn't feel guilty for taking their money.

And so as I left the stage, my "walk of shame show" started as I wandered through the entire production crew, who tried not to make eye contact with me. If they didn't see me, they didn't have to acknowledge my act. I just kept my head down and looked up only to try to find a person to pay me. Then we could all just go our separate ways and pretend this never happened.

I circled for about five minutes, then found the man who pushed me out onstage.

"Hey, how ya doing?" I sounded like a rookie hooker, sheepish and ashamed. "Do you know how I get paid?"

"Yeah." He never looked at me, just kept monitoring the stage. "Frankie *himself* will pay you after the show."

This was supposed to be an honor.

"*After* his show?"

"Of course," he said in a cartoonish mob deadpan.

Defeated, I cowered in a corner offstage and watched the ladies in the audience swoon to "My Eyes Adored You" and "Oh, What a Night." It was what I expected. But then, *then* came something quite unexpected.

Frankie announced he was going to "take the vibe down" or some phrase equally cheesy, and if memory served me correctly, all of a sudden a faux brownstone stoop kind of thingy was rolled out onstage. He took off his bolero jacket and sat down on it to chat with those three thousand people. Just like they used to do "back in the neighborhood." On the stoop. He talked about the greatness of America, patriotism, and how proud he was we won the Gulf War.

The audience was cheering wildly. I actually tried to crawl inside myself and disappear. The reaction explained the tepid response to my "Who are these idiotic people who got suckered into supporting this war?" material.

They *were* those people.

I watched the remainder of the show. I was still mortified, but now at least I had a little clarity. I even sang along to the theme from *Grease*.

When it was over I waited. And waited. The entire backstage was now full of what looked like second-string wiseguys. I was in Frankie Valli after-party hell. I was too scared to ask for my money, so I sat and watched all the blond Italian women and the men with pinky rings talking and laughing with the star of the night.

Finally, an hour after his show was over, the stage goon found me. I had been summoned to the dressing room. Frankie was there with a few people.

He paid me my five hundred bucks cash in a handshake.

"You new to this business?"

"I'm about eight years in."

He kept holding my hand.

"Lemme give you a piece of advice."

I would take any advice as long as it involved me getting cash at the end of it.

"Sweetheart, always let the audience know you love 'em." He released his grip and gave my hand a tap. "Good luck, kid."

"Thanks. Thanks for having me."

I didn't know what to say. Tonight, I didn't love 'em. Sometimes I just don't love 'em.

But thanks to Frankie, I realized I could no longer work venues where I was tossed in front of just anybody's fans for a random comedy show.

So how would I pay my bills?

It was one of those lean times when I didn't even have two dollars for a slice of pizza, so I pulled out my credit card and charged a fifteen-dollar lunch. My favorite poor trick was taking out a cash advance on my credit card so I could pay the minimum payment on the same credit card. You know, like the government does. With that kind of ingenuity I scraped by, but not without the help of family and friends.

I would still get a smattering of club dates from time to time. Caroline Hirsch, owner of Carolines comedy club, and Lucien Hold from the Comic Strip were my biggest champions in New York. Caroline loved my feminist material and Lucien loved to talk politics. They both wanted their audiences to hear challenging material, even if it didn't get the huge laughs. Jon Stewart had a gig hosting a Comedy Central show called *Short Attention Span Theater*, and when his cohost was on vacation, I earned a few bucks filling in. My friend Hank Gallo was the king of booking those cable stand-up shows that cropped up in the early '90s, so he always gave me a slot that paid a thousand bucks here and a thousand bucks there. And then he'd lend me a thousand bucks here and a thousand bucks there. My sister Mary sent me care packages of food. She was a one-woman WIC program, minus the *IC*.

It was not a living, but more of a living paycheck to paycheck— sometimes off of someone else's paycheck until I got one. As I tried to make all of these ends meet, I didn't know if I would be able to survive financially. But I knew that I couldn't survive doing material that didn't matter, either.

I was paralyzed: with fear, with indecision, with self-doubt. So I did the most logical thing to combat all three of these: I took my last thousand dollars and left my apartment to buy a computer. This would solidify my commitment to writing.

Well. Instead of buying that computer, I came home with a chair. An overstuffed, two-tone, striped beige-on-beiger, double-wide chair.

The Chair was like an island. For a good portion of the early 1990s, I curled up in it and lined up my newspapers, magazines, takeout menus, cigarettes, phone, and remote control in a semi-circle at the base of it. I watched TV nonstop, unable to get enough of what America was absorbing as information, news, or entertainment. I would only get out of The Chair to get delivery food, use the bathroom, and of course to perform.

The Chair was a down-filled oasis that became the cornerstone of my life for fifteen years. I used it for writing, laughing with a sister, bathing a friend in my tears, napping, fucking, and dog bonding. It was a not-so-subtle metaphor for my life.

If The Chair could have talked, it could have ruined me.

The Chair became legendary to my inner circle, and every friend of mine has a story about The Chair.

Years after I got it, Sarah Silverman shot her segment of the movie *The Aristocrats* in The Chair. At least a dozen friends called me to say, "I saw The Chair in *The Aristocrats*!"

"Yes," I would say with a sigh. The Chair had been in more movies than I had.

Many thought The Chair was bad for me, like it was my emotional kryptonite, and talked about it like it was an abusive boyfriend. "Lizz, The Chair is sucking the life out of you." Or "You haven't been out of The Chair for days." Or "You need to start seeing other furniture."

Other people thought it had powers over all who sat in it and refused to go anywhere near it. They assumed when I fell into this down-filled womb, I would lose all motivation. But I wrote my ass off in The Chair. People mistook The Chair for my Achilles' heel, but I had notebooks full of material written in The Chair, and my spots and Carolines, the Comic Strip or my ten-minute Monday night sets were not enough time to say everything.

One person who understood The Chair was Claire.

My roommate Claire was part of Christine and my Punk Rock Ghetto girl gang from back home, and she landed in New York to work as the managing editor of the Buddhist magazine *Tricycle*. She looked like a redheaded Andie MacDowell and was a born caretaker. Maybe it was the Zenfluence at the magazine, maybe it was for-real Minnesota Nice, but twice a week, Claire came home from work, cooked me dinner, and we curled up in The Chair together and watched old movies.

She was a champion of the Lizz cause. And to this day, with two kids and a husband, she still finds time to make me dinner.

"If people came to our house and saw you work in The Chair, they would get it," Claire would say with all that spiritual hopefulness.

"I know, I wish I could just do my show from The Chair," I would say with a sigh.

And then it hit me: "Why don't I?" I am going to bring The Chair to them.

I was so excited! I called my new manager: "I want to do a theater show from The Chair. I will tell my stories about all that I am observing just like I do at home every day! Except instead of just yelling at the TV, I will tell actual people."

"Who would pay to see that? Who would pay to produce it?" he asked, as if I had just handed him a Steinway to carry up five flights of stairs.

"I'll launch it in Minneapolis. I have a following there and I'll get friends to help."

"It just seems like a lot of work, and people just don't care about . . ."

I stopped listening. I hung up. But I was not defeated. I was too excited to be defeated. I had something to say and somewhere to say it from.

I decided to do it on my own. Every step of the way as I explained what the show was, people wanted to help make it happen. I found a theater in Minneapolis that took a cut of the door. I called in every favor. A friend helped produce the show, and my cousin gave me a deal on posters and postcards. They looked great. A gold and black background with my huge face, screaming, surrounded by icons of bombs and news logos and Jesse Helms, with the name of the show bursting off the paper: DON'T GET ME STARTED. Every phone pole and bus stop in the city was plastered with my mug.

Each time I told my story to a TV or newspaper reporter, we sold more tickets.

There were people who cared. And they didn't go to see Frankie Valli, but they came to see me.

And after just two months of preparation, there I was on opening night in front of three hundred people in my hometown on a set that re-created my New York City apartment. I sat in a big overstuffed chair in my pajamas and talked about the media, feminism, war, politics, gay rights, and my own struggle with relevance.

The reviews were sensational. Caroline Hirsch flew in to see it. Months before, she had taken that little Monday night show and produced it in her club. Now it was a bigger Monday night show. Caroline was looking for a new way to make some noise. A year later, "Don't Get Me Started" was renamed "Scream of Consciousness" and she produced it in Boston. We sold it out for six weeks. The plan was to bring it to New York.

But you know what they say about plans: They make an ass out of you and me. Wait, that isn't what they say. At any rate, plans tend to change.

And change they did.

I RAISED YOU TO HAVE AN OPINION

I t was around 1999 when Dad's hospital episodes started to happen with some frequency. Whenever I got a call that he was admitted, I would rush to Minneapolis from New York, because having four siblings with four different opinions about the seriousness of the situation made it impossible to know its actual gravity. Was Dad "down for a few days," "on his deathbed," or somewhere in between? The possibilities were staggering. The odds of hitting the lottery were sometimes better than getting an accurate read on Dad's health status.

In the best-case scenario, my brother would be the one to reach me. He always made me feel like I could calmly prepare my trip with something simple like, "Dad is back in the hospital again and I'm going to check in with him after work." Clear and calm.

The worst-case scenario was if one of my sisters called me from the dire train: "D-D-D-DAAAAD-D . . . *sob . . . blubber . . . blubber . . . deep chest draw* . . . hospital . . . *chest draw blubber blubber* . . . you should get home."

Those were the calls when I would lose it, which, as it would turn out, had a direct correlation to how efficiently I packed. I would emotionally shut down and start to packuum.

packuum: /ˈpak-yüm/ v. *To pack luggage in a panic-stricken vacuum.*

And whenever I packuumed, I would open my suitcase in Minneapolis to find I'd made irrational choices, like bringing two pairs of Tevas and an old bridesmaid dress. But no sweater. Or underwear.

Eventually I just left clothes there.

I think Dad secretly loved going into the hospital, as it gave him the freedom he really never had at home: full control of the TV remote. He didn't have to sit through "As The World Turns" or "The Guiding Light," Mom's stories, and he could surf and bitch about how much he had to surf. And then he would interject ad hominem grumblings about the shit he saw in his twenty seconds of staying on each program. He was constantly editorializing—a nonstOp-ed.

"If Oprah Winfrey is so inspirational, why doesn't she 'inspire' people to turn off her show and go out and do something?" he barked at me as I entered his hospital room on one of my visits. "If she were any good at this motivation racket, her ratings would be in the shitter."

He had a point.

I must confess, I also secretly liked when Dad was in the hospital, too. When he was, I timed my daily visits for three P.M. That was the time that *Jeopardy!* (the exclamation point is for effect and also part of the trademark title of the show) aired locally. I would climb onto the bed with him, he would rub my hand, and we'd watch *Jeopardy!*

Watching *Jeopardy!* together was a ritual I started in college when I tried to find a way to avoid talking politics with him. He was endlessly frustrated at my liberalism, and I thought his Reaganitis was, well, acute. Our common ground was *Jeopardy!* We sat and watched the show, and for thirty minutes we screamed at the TV, not at each other. By showing off our general knowledge prowess, we proved to each other that even though we disagreed on a fundamental life philosophy, somehow shouting "What is the Sudetenland?" simultaneously and being correct meant that neither one could call the other stupid. It was the perfect détente.

But it left me perplexed.

When he beat me at *Jeopardy!*, I always thought to myself, *He hates idiots. How can he know so much stuff and still like Reagan?* When I won, he tossed out one of his many theories about how I turned out the way I did. In my early twenties he blamed it on the fact that I was brainwashed by the "bearded women's libbers" who taught "man-hating 101."

As I got older, we started fighting about issues, like the Iran-Contra Affair and the First Gulf War. That's when he added a new theory: "Maybe it's because you were conceived the night Kennedy won the election."

I liked that one. I counted back nine months, and it was totally plausible. I had no idea! How cool!

Then I foolishly asked, "Dad, how do you know that? How can you be sure?"

He simply replied, "I just know," in a voice that conjured up a visual I dared not wonder about further.

I didn't need any more details. And after I thought about it, I really didn't need *that* detail.

But it was when my comedy turned more political that he had the aha moment that made the most sense to both of us, because it was a combination of one of his twisted truths with our shared sense of humor. "Spook," he said—he called all of us kids spook; I had no idea it was also a bad word until I heard Archie Bunker use it—"I screwed up. I raised you to have an opinion, and I forgot to tell you it was supposed to be mine."

He said this quite a bit.

It was the way he called uncle, no matter who seemed to have the upper hand in the fight. It always made us laugh. And it helped me see that even though we fought bitterly, he loved the fact that he instilled the fight in me. He was proud I had an opinion, and he baited me to show it because when I was at my most passionate, he could most see himself in me. And the more political I got, the more I saw it, too.

But it wasn't until I overheard him on the phone one day that I had my own aha moment and realized how proud I am of being so much like him and how I had an obligation to live up to who he was.

I was in Minneapolis, booked to perform at a fund-raiser for a local pro-choice organization. In 1999, my folks had moved into a senior high-rise in Bloomington, Minnesota, a city just fifteen minutes from downtown Minneapolis. It was some sweet digs. The building had an exercise room, a library, a big sun porch, and a "party room." It was the kind of place you move to when you've sold the house but still wanted to live independently. I called it Club Medicare, or Club Meds for short.

I always stayed at Club Meds when I visited, and I always slept in my dad's bed because he slept in the recliner in the den. As his emphysema worsened, it was easier for him to breathe sleeping at a slant. Plus he could watch *Def Comedy Jam* late at night. He loved *Def Comedy Jam*. I often woke up in the middle of the night to the sound of his coughter at comedy material that made me blush even from a room away.

coughter: /ˈkawf-tər/ n. *A laugh that starts out from the belly, then transitions into a frightening cough.*

My dad's coughter started back when he was a three-pack-a-day Pall Maller. As his lungs got worse it became less laugh and more cough. It used to scare the shit out of me, then I learned to let him ride it out as he regrouped for fifteen minutes on the nebulizer.

And the *Def Comedy Jam* coughter was intense. I once made the mistake of asking him what it was about *Def Comedy Jam* that he loved so much.

"There's nothing funnier than a black guy begging for pussy," he matter-of-factly explained.

I will be honest and tell you what bugged me most about that comment wasn't the weird racism behind it, but the fact that I will never be a black guy begging for pussy. So in his eyes, my comedy would always be inferior to anything on *Def Comedy Jam*.

I have come to terms with this.

When I stayed with my folks, I usually woke up to the seven A.M. alarm that was Mom laying in bed saying the Rosary while simultaneously doing her leg exercises. "Oh, I'm sorry, did I wake you?" she would ask, knowing the leg bouncing and Hail Mary incantations were so loud, she could wake the whole building.

This morning was different.

I woke up to the deafening power of a pair of eyes staring at me. As I slowly opened one eye, Mom was standing over me, holding the local paper open to an ad for the event I was performing at. She had something to say. And I think had had to say it for about two hours.

"Why do you have to advertise your deal?"

"So we can raise money."

"To pay for abortions?"

"No, to pay for ways to torture you. Whatever is left over goes for abortion."

"You don't get it, do you?"

"You don't get *me*, do you?'

This was one of our typical aggressive-aggressive exchanges on the subject. We stopped talking. She went into the TV room and I needed to get out of the house.

Every time I spoke out publicly on the subject of abortion, I knew my parents died a little inside. They didn't hide it. They knew I went through "The Incident"—as my mother always called it—in high school, and if they had their way, it would have been an experience that was a private family matter, never to be spoken of again; something that would have been an endless source of self-evaluation that solidified my devotion to Catholicism.

I went in a different direction.

I tossed on some clothes and harrumphed into the TV room. Mom and Dad were doing something on the WebTV. Probably forwarding shitty joke e-mails to me so I would have them to look forward to when I got back.

"I'm going to get a Starbucks and *the New York Times*. I'll be back in a—"

This jarred my dad into a brief tirade. "For what? *The New York Times* is an Israeli-occupied territory. They should just print the Jerusalem public school lunch menus while they're at it."

"They already do, Dad." If nothing else, I can be very informative.

I got to Starbucks too late: Today's issue of *the Times* was sold out. I could hear Dad's voice in my head: "I guess all the Jews were up early today and beat you to it."

I didn't want to go back to Club Meds and sit in the thick humidity of anger and disappointment I had just left. But I had to. When I stormed out, I actually left my fucking purse in the kitchen. I don't leave the scene of an argument gracefully.

I drove home slowly and sulked back down the hallway to their apartment. I opened the door to hear Dad on the phone. He was angry. I could hear the red in his face from the front door.

"Who is this? Oh, you're not going to tell me your name. Well, let me tell you something. To call here and accuse my daughter of being a baby killer then not tell me who you are is cowardly horseshit. At least my daughter says what she thinks and doesn't hide who she is. I am proud I raised a daughter with some balls. Go to hell." I heard him angrily struggling to get the phone back on the receiver.

I took a breath before I walked into the TV room. Before I could say anything, Mom made the first move in our ongoing game of Let's Pretend This Never Happened.

"You forgot your purse. I made you some coffee."

"Thanks."

I kissed her on the forehead, then asked with great hesitation, "Who was that?"

"I don't know," Dad said. "Some broad who saw the ad for your show deal. She just called and started yelling shit and wouldn't tell me who she was. I hung up."

He just looked at me and took a hit of medicine from his asthma pipe. Then, as he pushed himself back into full recline, he said, "I raised you to have an opinion."

TWO DOGS, ONE CUP

I am a sucker for a rescue dog. I grew up with Susie, a cocker/ lab mix that lived to be fifteen. She was the last dog I had until I was in my forties because I couldn't justify getting another, as my life involved either being on the road forty weeks a year doing stand-up or working fourteen-hour days producing TV shows. I was well aware that caring for a dog was not responsible or practical, and so I resisted the urge. Then about seven years ago I started to crack. I noticed more and more homeless people in New York with mutts, never mind the endless footage of the stranded dogs of Katrina.

Then I discovered petfinder.com, that puppy porn website, and spent hours a day lusting after dogs I desperately wanted.

But what finally broke me was when that soul-wrenching ASPCA commercial hit the airwaves. You know the one: Dog after dog in those Abu Ghraib–looking cells, Sarah McLachlan's voice like a steak knife that had taken on a life of its own, stabbing and stabbing my heart. *"In the arms of the angel . . . "* *Dead*

Tears streamed down my face as those doe-eyed rib cages with fur mouthed messages to me personally: "Can I come live with you? Please?"

I would mouth back, "I can't. I have two shows in Canton, Ohio, this weekend."

But finally one day I caved.

Forget about the fact I was still working fourteen-hour days and was never in my apartment. All I needed was love, right?

Well, love and enough money for a dog walker twice a day. *I* had enough love to transform a dog's life no matter how hideous the previous living conditions. Dog fighting ring? Raised by the Taliban? Paris Hilton's purse prison? Distant memories.

And I had enough cash because I worked eighty hours a week! Yes! This was the ideal time to get a dog! Who cared that I hadn't had a dog since 1979? So what? Did I need to consult with someone for a second opinion? *No!* I had done this before. We got Susie when I was three and had her for fifteen years. I watched Mom raise her. That dog loved me. I gave her Arby's. I was sure that because I watched Mom raise a dog, I could do it again in a second. So yet again I indulged my knee-jerk know-it-all-know-nothing-ness, looked back at the TV screen, and said, "Okay, I give!"

Well, again, my heart was in the right place, but I jumped in way over my head.

Wearing a cement suit.

Holding a sleeper sofa.

And when I do this, I never, ever take even thirty seconds to gather the information responsible people get before making huge life-changing decisions, crucial information that one should *always* have to make smart choices when deciding to adopt a pet.

There were the obvious questions I should have asked, such as, "How much exercise do certain breeds need?" or "Does this dog shed a lot?" But more important, when it comes to a rescue dog, there are all sorts of telling buzzwords—code, if you will—I needed to be aware of when at a shelter. It's like knowing how to read between the lines a sleazy landlord feeds you when he's trying to rent you a crappy apartment.

Suppose the shelter volunteer said: "Oh, we love little Max. He is loyal, but also excitable, so he belongs in a household without small children, because they bring out his herding tendencies, which manifest in the form of mouth play."

What that really means: "We had to yank a newborn out of the clutches of little Maxie's jaw."

And this one is a classic: "Rex is a bit touch-sensitive."

Translation: "Rex will attack people who exhale near him."

I could have gotten all of this insight if I had made just one phone call to a friend who has rescued a dog, or worked at a rescue, or runs a rescue. I know all these people. I have performed at fund-raisers for animal shelters. *I know people who know what they're doing with dogs!*

But no. I decided love was all I needed.

Now, not only was I ignorantly impulsive, I took my ignorant impulsiveness one step further.

I decided that the ASPCA commercial had probably roped in enough blubbering suckers to give all those pups homes, and I didn't want to adopt from a cutesy place called something like Woofstock or A Paws, A Paws. Oh, no. I decided to go dogue rogue. I headed straight to the canine Green Mile: the Brooklyn Animal Care Center.

This was doggy death row. It made those cages in the Sarah McLachlan commercials look like Sandals Beach Resorts.

The volunteers here were hardcore. It was literally life or death for the animals there, so they poured it on. The woman who helped me was all of about twenty-three and walked me past rows and rows of cages, finally stopping at Candy, my first potential rescue.

Candy had caramel and white markings. She had big brown eyes and beautiful natural black eyeliner. When she saw me she hopped up from lying curled up on her bed of shredded newspaper to sit, and her ears perked up like one of those hats on *The Flying Nun*. But poor Candy had the frame of a sixty-pound dog and weighed about thirty-five.

The volunteer started her spiel as Candy pawed at me through the bars.

"Candy was received last night, dropped off by a homeless family who got into their own shelter. She is a four-year-old shepherd mix."

Mix is code for if the dog weighs more than thirty-five pounds, there is probably some pit bull in the mix.

"We have really come to love little Candy. She is passionate about the things she loves and cleans up after herself and others!"

Passionate and clean! I didn't even stop to think that, because Candy had been in the shelter less than twenty-four hours, any assessment about her should be met with some skepticism. I was too love-struck by her cocked head and attentive brown eyes to think clearly.

Then the volunteer dropped the bomb.

"If she is not adopted by the end of the week, she will be euthanized."

WRONG. WRONG. WRONG.

You are talking to Lizz Winstead, professional impulsive douche bag—a sucker! I will save Candy. Passionate, clean Candy will live!

"I'll take her," I said, like she was a cake I was bringing to a dinner party I was running an hour late for.

"Don't you want to see some other dogs, or walk her a bit, or think about—"

"No, I want her. She is exactly what I want."

That might have been the biggest lie I had ever uttered in my life. I hadn't the slightest idea of exactly what I wanted. And I had no idea what Candy was like.

I laid out my seventy-five bucks, and little Candy was mine. But let's be honest, the name had to go. *Candy* sounded like an underage stripper at one of those creepy New Jersey joints on a two-lane highway next to motels that rent by the minute. I wanted a name that would class her up a bit but still keep her edge, so I decided to go with Edie, after my favorite social misanthrope, Edie Beale, of *Grey Gardens* infamy. Never heard of her? Google it. Later.

Had I consulted someone with expertise prior to my impulsive trip to the Green Mile, I would have learned that the phrase *cleans up after herself and others* is code for *she eats poop*. And *passionate* means she's passionate about eating poop.

To coin a phrase, Edie was a shit-eating menace.

From the day I brought her home, every walk, every moment at the dog park, was a single-minded obsessive hunt for her to find shit and wolf it down.

Watching Edie's shitscapades is spellbinding. The carnal pleasure she derives as she gobbles it up is both repellent and hypnotic. When I watch her score an errant turd, the clear ecstasy on her face is so intense, so voracious, so focused, that I can't help wonder—if only for a misguided split second—if eating poop could possibly be the single most enjoyable activity since enjoyable activities have been documented throughout history.

Clearly I was no Cesar Millan, but even I knew that this was not ideal canine behavior, so within a week I contacted a trained professional and tried to end this problem. Not someone trained in shit-eating, mind you; someone trained in treating animals. They are called *veterinarians*, and from what I have come to learn, they went to college for eight years so they can charge $150 to poke at a dog's gums, squeeze its haunches, then offer up wild speculation about what is wrong with said pet. Always plan on paying at least $150 for every visit. It doesn't matter if the dog has a mild form of eczema or has gnawed off its own leg. And with each squeeze and poke, the charges escalate faster than the national debt clock.

On my first visit I was embarrassed to tell The Veterinarian exactly what my problem was, so I tried to be adult and danced around the problem.

"Edie seems to eat things she probably shouldn't," I said, like she had a sweet tooth.

"Like electrical cords or furniture?" The Vet asked matter-of-factly.

Yikes. I hadn't checked my cords or furniture. Maybe I had another problem I didn't even know about. But I couldn't worry about *that* now as I struggled to spit this one out.

"No. More like eating stuff she has *already* eaten."

Please don't make me say it, lady, it's awful. This was worse than the disappearing tampon conversation I once had with my gyno. Much worse.

"So she eats feces?" The Vet asked.

Thank you, Jesus.

"Yes, feces."

"Her feces, other dogs' feces, the cat's, yours?" she again asked matter-of-factly as she checked Edie's gums and gave her tush a squeeze.

Mine? Ugh. Well, at least other people had dogs more fucked up than mine.

"Others'," I said. And then I felt that wasn't clear, so I launched into an incoherent elaboration. "I mean other dogs'. Not 'others' as in 'You haven't listed the type of poop she likes.' Just dog, no other kind of poop that I know of. She hasn't really been exposed to a wide variety of poop." God, I sounded creepy. I just said "other kind of poop." What other kind? Cool Ranch? I was such an idiot.

The Vet seemed to be listening to me as she spent what I felt to be an excessive amount of time on Edie's gums. She didn't ask any more questions, but somehow from my meandering description and her gum inspection, she confidently made a diagnosis.

"Edie is eating poop because her diet is lacking . . . *something*."

Lacking what? I thought to myself. *E. coli?*

"I think if we move her to a raw meat diet she will start getting the nutrients she is craving, and this should stop her desire to get these nutrients in the way she is doing so currently."

Wow. You learned all that by poking around in her mouth? I knew I had zero information to draw my skepticism from, but eating poop seemed like a huge problem that a simple gingivitis check wouldn't detect.

I was now frustrated at myself for being so dog dumb and impulsive and tried to suppress an ugly tendency I have to blame someone else for my stupidity. I did not want to unleash Lizzilla on her.

Lizzilla is part of my type-A-hole personality. I latch on to something someone says that isn't *exactly* what *I* think, and within fifteen seconds I heap mounds of judgment on the alleged perp. It's hard to suppress and makes me feel the same way I do when I'm on a diet and cry while eating a family-size bag of Ruffles: I know it's wrong and bad, but I can't stop, and then I keep crying because I can't stop.

I have developed a self-awareness about it. I manage it by forcing myself to sit, hands in plain sight to make sure they remain implement free. Then I reevaluate. I breathe and think of all the positives in the situation I can muster.

This usually accompanies an internal screaming match with Lizzilla that, with each passing year, I win more often than she does.

This time, Lizzilla was set off by hearing yet another "expert" concoct a solution that felt like a bill of goods that up until this point she hadn't been able to sell to the average gravel-brained pet owner. Just like Father Hansen and that psych teacher. Combine this random diagnosis with my knee-jerk know-it-all-know-nothing-ness and round one with Lizzilla begins.

She is a doctor. She has degrees. Why couldn't it be a nutrition problem? It's someplace to start.

But Lizzilla fired back, mocking me. *A* doctor *of veterinary medicine. A* degree *that earned her the scientific prowess to conclude that eating raw meat would stop a dog from eating shit. You go with that, Lizz.*

I didn't have a clue what to do, so why listen to my inner bitch? Besides, I knew this vet had more education in her cuticles than I had in my whole DNA, so if she said raw meat is the solution because Edie's diet is lacking, um, *something*, then I was going with the professional on this, not Lizzilla's knee-jerk know-it-all-know-nothing-ness.

Bam! Lizzilla. Is. Served.

So off I went to the holistic pet food store to start Operation Fresh Breath. I plopped down two hundred bucks for the first month's worth of meat and headed home to begin Edie's wellness program.

It took just one day of raw meat madness to realize this time, Lizzilla was right. All this had done was turn my dog into a meat machine. She ate pure meat, pooped pure meat, then immediately ate the "meat" again. Seriously, they could have served her shit at Morton's. And while I couldn't tell for sure, I think with Edie's second poop on this diet she actually tried shitting right into her own mouth. The only silver lining was that for one whole day, she looked at me like I was the greatest mom ever.

It was the very definition of fresh hell.

I stopped that diet at once, and now, two hundred bucks down the drain, I had to fork out another $150 to see if *maybe* the good doctor had a plan B.

During the second visit I explained that the new solution just added a new chapter to the problem, and the $150-erinarian seemed nonplussed. She performed the obligatory gum and bum check again, but this time offered a very different expert diagnosis.

"Well, if it isn't an issue with her diet, it's probably psychological. Maybe Edie is eating her feces because she is . . . *bored.*"

Wow. Unbeknownst to me, my $150-erinarian was a pet vet *and* a pet psychiatrist. God, I wanted to be positive, but Lizzilla had other ideas.

Maybe she is a better shrink than a vet, I tried to convince myself.

But Lizzilla piped up, *Hello?? She used the same gum/bum trick to make a totally different diagnosis. If our shrink squeezed our ass and told us we had a little ennui, we would have her arrested.*

Then Lizzilla began to quack faintly but relentlessly. I thought that, too. But before I concluded that The Vet officially didn't know what she was talking about, she offered her prognosis: "You may want to get another dog to entertain Edie. You are very busy, and Edie would have a playmate that would distract her from eating poop. Smaller, younger, and male would be the best fit."

I wanted to bow at her feet. She, an expert, wanted me to get another dog.

She was a better shrink than a vet. I forgot my annoyance about the meat and rejoiced in her wisdom. My vet, an expert, during a consultation, *implored* me to get another dog.

Lizzilla stopped quacking and piped in, *I am sure the fact that this $150-erinarian will become a $300-erinarian has nothing to do with her recommendation.*

This is for Edie, I said. *I have to get another dog. I mean, a doctor—*

And before I could finish, Lizzilla interrupted: *Of veterinary medicine.*

—*ordered it. I am obligated. It's almost a law in some states.*

I went home, and plan B for Operation Fresh Breath began.

I got Buddy about two weeks later while on a trip home to Minneapolis. I couldn't spend one more extracurricular Target outing with Mom, so I suggested a trip to the local Humane Society to visit dogs.

It was a muggy ninety degree day, and Mom agreed. With conditions.

"I am not getting out of the car; you have to bring the dogs to me." And "You are not going to take home one of these dogs. It's impractical and stupid."

Who needed Lizzilla when you had Momzilla sitting next to you in your rental car?

So I brought a few dogs out to the car for Mom to see. She pet them, noncommittal but enjoying them.

Then I brought out Paco, a little spaniel/corgi combo, who jumped up on her lap, licked her face, then curled up and fell asleep.

"The lady inside said he is protective and curious," I told her.

Mom pet his head and he nestled further into her and sighed. "You should get this dog."

So much for being a voice of reason. Momzilla was bitten by the rescue bug. She didn't even have to see the ASPCA commercial.

So this time I forked over a hundred bucks—it's more expensive when you don't rescue from death row, and a tad more thorough. I had to fill out some paperwork saying I was fit to be a dog owner—*ahem*, I hoped nobody at the shelter noticed I'd left an eighty-five-year-old woman in a hot car while I filled out the papers saying I was a fit caregiver.

Paco became Buddy, as in Edie's buddy. He was *protective* and *curious*: more code. *Protective* = barks constantly. *Curious* = will dig in your hamper, drag a thong into the living room, and chew the crotch out in front of friends at a dinner party.

Bud enjoyed the undies; so what? He doesn't eat poo! Yay! But he makes poo! Boo!

When I brought Buddy home, almost instantly he and Edie fell in love with each other. Not because Buddy alleviated Edie's boredom, but because Buddy was Edie's personal soft-serve shit machine. Now Edie was really convinced I was the greatest mom ever.

She was in heaven.

I was in an even fresher hell.

And so I returned to The Vet, even though Lizzilla's quacking was on a loop. If you are keeping score, The Vet is 0 for 2, Lizzilla 2 for 2. With these stats, I had no choice but to listen to Lizzilla *and* take a closer look at The Vet's diploma. I mean, seriously, did she study at Make-Shit-Up-As-You-Go-Along Community College?

Mustering up the last of my civility, I informed her Buddy wasn't distracting Edie, but playing a more "friend with benefits" role.

"Wow, it's usually one of these two things," the $300-erinarian said as she reached for Edie's mouth for the gum check.

"Don't bother," I snapped. "They're probably brown, and her haunches are fine."

"Well, I am out of medical ideas, *but* I have had some clients tell me they have had luck with a home remedy."

What? Now we had gone from only two "medical" possibilities to suggestions from other stupid dog owners who fell prey to Sarah McLachlan's caterwauling? That was all she had? And I bet this will cost me $150.

Well, I was desperate. So against my better judgment I asked—

"Do you ever have good judgment?" you ask. "Fuck you," I say.

The Vet: "And that is?"

"Well, some clients *have* had luck sprinkling Tabasco on the feces whenever they see them."

What . . . the . . . fuck.

After three visits and hundreds of dollars in failed diagnoses and expensive meat, this vet's final solution was that I was to walk my dog on the streets of New York, and every time I happened upon an errant turd (which is about every three feet) I should pull out a bottle of Tabasco and season it? It's bad enough that my dog eats shit; now this ripoff-erinarian wanted me to become someone whom mothers pull their children away from and scurry across the street because I am the crazy neighborhood lady who is the shit sous-chef?

Well, believe it or not, I still had a shred of dignity, so I rejected that idea completely and rejected this quacktor of veterinary medicine as well. I have resigned myself to the fact that I own a shit eater. A lovable, adorable shit eater. And after running out of professional ideas, I came up with one of my own.

The $5.99 doggie toothbrush.

So I never discovered a cure for Edie, but I did find a means to tolerate her behavior, and there's a life lesson in here somewhere, I think.

M eanwhile, it turned out that cute and sweet-tempered Buddy was an undiscriminating pisser. He couldn't really differentiate between indoors and outdoors, a table leg from a hydrant.

I needed to find a new veterinarian to help. Actually having learned something from this experience, this time I asked some pet-owning friends to suggest someone, and after getting a lot of different suggestions—all of which came with the same unhelpful selling point ("My vet really loves animals!")—I realized it's all a crapshoot. So I went with convenience. I chose the vet closest to my house.

I explained the whole peeing issue and, after much cooing and fawning over Buddy, the gum and ass squeezing, this new $300-erinarian said, "It could be a number of things: bladder infection, kidney stones, bladder stones." *Or any other combination of those two words,* I think to myself. But then she startled me by saying something that made sense to me. "We are going to need a urine sample to figure this out."

Wow, a test to see what's wrong! How novel. Now I was kind of psyched. These are all problems that maybe can be treated! *I* have been treated for all these things, *and* I didn't have to get a third dog to cure them!

My excitement, however, was short-lived.

The $300-erinarian matter-of-factly explained I have to bring in not just a urine sample, but a "clean" urine sample.

"How do I do that?" I asked, dreading the answer.

"You simply have to place a container under him and catch the urine midstream, then bring it in for the test."

It wasn't just what she said, but the way she said it—as if every good pet owner should already know how to do this. And I, with my embarrassment about being such a terrible owner, failed to ask for instructions, plopped down another $150, and headed home to figure out how to catch urine from a male dog without ending up coated like a porn fetishist.

To my great surprise, there was nothing obvious in my apartment appropriate for catching dog piss midstream. So I put on my crafty hat and, after digging through some kitchen drawers and my recycling, I fashioned together a pee-catching contraption by duct-taping a small plastic cup that soy sauce came in from my favorite Chinese restaurant to a wooden spoon. I became the MacGyver of urine extraction.

Off we went, Buddy and I. And whatever shred of dignity I had salvaged by refusing to spice up turds like they were fingerling potatoes? It disappeared as I sheepishly inserted my cup-on-spoon into Buddy's urine stream. In front of a babyGap. I get about a thimble full. *Good enough,* I say to myself and fumble in my pockets to find the . . . *Jesus, I don't have the lid.* So I was forced to walk through the East Village with a cup of pee taped to a spoon, trying not to spill it. Now I *am* the crazy lady in the neighborhood taking some pee for a stroll.

I decided to go directly back to the vet, as I didn't know the shelf life of clean dog urine, nor did I know the open container laws in New York City for urine, although I suspect they are very liberal.

"I have Buddy's sample," I said as I tried to hand it to the receptionist.

"Oh," she said as she tentatively reached for it. "You made this yourself?"

"Yes, I did," I said, beaming with pride at my craftasticness.

"Was there something wrong with the urine collection kit we provide?"

Ugh. I wanted to throttle her.

"Well, we'll run tests on this, and the doctor will call you in twenty-four hours with the results," the receptionist said.

When the phone rang the next morning, the $300-erinarian was all business.

"Buddy's urine has a high white count. Combine that with his frequent urination in the house, and we think he has bladder stones."

"What's the next step?" I asked reluctantly.

"We are going to place him on a prescription diet, food that breaks up the crystals, and after two weeks, we look at another clean urine sample to check his progress."

"And where do I get this food?"

"You have to buy it from us, and it's twenty-five dollars a case, which should last about ten days. Then you should blah, and then blah, and if you blah . . ." As she droned on, I tuned out, trying to figure out how much money I can get for my plasma to offset Buddy's new gourmet diet.

". . . so come on in and pick it up after three."

"K. Thanks." And then I remember. "Can I pick up one of your collection kits?"

"Sure. But if you bring him here in a cab, we can extract it for you. Unless you would prefer to do it yourself."

Lizzilla, I'm way ahead of you.

After two weeks on his medical gruel, whaddaya know, Buddy had stopped peeing in the house. We hopped out of the cab and I gleefully professed to the now genius vet that Buddy is much better. A-okay. So after a quick gum and rump check, she takes him away to do the "extraction" and would have the results for me in "minutes," which turned out to mean sixty minutes, give or take ninety minutes.

After sitting in the waiting room for two hours with Buddy, I was called back into the examining room. The results weren't what we had hoped. Even though Buddy had developed a keen sense of what objects are deemed appropriate to pee on, his white count was still high.

"Soooo," starts the $300-erinarian, "it looks like we have the crystals under control, but because the white count is still high, he may have a bladder infection. So we should start him on ten days of antibiotic *a-ching, ca-ching, ca-ching, ca-ching* . . ."

All I heard was the sound of my savings account depleting. By my calculations, I had hemorrhaged close to a thousand bucks on canine waste issues, and this was when I realized I was utterly beholden to the diagnostic whims of these doctors of whatever. And yet I agreed to do whatever it took, pay whatever it cost for Buddy's and Edie's theoretical analysis, because I had fallen prey to the Sarah McLachlan syndrome.

I raised my personal debt ceiling another four hundred dollars for my office visit, lab results, and ten days of some pill called Zeniquin, and for the next week and a half Buddy's life consisted largely of ingesting prescriptions. Breakfast and dinner, I crushed up his antibiotic, put it in his prescription food, and watched for I-don't-know-what because he seemed fine now. Ten days later he still seemed fine, with the added benefit that he'd developed an affinity for cab rides.

By now I felt like a regular at this place, and the whole experience had become rote, like sex in a loveless marriage. Hi, hi, squeeze, squeeze, let's get some pee, wait, wait, can we just get this over with?

Apparently not.

"So, the crystals are still under control, there is no infection, but he still has white cells in the urine. We need to do an ultrasound to see how we can spend all the money you were saving for those boots you really wanted, that new couch you had your eye on, your own health insurance, a bottle of wine, the occasional . . . It'll be around six hundred dollars for the test, the X-rays, and the shave."

I guess I can forgo my mammogram this year to see what's up with Buddy's bladder.

Take him, shave him, sonogram him, blow him, I don't care, just find out why he is not acting sick anymore, I thought to myself. At this point, I was utterly defeated.

"And," adds the who-knows-how-much-this-will-run-you-erinarian, "if the sonogram doesn't show us anything, the next option is surgery."

Just before I asked how much of a home equity loan I should take out for this procedure, the vet said, "We will discuss those costs if the time comes."

With that, I dragged myself to the waiting room, and after about forty-five minutes, some twenty-year-old who-knows-how-much-this-will-run-you-erinarian-in-training came to find me. "We found the problem, and we need you to come to the back with us."

I was scared, but not too scared, because they didn't take me to the room with no window. Be forewarned: If any who-knows-how-much-this-will-run-you-erinarian brings you to the room with no windows, it's curtains.

I was expecting to be looking at an X-ray, but instead there was Buddy, lying on his back with a fully shaved abdomen.

He looked so vulnerable.

"What was the problem?" I asked. "Does he have a tumor, or some other problem that involves the word *tract*?"

"No." And with the straightest of faces, the aide said, "Buddy's penis is covered in smegma, and it was flaking off into his urine samples, causing the high white cell count."

Did I just hear that?

"Flaking off?" I repeated.

Again, without so much as a smirk, she said, "Aren't you happy?"

I didn't know what I was besides totally nauseated.

When I asked her why, for the love of God, he had smegma on—no wait—*covering* his penis, she replied, "Well, obviously because he doesn't lick his penis."

Right. Obviously.

Now I have to sit down, because after scouring all those fucking websites and falling in love with a zillion dogs, all of whom I wanted to give a loving home to, how is it that I chose the only dog in the history of dogs that doesn't lick his dick?

It's because my mom picked him out, I know it. I shall blame her.

Just then, the who-knows-how-much-this-will-run-you-erinarian walked in. Unluckily for her, the amount of patience I had left equaled the amount of money I had left in my bank account.

Before she said a word, I barked. Not Lizzilla, me. "I have brought my dog here four different times to treat a peeing problem. You personally extracted urine from him twice, and no one ever thought, at any one of those junctures, to actually look at his penis until now? You checked his gums four fucking times; did you think he was *pissing through his mouth*?"

And she came back at me with this: "Well, some things are the owner's responsibility."

I stared at her blankly, seething that she accused me of being the only dog owner who was not doing a regular penis check on her dog. I hated her. Again, not Lizzilla. Me. The amount of money I spent should have bought me at least *one* cock exam.

"But I have a solution," she said. There was that matter-of-fact tone again! They must all learn that in school. How did this fucking doctor of veterinary medicine have the balls to tell me, after all this, that she had a solution? Put Tabasco on his wiener? I wanted to punch her, but then I saw something in her hand. It was a bottle full of liquid—not Tabasco, but a literal solution as the solution.

She handed it to me. "It is a special cleanser. You just squirt some on a cotton swab and then twice a day clean off the smegma."

Twice a day! I have to wash my dog's cock twice a day? Am I being *Punk'd*?

"So," I asked begrudgingly, "just how long do I have to do this? And how much does this cleanser cost?"

"I told you, every day, twice a day. A bottle should last you about six months and is $270. You can pay up front."

A bottle of cockwash. The cleanser I use on my dog's wiener costs $270, and the cleanser I use to wash my face costs $20. What is the secret of this stuff? Can I use it on *my* face? So many questions that would go unanswered.

I wandered up to the reception desk and cashed out the $545 for this round: the visit, the lab work (they had the gall to charge me $50 for the shave), the cockwash, and Buddy and I strolled home poorer but wiser.

I finally took a moment to be thankful that Buddy was healthy, albeit a bit funky. And I'm even more thankful for the person who invented cockwash, because if someone hadn't, that office visit could have ended with the phrase "Since Buddy doesn't seem to lick his penis, you are going to have to do it for him." Sure, I would have saved $270, but I would have cashed in the last of my dignity. Dog owners always say we would do anything for our dogs. I learned that day where I would have drawn the line.

I AM
MRS. WINSTEAD

Never having had kids, I learned most of my skills at dealing with really tricky emotional situations from my relationships with dogs or men who behaved like dogs. But as my parents got older, I had to learn a new emotional game I call "The Role Reversal of Fortune." This is when the child must become the parent and tries to do so without the parent catching on. Prepare yourself; it happens to everyone.

For some families it starts when you have to take the car keys away or convince them to sell the house. My folks sold our childhood home in good health, and my dad decided all on his own not to drive anymore and replaced his car with a fancy-ass cherry red scooter that he hung blue fuzzy dice on. For the Winsteads, it was wrestling with the next phase of life, dealing with the question "How do you know when it's time to talk to your parents about assisted living?" The signs are different for every family. For some it becomes clear when one parent has trouble with simple clarity, such as not being able to differentiate between the phone and the iron, or maybe their spouse and the iron.

For my siblings and me, one important sign was the day we found out a thirty-year-old homeless crack addict had entered the second floor apartment of Club Meds and robbed them.

In the middle of the afternoon.

While they were both napping.

Upright on the couch.

During *Jeopardy!*

My parents had spent many years at their transitional apartment, Club Meds. The occupants of Club Meds ran the gamut of Minnesota diversity: Swedish, Norwegian, German. All of the stoic European fair-skinned ethnicities were represented.

Anyone roaming the halls under the age of fifty stuck out like a sore thumb; anyone darker than a Dane set off alarms.

The double doors of the building's main entrance faced the office and were equipped with the same security system used by the CIA at Langley. From nine A.M. to five P.M. the office was occupied by the manager, and there were always a few tenants in there getting a replacement mail key or trying to find out if the $3.50 bus ticket to the Mall of America included lunch. There was also the unofficial border patrol, whom I not so euphemistically dubbed the Coffee Comitatus.

This watchdog group, made up of four or five stalwart seniors, would gather every day at a table a few feet from the entrance and while away their afternoons chatting about the weather, the war—*their* war, mind you—and the weather during *their* war. (Tom Brokaw really opened a Pandora's box of egomaniacs with that whole "Greatest Generation" thing.) They quipped and sipped every day from mugs with sidesplitting slogans like I'M TOO SEXY TO BE 75! or STOP ME BEFORE I VOLUNTEER AGAIN.

One afternoon I noticed one that simply read ZYPREXA ZYPREXA ZYPREXA. I didn't get the joke, so I Googled *Zyprexa* and found it was "The most popular antipsychotic drug on the market." I guess it goes well with coffee.

But as soon as someone approached that front door, their conversational strolls down memory lane came to a screeching halt and they turned their attention to watch as some poor soul struggled to get in. Whether it was the mailman fumbling with his sixty-pound key ring or a deliveryman trying to keep his pink invoice tucked under his chin as he hauled a few milk crates full of bread, none of the posse got up to let anyone in. It would only be a four-step walk and one cane push on the big silver disk engraved with a blue wheelchair to magically make those big glass doors open and unburden those bringing them *their* supplies. But even Minnesota Nice had its limits.

It was maddening. And it was worse if you weren't a delivery person, because if you weren't sporting some kind of uniform indicating you were there to bring them stuff, once you got through the doors, you faced an inquisition.

One exchange I struggled through went like this:

"Who are you here to see?"

"I am Ginny and Wilbur's youngest, Lizz."

"Are you the comedian from New York or the other one?"

Ouch. There are four "other ones."

Maybe that's how Crackula got in, claiming to be the "other one."

Maybe you start doing crack because someone in your life referred to you as the "other one."

So how in the world did a thirtysomething African-American crack addict penetrate this force field? Mom swore she didn't buzz anyone in. I kind of believe her. Had the robber used the intercom system, the frustration of trying to get buzzed in probably would have momentarily overridden her desperation, as it involved talking (read: shrieking) at the resident through a giant speaker that had the sound quality of a Taco Bell drive-through, and patience is not a virtue of most crackheads.

The actual dialing system involved searching a directory that had an endless scrolling process with codes and # signs that seemed more conducive to a Stephen Hawking theorem than letting my folks know I was downstairs with their lemon drops and Kleenex. The Kleenex they forced me to buy at the Target ten miles away because it was fifteen cents cheaper than the same Kleenex at the Walgreens, which was located on the ground floor of their building. The cube-shaped Kleenex that fit in the peach-and-blue stenciled Kleenex box cover in the bathroom. That matched the peach-and-blue finger towels.

That Kleenex.

Once I connected with them through the intercom, some variation of this back-and-forth took place:

"Yah, hello."

"Mom, it's Lizz."

"Who?"

"Lizz."

"Who?"

"Your great source of disappointment."

"Oh, Lizz, are you here?"

"Yes, buzz me in!"

"Let me turn on channel 7 and watch you come up."

Channel 7 was the in-house TV channel that showed a split screen of both the building's front and back entrances. My parents watched it for hours on end to see who got their oxygen tank refilled or who got hauled away in an ambulance. Mom liked to continue our conversation while she stared at me on the TV.

"I'm not sure I like this hairstyle on you."

Five seconds ago she couldn't even tell it was me, but that doesn't stop her from starting in.

"Just let me in! You can insult me when I get up there."

"Okay, hold on. Wilb, do I push five to let her—"

Buzzzzzzzzzzzzzzzzzzzzzzzzzzzzzzzzzzzzzzzzzzzzzzzzzzzzzzzzzzzzzzzzzzzzzzzzzzzzzzzzzzzzzzzzzzzzzzzzzzzzzzzzzzzzzzzzzzzzzzzzzzzzzzzzzzzzzzzzzzzzzzzzzzzzzzzzzzzzzzzzzzzzzzzzzzzzzzzzzzzzzzzzzzzz I was through both doors, walking down the hall to the elevator *buzzzzzzzzzzzzzzzzzzzzzzzzzzzzzzzzzzzzzzzzzzzzzzzzzzzzzzzzzzzzzzzzzzzzzzzzzzzzzzzzz* walking past the decorative teapot collection *buzzzzzzzzzzzzzzzzzzzzzzzzzzzzzzzzzz* walking into the elevator *buzzzzzzzzzzzzzzzzzzzzzzzzzzzzzzzzzzzzzzzzzzzzzzzzzzzzzzzzzzzzzzzzzzzzzzzzzzzzzzzz* stepping off the elevator on the second floor *buzzzzzzzzzzzzzzzzzzzzzzzzzzzzzzzzzzzzzzzzzzzzzzzzzzzzzz* walking down the hall past six doors that each have a fake flower arrangement tacked to it *buzzzzzzzzzzzzzzzzzzzzzzzzzzzzzz* into their apartment *buzzzzzzzzzzzzzzzzzzzzzzzzzzzzzzzzzzzz*

"Oh, you're here" *buzzzzzzzzzzzzzzzzz*—dial tone.

You would have thought that with all the codes and buzzing and interrogations you needed to gain access that the actual apartment doors would have dead bolts and card keys and force fields, right?

Maybe some of them did.

But not my folks'.

Oh, no.

Once past the javarazzi, anyone could waltz right into their apartment and help themselves to a few Werther's from the bowl on the living room coffee table and then just saunter into the bathroom and grab as much jewelry as they could fit in their pockets. It usually sat there on the vanity, spilling out of a box, right next to that peach-and-blue stenciled Kleenex box holder and the bowl o' floss picks.

Neither of my parents had a clue what had happened the day they were robbed, so the following is a piecemeal recounting from a conversation (or rather, the traditional Winstead interrupt-a-thon) I had with them as they both tried to explain how the break-in—er, stroll-in may have taken place. As these are Wilbur and Ginny Winstead, there will be a few digressions.

"Okay, Mom, how do you think this happened?"

"Well, between your father and I, we get about four hours of sleep . . ."

My folks always complained they could only sleep a few hours at night. I have a sneaking suspicion that might be due in part to the fact that they took afternoon naps so intense that they had to nap after the nap to feel rested.

"... and we must have left the door unlocked on the off chance one of you kids might stop by ..."

Notice the dig? The "off chance." That door was *never* locked.

"... so we both had dozed off for just a minute ..."

A *minute*? Let the under-exaggerating begin.

Now Dad chimed in, patting his right side.

"And I always keep my wallet in this pocket."

Are you still with us? This minute-long nap of my dad's was so deep and so powerful that a ham-fisted crack addict was able to steal his wallet from the pants he was wearing.

At this point I have to admit I have had some interaction with the crack-addled in my day—I live in New York City, after all—and in none of my experiences did they possess that catlike finesse of Cary Grant in *To Catch a Thief*, silently slinking in and out of the shadows and blending into the scenery, artfully snatching valuables with nary a peep or disturbing a thing.

No, the permeating stench of a crack addict's lips alone should be enough to rouse a brown bear in February. Add to that, the carpeting in every room at Club Meds was littered with petrified toast droppings mixed with more than a few dropped pills. Not even the most balletic burglar could have silenced the crunching on the Winstead wall-to-wall.

Any one of these things should jog you out of your post-nap nap. Not Wilbur and Ginny. They slept right through the stench, the crunching, and the rifling, so the thief got away with *both* of their wallets and some jewelry. The fact that it was so easy to rob them set off the dreaded first "Maybe it's time to talk about assisted living" thought in my head.

I had a pretty good working knowledge of their routine; eating, napping, TV, spamming me with e-mails, eating, more napping. I tentatively asked my next question: "So when did you realize you had been robbed?"

Mom jumped on that one. "Well, it wasn't until the middle of the night when the phone rang. Your dad finally answered it, but he was clearing his throat so I couldn't hear anything."

My dad's emphysema and asthma had gotten really bad at this point, and extensive clearing of his throat had now become part of his speech pattern.

Dad now continued the story. "So I—*clearing throat, CLEARING THROAT*—picked up the phone: 'Hell—*clearing throat*—o?'

"'Is this Mr. Winstead?'

"'*clearing throat*—Yes.'

"'Yo, this is your bank and I need your PIN number.'"

Now my exasperation was slowly turning to concern. "Yo, this is your bank" in the middle of the night didn't cause him to hang up.

Luckily, one of the many twentieth-century breakthroughs my parents never embraced was an ATM card, and forget about the concept of a PIN. My mom wrote checks for everything—cab fare, lunches, the beauty shop. The problem here was they were from that era of people who put every single piece of personal information on their checks. Name, address, date of birth, driver's license number, Social Security number, AARP number, Medicare number, children's addresses, a few saints' days, and, of course, their phone number. They were an identity thief's wet dream.

"But wait, Dad," I interrupted. "This guy didn't give you his name. Didn't you wonder why the bank was calling you so late?"

"Well, I was dozing off and on and I—*clearing throat*—wasn't sure what time it was. Plus, I was trying to figure out what a goddamn PIN number was. I wasn't gonna give it to him if I didn't know what it was!—*clearing throat, clearing throat.*"

Um, right. I was so relieved.

"I kept asking, 'What's a PIN number? What's it for?' I kept asking this—*clearing throat*—banker. So he tells me it's some kinda code."

Mom had been sitting there not interrupting him and could no longer bear it. "So your dad called to me from his recliner. 'Ginny!' Now I'm up and worried. Is someone hurt? Is it one of the kids, is it—"

Dad was now frustrated that she was helping tell the story.

"I was trying to get your mom to listen. She never listens."

Um, she's sitting right here.

"No—*clearing throat*—I tried to tell her, but she kept listing off all you kids to see if one of you was hurt. So I finally got her to stop yapping and told her the bank was on the phone and they needed our PIN number and I didn't even know what the hell it was."

Their bickering was a welcome piece of normal, so my dread stabilized. Then Mom offered up the most reasonable part of the story so far.

"I didn't know what this PIN was, either, so I shouted back to your dad, 'Tell them to call back in the morning.' And I do too listen."

For the record, neither of them were great listeners.

"Your mom was no help, so I tell the guy, 'Call back in the morning so I can figure out what the hell you want.' Then I hung up."

Then there was a bit of a setback as Mom innocently chimed in, "We forgot all about that call until later the next day."

The fact that they forgot all about the call was, oh, more than a bit troubling for me. I thought for sure my dad would have gotten up at five A.M., called the bank to get to the bottom of what the hell a PIN number was. But no. He was busy. The coffee club was meeting downstairs, and lunch, then of course *Jeopardy!* was on at three, so all the day's activities had relegated the three A.M. call from last night to a distant memory.

So I pushed Mom for the details.

"When did you start to figure out something was weird?" I asked, hoping for a glimpse of clarity, because apparently receiving a late-night call from someone slurring, "Yo, this is your bank and I need your PIN number" triggered nothing. "Did the crook call back?"

"No, but Target called."

"Mom! I already picked up your prescriptions at Target. Please tell me what happened next. This is scary!" I was on dread alert at how nonplussed my folks were while telling me the story. Maybe it was because they slept through the whole robbery and didn't realize what would have happened if they woke up. All I thought about was what would have happened if they had.

Did the thief grab a knife from the kitchen before he walked into the TV room? Would he have cracked my mom over the head with her statue of St. Jude? Rip Dad's oxygen from his nose? I hoped these things never would occur to my parents.

And now Mom wanted to talk about Target.

"Don't interrupt me, Lizz! This thief went to Target, they smelled a rat and called us!"

For the record, sometimes I, too, am not a great listener. It is genetic. We are a family of Winsterrupters.

I thought Dad had dozed off, but he was listening, waiting for just the right move back into the convo.

"Tried to buy up the whole store!" Then a big grin came over his face and he began to chuckle, shoulders and belly bouncing up and down. His recliner shook a bit and he had to sit up. "She wrote a check for the haul from your mom's account and signed it *Mrs. Winstead.*"

Then he started in with the coughter.

Now I was totally confused. "She?" I asked. "I thought a guy called you last night?" Mom took the coughter as an opportunity to continue.

"It's all very confusing. The guy on the phone was working with a woman. She's the one who broke in, then went to Target. The checkout girl thought signing the check *Mrs. Winstead* was a bit odd, and she asked this girl for ID."

More under-exaggeration.

This was where the story got pretty great.

The crackpot, without any hesitation, proceeded to pull out Mom's Discover card and photo ID. Upon examination of the ID, our clever clerk's suspicions were heightened.

The woman standing before her was an African-American woman in her thirties. The woman pictured in the photo ID was a Swedish woman in her eighties.

Now, we all know crack ravages your face. But I, and obviously the gumshoe at the register, had never seen effects so severe that someone ages fifty years and their ethnic makeup changes from white to black. Not even on *Dateline.* Not to mention that no one under seventy-five has a Discover card.

Leave it to Ginny to sum it up a bit more succinctly.

"Well, the girl writing the check looked nothing like me!" That may be the biggest under-exaggeration ever uttered. "So I get a call from Target security. Thank God my phone number is on the check." Yes, thank God. "I thought it was the pharmacy."

Mom went over every friggin' detail.

" 'This is Target calling, to whom am I speaking?'

" 'Virginia Winstead. Oh, are my prescriptions ready?' "

Then Mom switched out of dialogue with the Target person and continued in her words, clarifying that it was Target *security* and that they asked if she had her checkbook. But her excitement launched her back in:

" 'Well, I haven't left the house for two days,' and then she said, 'Well, I have someone here who has just written a check with this phone number printed on it. Do you have an African-American daughter who may be picking up a few things for you?' " She switched out of dialogue again. "A black daughter? Can you imagine?"

This kind of verbal spin cycle while recounting a story was also a sign that the assisted living chat was closer than I thought.

"So I had her hang on while I went into the bedroom to get my purse."

Mom kept her purse on the bedroom nightstand on top of her mound of prayer cards and rosaries. I've never understood this. Who needs a purse in the bedroom? Who needs a little lipstick before lights-out? And no one smokes in bed anymore. I suspected it was in the hope that one of those times she asked me to go get it for her, I would see that massive statue of St. Jude and be inspired to rejoin the flock.

"Anyway . . ."

Uh-oh. She just said *anyway*, the adverb that leads to the kind of meandering detail that drives daughters to have sex with dangerous men.

"I looked through every pocket of my purse. The outside one where I only keep hand lotion and tissues, the interior zipper pocket where I keep a compact, a few lemon drops, and some tape, both the slot for my keys and . . ."

As she yammered about the sum of her pocketbook contents, I zoned out imagining sex with one of those guys on *Lockup* and then picturing ole cracky lifting Mom's wallet and popping one of those fur-coated lemon drops in her mouth as she tried to spit out the mystery fuzz.

Finally Mom started *nearing* the point.

"I picked up the extension in the bedroom. We have to get a new phone; white phones get dirty so fast, it's terrible. Where were we?"

You were describing the bowels of your purse and I was bent over a visitors' table at San Quentin, I said to myself. I reminded her with a bit less detail. "You were just about to get back on the phone with Target."

"My checkbook was gone, my credit cards were gone, and so was my identification card. I don't recall giving them to anyone." (Translation: "I don't know any black people.") "The lady from Target said she would take care of this and call me back. So I walked back into the TV room and woke up your dad. 'Windy'"—this was Dad's nickname, as he was a bit of a talker—"'I think we were robbed while we were home,' and I asked him to check for his wallet."

Dad had now returned from the nebulizer just in time to take over the story.

"'Whaddaya mean—*CLEARING THROAT*—check? It's in my pocket.

It's always in my pocket.' But I checked anyway to make your mother happy, and guess what?"

I decided to go out on a limb. "No wallet?"

"No wallet. Maybe I left it on the kitchen counter. Sometimes I did that."

Now, he may very well have left it on the counter, but even thirty years ago, as a teenager, I had no trouble reaching into his pockets while he sawed logs, snatching a fiver from his wallet, and putting it back without his making a stir.

"I just couldn't for the life of me figure when we could have been robbed."

And then, finally, the late-night phone call from his "bank" came back to him.

"So I started to think, maybe it wasn't really the bank that called us last night."

This reminded Mom. "Oh, you know, I never called them today about that PIN deal."

"Mom! The bank didn't call you!"

Dad shared his lightbulb moment: "I think it was the thieves," he said, mastering the obvious. "But what's a PIN number?"

"Dad, it's a code for your bank card or credit card to take out cash withdrawals."

My mom perked up. "You can take cash off the credit card?"

They indeed were robbed.

Surprise!

My folks called Target back and the Bloomington cops arrived and hauled this Fulbright Scholar masquerading as Virginia Winstead down to the station. The crack addict still insisted she was "Mrs. Winstead" during her questioning, even though she couldn't immediately recall her first name, which to be fair is behavior that a crack addict might share with my mom.

But the last twist to the story was what dealt our amateur identity thief her final blow. You see, the Bloomington cops were familiar with the name Winstead, as it was also the surname of the mayor, the fifty-two-year-old son of one eighty-two-year-old Virginia Winstead. The same eighty-two-year-old woman pictured in the ID.

Oops.

By now, even if she had given an Oscar-winning performance convincing the cops she was Mrs. Winstead, nature would be the final judge and jury, as it had never produced a son twenty-two years older than his mother.

The crack addict finally realized this was the end of the line and explained to the cops how she followed in a delivery guy, then dashed down the hall and up the back stairs to escape the "old white folks just sittin'." I knew how she felt. The second door on the left was not only open, it was ajar.

She waltzed in.

In the middle of the afternoon.

While they were both napping.

Upright on the couch.

During *Jeopardy!*

I didn't ask if the wallet was on the kitchen counter.

It was time to talk to our folks about assisted living.

THE TWENTY-FIVE-CENT SPA

When it comes to travel, if you are one of those people who try to sound interesting by saying things like, "I want to experience the pure culture of every country I visit," stop it right now.

Why? Because guess what: Sometimes you really don't.

At least not for the reasons you think. And how one handles the shit outside one's comfort zone is how a person should be judged as a traveler. Maybe even as a person.

It's so easy to toss around that kind of travel babble. Just don't confuse the fact that simply because your inner Bourdain would never dream of drinking Starbucks in Rome that you are going to be willing to feast on the pituitary gland of a monkey's brain in some far-off land.

When you really decide to immerse yourself into the daily life of another culture, don't be disappointed if it's a very different experience from the one your little Western fantasy promised you it would be. And if it completely shatters your fantasy and challenges you to rethink your values, take it in and maybe you will discover all your know-it-all worldliness is a complete load of crap.

I can say this with confidence because I could repave the streets of Brooklyn with the self-important bullshit I have spewed over the years. Such lessons came to me from a vacation I took to Spain and Morocco several years ago.

One of my companions was my old friend Sharon, a jewelry designer, yogi, and photographer, who kind of looks like a bohemian version of Carrie Bradshaw. Our other fellow traveler was her friend Meredith, whom I had met briefly before we left for the trip. Meredith was a rep for young fashion photographers. She has olive skin, light eyes, and I would love it if she let her brown hair go wild instead of blowing it out. She has a vibe that is equal parts fashion magazine editor and Bridgehampton weekender. She seemed fun, and who doesn't like to talk about the great score they got at the Barneys Warehouse Sale every now and again?

Oh, right. Me.

Before our adventure, the three of us met for dinner to talk about the trip and to make sure it was understood that "we must experience the pure culture of every country we visit." I'm sure we sounded like assholes at the Moroccan restaurant in Tribeca we met at.

The plan was Sharon and I would start the trip alone, travel around northern and eastern Spain, and Meredith would catch up with us in the southwestern part of the country. Sharon and I had started prepping for the trip months in advance. We went to extra yoga classes to strengthen our muscles for the massive backpacks we would be carrying. We grew our hair long enough to keep it in braids for days without having to wash it. We invested in a lot of cotton drawstring pants. We were going to rough it. Or at least Rough Guide it.

The red-eye flight to Barcelona left JFK on time. Sharon buckled up as soon as we boarded and promptly passed out. I was praying for a decent in-flight movie (this was back when it was one movie per cabin. Remember those golden days?). That was when a steward with gelled black hair, thin pointy sideburns, and a thick Spangayish accent came over the intercom: "Today movie is a romainkick comedy starrink Tom Hank and Mag Ryan called *Joo Got Any Mail?*"

Prayers dashed.

Like all loud funny women who wear a lot of vintage coats and have chronic hair issues, I am the kind of gal openly gay men hunt down and give tips to on how to be a better woman. Closeted gay men usually date me for anywhere between two and six and a half years. Then they come out and give me tips on how to be a better woman.

And like clockwork, I felt the flight attendant looming.

I looked up at him and waited for my tip. But instead he gestured wildly at the movie screen. "I am so over Mag Ryan in those yumpers. Chee is nearling forty. Joo you know what the biggest threat to a woman nearling forty is? Unsightly swollen ankles."

Huh. And I always thought it was breast cancer.

I looked down at my own ankles to see if that was my tip. They seemed relatively deflated, so I assumed this was just some kind of awkward icebreaker. But no, he was adamant. He wanted me to understand, dammit!

"Look at Heellary Clean-tone's ankles!" he shrieked, as if that should be the single example anyone would ever need to give to prove his theory. "Ninety-seex inauguration, powder blue suit, black hose, ankles like raidwoods. Tail me I'm wronk."

And with that he handed me two little blue pills from his private stash and a mini bottle of Robert Mondavi red.

He continued: "Joo should always carry Paimprin and wash it back with a little caybernay whenever joo fly. Get drunk, pass out, and joo don't balloon up. It's a ween-ween."

Leave it to a gay man to figure out how to turn Pamprin into a club drug.

I never noticed Heellary's ankles before this, but the picture he painted was so scary that I started popping Pamprin and swilling red wine at a rate only Judy Garland could truly appreciate. I've always admired Garland's commitment, so six caybernay-Paimprin cocktails later, we arrived in Barcelona at the crack of three hours too early to check into the hotel. So Sharon and I gathered our backpacks and our wits and did what everyone does in Spain in the morning: ate some ham . . . and proceeded to swell.

Sharon was refreshed from her sleep and suggested we go to a museum to kill time. I was coming down from a fuzzy buzz and felt miserable, but reluctantly agreed. The problem was that the only museum open at nine A.M. in Barcelona was the Museu de l'Eròtica. It's open twenty-four hours.

So loaded up with pork and booze, I was off to get some culture.

Turns out, the Museu de l'Eròtica was a relatively new museum, and the curators needed to work out some of the bugs. I don't mean to judge, but first impressions do mean everything. Right off the bat there should have been someone even marginally erotic taking our money at the door. Instead, we were "greeted" by a morbidly obese disenchantress coughing up a Salem Light and what was left of her dignity. She exhaled in my face, pointed at the admission sign, and held out her hand. She needed a little work on her people skills. I have found that most people who smoke menthols do.

I am not sure who the curator of the Museu de l'Eròtica was, but there was an absence of variety in it. I found a painful redundancy when viewing glass case after glass case of somebody else's ancient wooden dildos. For starters, there were no descriptions of how they worked, which was the first piece of documentation I wanted to read. Second, they were all anonymous dildos.

I would have liked to have seen at least one or two vibrators from some of Spain's glitterati. Something like "Queen Isabella's Magic Wand, circa 1492," or "This doubleheader once belonged to Pené-lope Cruz." Historical context really is very important.

The best part of the museum was the room dedicated to witch-craft. Apparently there was a period in Spanish history when the definition of a witch was a woman who acted on her sexual desires, and when her friends in the ancient order of the Christian Right found out about them, they remedied the problem by setting up brutal torture devices—in the town square, of course.

What about that "Love the sinner, hate the sin" rap those churchy types yammer on about? I guess that phrase wasn't created until the Christian Right started the American Inquisition of the twentieth century.

I did see two exhibits of note:

Aphrodisiac suppositories consisting of oysters wrapped in grape leaves. Two items still readily available at your neighborhood Costco. In bulk.

The Pleasure Ride: Think exercise bike circa 1600 with a cylindrical seat. I don't think the word "contraption" should come to mind when talking sex toys.

I have photos.

We spent all day at this place, mainly because I was truly interested, but also because at the time sex seemed like ancient history to me.

It was befitting that this sex museum was nestled among a bazillion Catholic churches. We all know the Spanish are pretty darn Catholic, and Catholics are obsessed with two things: sex and saints.

They love a saint. There is a holiday commemorating some martyr every other day in their Catholic calendar. If St. Augustine passed a kidney stone, the Spanish close the banks and have a procession in the street.

When we had gotten our filldo of sex memorabilia, Sharon and I headed to our hotel, and at twenty-six bucks a night, it seemed more conducive to fulfilling a suicide pact than actually providing a good night's sleep. It had two twin beds and a great view . . . of an apartment complex that looked like it housed Jerry Springer's international guests. In window after window I could see a mattress on the floor and a forty-two-inch TV screen. It was always nice to see the American corporate machine continued to enlighten cultures abroad.

We collapsed, fully clothed, onto the fifteen–thread count sheets and fell asleep to the faint sound of *General Hospital* en Español.

Sharon and I spent the next week making our way across Spain. Down the east coast and back around to the southwest, to meet Meredith in Granada. Eating, drinking, hamming, visiting churches, El Cid, skinny-dipping in the Mediterranean, more churches, more hamming, more drinking, and more drinking. We went to bed late and woke up when we woke up. Usually late.

Showering happened only on the days when the water didn't exacerbate our rosé hangovers from the night before. "Can you smell me?" one of us would ask the other. If the answer was "Not from here," we braided our hair and hit the road. We were on the same wavelength.

Meredith showed up ten days into our trip to finish up southwestern Spain with us, then we continued on to our biggest leg, Morocco. The day she arrived, Sharon and I were sitting on the rickety wooden deck of our hotel, dressed in whoknowsterday's clothes, pounding a cheap rioja. The flowering jasmine and intricate ceramic tables that reflected the Moorish influences of Granada only somewhat masked our view of the, oh, *cómo se dice en Español? Landfilleria?* Probably not.

Meredith breezed in wearing a crisp white tank top, a little pencil skirt, and a pair of jangly "ethnic" flip-flops. Her red mini Prada backpack bounced to the beat of her enthusiastic stride. "You guys!"

she exclaimed, her arms wide open. We leapt up for the big three-way hug—then she recoiled. "Whoa, you guys reek!" Hmmm. She seemed a bit taken aback by our traveling style.

But how could that be? We had that trip-planning dinner! We figured out a lot of important stuff that night, right? I mean, we had decided what music we all wanted to listen to in our hotel room (yes on Moby, no on Coldplay) and who was going to bring the cigarettes (me), and then we went into great detail about . . . Oh, that cultural experience thing, and then, um, well . . .

Oh, shit. We didn't sort anything out.

That was pretty much all we talked about. I was scrambling in my mind to make it okay, so I ran the checklist in my head.

We all agreed we wanted that pure cultural experience. That was key. That meant backpacks and creative hygiene. And we *all* hated Coldplay! Also key. Someone who could sit through that song "Yellow" without Klonopin would not be in sync with our plans. I mean, we slurred about our hatred of Coldplay in great detail! And I committed to carrying the carton of cigs—that was some serious planning—so I just assumed Meredith would be psyched to hop right on the funky bus with us. But judging by the kicky footwear, it seemed like she spent her pretrip time making sure she had the perfect impractical sandal to go with her perfect impractical hand-bag. My purse was a money belt that was now glued to my stomach with a natural adhesive made from body drippings and a variety of soils collected from many Spanish cities. I mean, seriously, we were going to climb ruins. Ruins, meaning ancient crumbling rock with sharper pieces of crumbling rock sticking out of said crumbling rock. Not exactly a flirty skirt/open-toe activity. The last people to visit the ruins in sandals did so *before* they were called *ruins*. Just sayin'.

She plopped down and poured herself a glass of wine.

"Where's your bag?" I asked.

When she told us it was being brought up to the room because she could barely lift it, I felt Lizzilla bubble up, convinced Meredith and her coin-encrusted flip-flops would destroy any and all joy, not only on our trip but also for every inhabitant of planet Earth with an intention to travel now or in the future.

I promptly put my hands on the table, took a deep breath, and on the inhale I said to myself, *It's always fun having new blood on a trip, and we all hate Coldplay!* And sure enough, on the exhale, a clearer-headed Lizz prevailed as I realized this poor woman had done nothing except show up with a smile and a justified desire not to get any of me on her.

I rewarded my self-control with a sip of wine and a cigarette. I soon forgot about the suitcase, and the Prada backpack, and the jangly shoes. The next few days we powered through Granada and Seville with no problems. They were cities filled with a lot of cafés, more museums, and churches. Seville Cathedral was the most unsettling and is one of the largest churches in the world, a sixteenth-century gothic gold-plated, dizzying maze. It proudly boasted in the brochure, *Burial place of Christopher Columbus* and *This cathedral was specifically designed in such a grand scale and with a labyrinth-like quality so all who enter will feel as though they are insane.* Who says organized religion is manipulative? At least it was kicky skirt—friendly.

Then it was the road to Morocco.

I t was nine A.M. and 115 degrees on our first morning at the Amanjena Hotel in Marrakech. This was our splurge hotel. Our coffee had been delivered to our private patio, and as we sat lounging on the oversize outdoor canopy bed, the ivory sheers blowing in the wind, I felt more like I was in an authentic Chris Isaak video than an authentic trip to North Africa. But that was to be expected from a hotel that described itself as "a resort secluded in a private lush haven near the pulsating Medina of Marrakech."

Okay, so we were staying "near" the authenticity, in a hotel lousy with rich German gay men, but dammit, we were going to take day trips to authenticity.

So let the planning begin. As Sharon plopped down our *Rough Guide to Morocco* on the bed, Meredith tossed out the *Louis Vuitton City Guide*.

Holy shit. A Louis Vuitton guidebook? Who knew Louis Vuitton made anything but fake purses? Was this a guide to finding fake purses all across Morocco?

All the visions of Prada, jangly shoes, and the big-ass suitcase came rushing back.

We are fucked, I thought. Lizzilla wanted out. She also officially needed a shower, as the desert heat helped coat me in an aspic of travel filth that was just frosted with blind rage.

I slowly put down my coffee. Seething, I laid both hands back on the bed in plain view, subconsciously curling into the yoga rest position called Child's Pose.

Sharon sensed when Lizzilla was emerging the way an arthritic can predict a summer storm. Seeing the urgency to quell the beast, she quickly scoured the pages of the Rough Guide and found a "traditional cultural experience" that all three of us could enjoy: the hammam. She read aloud from the guide: "You can order a massage, in which you will be allowed to sweat, pulled about a bit to relax your muscles, and then rigorously scrubbed with a rough flannel glove."

Lizzilla needed a bath and was excited for a "traditional cultural experience," so this was sounding pretty good. However, Meredith, being Meredith, was skeptical of anything in the Rough Guide. And I will say her doubt was not entirely unfounded.

Truth be told, the Rough Guide was at its best if you needed to find a place in any city in the world to score hash. But Sharon, who knew failing was not an option, gave the performance of a lifetime to keep the peace between Meredith and Lizzilla. She convinced us that *steam bath* was synonymous with *spa* and *rigorous* was synonymous with *exfoliation*, so we were all sold on our first "traditional cultural experience" at a Moroccan "spa."

Lizzilla was calmed. For the moment.

We hired two guides, Shada and Amina, who arrived at our hotel around noon. They were two beautiful sisters in their early twenties who sort of spoke French and sort of spoke English, and Sharon and I sort of spoke French, so through a lot of sort-of and error we sort of got our point across.

We explained we wanted a hammam experience, showed them the Rough Guide, and they said, "So you want spa," and we said, "Yes!" They talked with each other in Arabic and told us we were heading to "the Ramadan." It sounded perfect! Authenticity awaited.

But as the taxi pulled up to the Ramadan, a steady stream of

American tourists wearing Jägermeister T-shirts and baseball caps emerged from the revolving door. We realized we had our first failure to communicate. The Ramadan was actually the Ramada Inn.

Fail.

We explained we didn't want an Americanized anything or an all-you-can-eat everything. We were looking for a place preferably free of people like us. We wanted to go where *Moroccan* women went to have their ladies' day.

Our two guides again had another confab in Arabic and then replied, "Oh, okay, um, but where we take you, you pay cash. No credit card. No points."

Points? What was she talking about?

In our broken Franclish, we determined that most of the Americans they had dealt with insisted on going places only where they could pay with points or use credit cards so they could accrue points. But it was never explained to them what points were.

"Maybe you can teach to us points?"

Trying to explain, in a language you are butchering, the American obsession with wanting to get points for credit card purchases to exchange them for an Xbox or a J. Crew gift card seemed daunting. We just said we didn't know what points were.

But we had cash.

And so, as round two of our spa hunt began, we hoped we had cracked the language barrier. We continued on, traveling about ten minutes from sanitized to traditionalized, yielding only to camel crossings and men pushing carts of fruit until we arrived at the entrance of the medina. This is the walled part of the city that's made up of a labyrinth of narrow ancient pathways, unmarked and navigable only by a local. The streets are unmarked and only an arm's length wide, so the only "vehicles" allowed to transport goods are mules. We were going in on foot.

Communication win. This was authentic.

Our guides walked at a pace that felt as if we were trying to ditch the bad guys in an Indiana Jones movie. It's as though they didn't want us to retain anything we had seen. Probably an old guide trick. If we knew where we were going, they were rendered useless.

So we weaved around, past carts of food, small booths that sold traditional robes, fruits and vegetable stands, and a lot of hanging chickens and unidentifiable four-legged animals that had seen better days.

It felt as if we were going in circles, down alleyway after passageway that seemingly led to nowhere.

Finally we turned down a long, dark, covered alley, and at the end we saw a woman sitting against a door. As we approached we noticed she was one of those sun-faced people who could be thirty-five or sixty. She had long gray hair to her waist and wore a very faded oversized Seattle Seahawks tank top.

And nothing else.

Next to her were piles of clothes: slacks, blouses, bras, panties, and a lot of abayas, the traditional black covering worn by some Muslim women. Pairs and pairs of shoes lined the wall.

"Is she homeless?" I asked Shada.

"No, she is the owner."

"Owner of what?" I asked. "She doesn't even own underwear."

"Owner of the spa," Amina chimed in.

"This is the spa?" Sharon asked. "The bathhouse?"

"Oui," Amina said. "You want the traditional hammam treatment, yes?"

"Oui, oui!" Sharon and I said, clapping with equal parts fear and excitement, as the color ran from Meredith's face.

As the guides negotiated the fee with our ageless aesthetician, she looked up at us and gave us a big toothless grin. They finalized the price and Shada and Amina gave us the news.

"For the traditional hammam experience, it will cost two dirhams each."

The three of us pulled out our laminated currency cards.

"Um, that's a quarter," Sharon whispered to us.

"Damn!" I said with fake exasperation. "I really wanted to pay with points!" That even made Meredith laugh, if only for a moment.

Our guides told us they would be back in an hour and a half to "pick us out." And with that, we gave our two dirhams to the gummy Seahawks fan. By then I was kind of psyched. I mean, what was the worst thing that could happen to three American women in a spa that cost a quarter in a Muslim country?

Oh, Lizz.

The first thing that happened was that the Seahawks tank top came off in the alley and our proprietor revealed her bangin' bod. And by *bangin'* I mean her boobs were bangin' against the top of her thighs. She pointed to the pile of clothes.

We stared at her and tried to speak French. Clearly, she didn't speak anything but Arabic, so she just shook her head, tugged at Sharon's shirt, and again pointed to the pile. Still dumbfounded, we looked at one another, confused at what we should do.

Exasperated, the spa keeper gave us a demonstration. She put her tank back on, then took it off and tossed it onto the pile. This apparently was the entrance *and* the changing room.

Meredith realized she was wearing her designer jangly sandals. She turned to me in a panic and whispered, "Do you think they have lockers?"

Ignoring her, Sharon and I decided to roll with it. We stripped down and tossed our clothes onto the pile. Meredith followed suit but refused to take off her panties.

What was she worried about? What could go wrong being a naked Western woman in a dark alley in a Muslim country?

When we finished undressing, our hostess opened the door and we walked into a dark, steamy ancient bath scene. It was a huge, cavernous, intricately tiled space, with ceilings thirty feet high. The floors were old cracked stone and pitched at an angle so the water could flow to one of the many drains provided for the fifty open showerheads that lined the perimeter of the space, about ten feet under rows of windows. They provided the only source of light in the place.

As we walked in, we noticed pairs and groups of naked Moroccan women everywhere, talking, laughing, showering, and having fun. *This must be where you relax before and after your treatments*, I thought.

It seemed pretty mellow. Why were we so uptight?

All of a sudden, Elizabeth Arden stopped dead in her tracks, squatted down, and gestured for Meredith and Sharon to squat and for me to step forward. We understood this was going to be spa charades, so we all obeyed. I don't know why I was still standing, but I quickly decided that it was okay with me. The thought of sitting my bare wageena on what looked like a thirteen-hundred-year-old "spa" floor kinda skeeved me out.

It didn't take me long to realize this was the "treatment" room and I was first for the "treatments," and apparently the bonus was that, when you pay a quarter, the owner took care of you personally. So as the gals squatted, *SURPRISE!* From behind me, I was doused with a bucket of what I hoped and prayed was water. It was the temperature of pee. Maybe it was pee. Who knew? Whatever it was, it was a surprise.

I don't have to tell you that it was unsettling when an unknown warmish liquid pounced on me from behind like water rape. And when you've spent twenty-five cents at a spa in an alley where no one speaks English and no one in the Western world knew where you were, you *really* like a fucking surprise. I guessed there was no sneaking up on you at Canyon Ranch.

Now Seahawky started up again with the motions.

Her gestures were a cross between that "rub your belly and head at the same time" coordination test and a "get these spiders off me" acid flashback. Which meant, I realized after a while, *I scrub you now.* I nodded with a pleading *Yes. Please scrub me. Please scrub off the mystery liquid that you just doused me with.* And so she pulled out the aforementioned "rough glove," or rock, or burlap bag full of broken glass, or whatever it was, and started scraping my arms and legs in what I suspected was the same technique used in the outtakes of that shower scene in the movie *Silkwood.*

I now had very little protective dermis left covering my muscle tissue.

But surprise again! Another water rape and then she made a gesture like an umpire calling a runner safe at a baseball game.

Am I safe? I didn't feel safe. I felt like I was stuck in a *Scared Straight!* program for spa addicts.

No, the gesture didn't mean safe. It meant *lie down*. Facedown. On the floor. This thousand-year-old, plague-infested floor.

That seemed the opposite of safe.

As I hit the floor, I had a chance to look over at Sharon and Meredith. They were still in a crouched position, and had now wrapped their arms around their knees and were rocking back and forth like abused psychiatric patients. It was at that moment that I realized that I was on a slant. And that I was downstream.

I looked longingly at all of the happy women in the showers, wondering why I couldn't have just gone that route, when instead I'm lying in a tributary of the Love Canal.

Then I noticed something: All of the women in the showers were doing the same thing. (No, not that thing.) Shaving. They were all shaving. Armpits, legs, all of it. It was shaving day. Maybe that's why the fee was so cheap!

As I averted my eyes from Shavapalooza, I saw in the distance that all the hair from all the showers had started to gather, forming a tsunami of hair that was cascading in ever higher waves as it picked up speed with each shower it passed. And it was headed right for me.

I was lying on the floor, not knowing what was about to happen, but I was trying to avoid the hair, so I started sliding side to side on my stomach like I was in the worst game of Asteroids ever.

The ever-diligent masseuse thought it was part of our gesture game and interpreted my movements as a request for a stomach exfoliation. So she summoned an "assistant" to help her. Another naked woman came over, this one so big and strong, she could have actually played defensive tackle for the Seahawks. So Toothless took my arms and the defensewoman took my legs and they pushed and pulled me back and forth on this craggy stone floor like a brick of cheddar on a grater, exfoliating my boobs to the point where they looked like utility-grade meat.

But before the unendurable stinging set in, I was treated to the bonus of something I will call "the anal polish," more commonly known as "having a bar of soap shoved up my ass."

I don't know what the soap was or where it came from, but my survival instincts convinced me it must have been a bar of that celestial Middle Eastern black soap that I saw in all of the fancy stores in the US. I had to believe that at this point. The other options were too scary to think about.

But moments of doubt crept in. Did this soap start out black? Of course it started out black. I didn't actually see any wrappers or anything, but that was all I had to cling to at this point. I did not want to believe this was some sort of community bar. I had no interest in being part of the Sisterhood of the Traveling Soap. I just kept telling myself this was some exclusive ritual, ancient and mystical, and that my anus will be full of . . . mysticism? Yes. I stuck with that. Very, very mystical. In fact, this soap was so mystical, it was also the soap the women used to wash my hair with.

So with no skin left on my limbs and boobs, and my ass as shiny as a new dime, Elizabeth Arden gestured me to step back and crouch.

I guess I just had the traditional hammam experience.

But where did Sharon and Meredith go?

I was now crouched alone, and as I looked around the room, in that sea of brown bodies showering, I spotted two very white women.

Showering with dignity. And with their own bars of soap.

They decided to forgo the "traditional experience of the rough glove," opting for the public showers, finding safety in the multitudes.

Could it be that it looked worse than it felt? Probably. So exhausted and defeated, I plopped my polished ass down on the floor—it was the only part of my body with some skin intact—and waited for the girls to finish.

I looked around again and watched all the groups of women who laughed and washed one another's hair, and then I realized: I didn't have the traditional experience at all. They were having it.

These women came here with their friends, tossed off their clothes, and took care of one another. They bathed one another, massaged one another, all while laughing, talking, and listening to one another. They had a deep trust and a bond of intimacy that American women lost when we transitioned from having slumber parties and scratching one another's backs to judging one another at the gym or at the office. While these women developed relationships, Americans developed TV shows that pit women against one another for entertainment, nurturing the worst part of our natures.

I was suddenly jealous. Jealous that the three of us hadn't walked in, picked up a bucket, and started sharing intimate details of our lives while we scrubbed one another's backs and massaged one another's scalps. I wondered why I expected a woman I didn't know to scrub me instead of my friends. I wondered if she thought the same thing.

I would have laughed if Meredith had poured a bucket of water on me. I would have relaxed if Sharon had washed my back.

But we don't seem to do those things anymore. We had forgotten the most important lesson of being women: We are one another, and when all else fails, we have one another. And when we strip down naked, we remove the false barriers of clothing and attitude and are free to need one another. We need to get back to being part of the Sisterhood of the Traveling Soap.

Or at least give one another a few more back rubs.

JESUS
TRAPEZES

When my parents sold the house I grew up in and moved into Club Meds, unpacking them became an exercise in patience that is equal to feeding a toddler. In the dark. Through the eye of a needle.

All five Winstead kids desperately tried to find the delicate balance between honoring the unique organizational skills my mother developed over eighty years, a technique I call "single-tasking," and stabbing her in her sleep.

Why? Because Mom was a crap rat.

We sort of knew this, but it was only when we tried to pry the shoe box full of candle stubs out of her cold live hands that we realized just how challenging it was going to be.

The first test of our fortitude was indulging Mom's unflinching insistence that we move everything from their four-bedroom house with full basement to their new two-bedroom apartment with a full basement storage cube. Then we would sort through it and downsize.

The only reason I *didn't* stab her then is that her knives were so dull, they couldn't cut through Cool Whip.

There we were, five grown children and Mom (Dad was napping, upright on his recliner), with half a century of stuff covering every inch of floor space in Club Meds.

The second test of patience was watching as Mom prioritized what she should keep (everything that was hers), what she should toss (everything that was Dad's), and worse, what she insisted we should have (everything that was of undetermined use or broken). She was wildly unpredictable. She put in the toss pile the cool black-and-white photos of Grandpa's fishing trips (we kept them), but she saved the three unused fondue pots (didn't keep). Why did she? I doubted she held out hope that she would still have one of those key parties that passed her by in her seventies.

The 1970s.

And we never dared dream about tossing out that box of cords that belonged to . . . nothing.

And the air popper!! The worst invention ever. If you tried to salt the popcorn that came out of those things, it shot back into your face like a cluster bomb going off at point-blank range.

"Lizz, you like popcorn, take this back to New York with you and get it fixed."

"Mom, why do you have a broken air popper?"

"Your father keeps forgetting to take it in. Just take it."

"Okay."

It was too hard to fight about every little thing, so the way we kids kept our collective shit together was to fawn over everything Mom gave us and smile. We threw it away later.

And the stuff she was willing to part with, she made me promise to donate to Catholic Charities. I said I would. But Goodwill was closer. This whole exercise was the equivalent of "We are taking the dog to the farm" for children taking care of elderly parents.

Finally we got to the point where they were pretty much settled and all that was left to put away were their clothes. My brother packed up his new treasures to "take to the farm," and my sisters helped Mom finish putting her holiday sweaters into their own wing of the apartment's only walk-in closet. Since I had been living in New York, I'd become an expert at judiciously using every centimeter of space, so I crammed Dad's entire life into the space Mom had delegated him: one shelf, eighteen inches of pole in the closet, and two dresser drawers. At least they were the top two drawers.

This was for everything Dad owned (read: she allowed him to keep). Suits, belts, shirts, coats, shoes, and his huge hat collection had to fit into a foot and a half of space. Everything else—socks, T-shirts, underwear, sweaters, old watches, shoehorns (old guys love shoehorns)—had to fit into those two drawers.

So as I attempted to make it all work, I discovered Mom had pre-emptively decided that his two drawers would also host other miscellaneous items she couldn't bear to part with. So as I uncomfortably stuffed Dad's ginormous white undies into the top drawer, I noticed it already contained some miscellaneous ephemera.

A lot of miscellaneous ephemera.

"Mom," I said, hoping I didn't find scissors sharp enough to, well, you know, "why are you keeping old VCR and lawn mower manuals in Dad's underwear dra—"

As I pulled them out of the drawer, lo and behold, sitting on them was the creepy icon from my childhood: that cross on a cross on a cross, the sick call box that hung next to the front door. The one that flanked the "Scare Pair®." I hadn't thought about this thing in years, which made me wonder: Had Mom taken it down at some point and we never noticed? Why would she do that? Certainly not to make room for a picture of me.

I stared at him, in the drawer, lying on an old answering machine manual, Jesus on the cross preserved forever in resin. And then, with a "We're going down memory lane" tone in my voice, I announced, "Hey guys, I found that Jesus that hung next to the front door!"

My brother walked into the bedroom, and Mom and my sisters all looked up.

Mom lit up like a string of Christmas lights. "Oh, that's where He is! I need you to—"

I yanked him out of the drawer and held him up next to my face so that everyone saw him, the way people in the movies did to scare away vampires.

As I did, the unthinkable happened. Jesus kicked me in the cheek. Hard.

I was stunned for a second. I looked and saw five chins scraping the floor.

"Ouch! Jesus just kicked me!" I cried out. I looked at the cross and realized that the nails driven through his left hand and feet were missing, and now he dangled from one hand on the cross, loose, clearly dangerous, and ready to pick a fight.

My sister Ann grabbed it from me, and the motion spun him around like a one-armed gymnast on the horizontal bar.

"Oh my God, Jesus trapezes!" she screamed.

I grabbed him back and kept making him spin. It was so freaky, watching a plastic Jesus spin around on his one nailed hand, that we began to laugh. I couldn't stop twirling it, we couldn't stop laughing. But Mom had none of it.

"*LIZZZZZZZZZZZ!* Stop this at once! You need to find a nail and nail him back onto the cross!"

All of us stopped and looked at her.

"*What?*"

"Stop that and nail him back onto the cross. And then nail him back on the wall. This is blasphemy."

I, of course, was thinking to myself, *I have had an abortion, haven't been to mass in decades, and am running down the commandments at a pretty good clip,* so I was having none of it.

"Mom," I said earnestly, trying to get her to hear what she had just asked. "You are not seriously asking me to re-nail Jesus to the cross, and then re-nail him to the wall."

"Just do it. Just get the hammer and a nail from your dad's drawer and nail him back where he belongs."

I didn't have a clue how to talk her down from this height of ecclesiastical excess, and so I stood there and held the savior of the world, as represented in nonrecyclable plastic, as he slowly swung by one hand.

On the verge of laughing and crying, I stood my ground.

"Mom, I would do just about anything for you. I have been here for three days proving that. But the one thing I will not do is re-crucify Jesus for you. The Jesus you have been so reverently storing in Dad's underwear drawer."

Mom looked at me like she hoped Jesus would pull a full Bruce Lee on me. "You kids are all going to hell. Forget it. Put him back. I'll do it myself. I have to do everything myself."

There it was, the apex of Catholic guilt. Surrounded by her five kids who for three days have packed her, moved her, and unpacked her. It was never enough. She still saw life as "I have to do every-thing myself."

If only the "Scare Pair"® had reappeared. I'll bet they would have been happy to do it for her.

CREATED BY . . .

the DAILY show

356 W 58TH STREET
FOURTH FLOOR
NEW YORK, NY 10019
[TEL] 212.560.3084
[FAX] 212.560.6996

LIZZ WINSTEAD
head writer

I met Brian Unger nine months after the First Gulf War started, at a mutual friend's Halloween party. I was dressed as a flapper. He was dressed as himself.

He looked like an Italian matinee idol: olive skin, sandy hair, brown eyes. Almost too perfect-looking for my taste.

As we stood around chatting, he asked me what I did.

"I get on a stage and shit on politicians and the media for money."

He laughed. "Then I will beam with pride as I tell you I went to school to pursue a career in broadcast journalism and currently I am doing hard-hitting investigative pieces about obese people who have resorted to tying their mouths shut with bread twisties so they don't eat the entire contents of their freezers in their sleep."

"And for which beacon of truth do you produce said stories?" I asked.

"Currently for the heir to the Murrow legacy, Maury Povich."

To which I replied flirtatiously, "You know you are destroying America."

He flirted back, "One brain cell at a time."

We laughed and spent the rest of the night together doing traditional Halloweeny things: We dropped X and made out. A fairy-tale start to a romance. He was funny and smart. And he was part of the problem. The problem with the media.

Brian didn't want to be part of the problem.

It was the early '90s, and what he did *was* journalism. Or at least what seemed to replace most of it. Daytime TV was wall-to-wall talk shows: Maury, Springer, Oprah, Montel—a new one seemed to crop up every week. It felt like the network overlords found a way to add more hours to the day to subject us to more of these freak fests. It was hour after hour of parading the wretched refuse of America on national TV for the purpose of making a generation of mindless couch enthusiasts feel *just* that much better about themselves.

It was a bad time, that dark period in daytime talk before the invention of the DNA tests that finally classed up the Maury Povich show.

Brian often called me from work with utter incredulity—after, say, he lost a battle with his producer, unable to convince her that having five people with Tourette's syndrome onstage at once may not make for a fluid conversation.

At least I had a catharsis; I could talk about all of the insanity I saw in my act. But he was still trapped in the rotting belly of the beast, churning out slop and hating himself for it.

We decided to write a satire together about these shows. A behind-the-scenes look at a daytime talk show.

We got exactly one meeting to pitch it.

The executive actually said, "No one wants to see shows about how TV works. You know what I would like to see? A show about a hair salon. Very relatable."

We felt defeated, and not very relatable.

But one good thing came from writing that script. It made Brian realize that he could no longer exist in a world where he put his journalism degree to use feeding America's appetite for gawking at people with diseases like progeria (the rapid aging disease, basically aging those inflicted to eighty by the time they are twelve) or Thumbelina syndrome (you can guess what that is, but to crystallize it for the brain-salad Maury viewer, the producers made some small person living with it stand next to a cereal box).

I shared his frustration and even saw that these shows started to have an effect on *my* audiences. More and more it seemed club goers had been schooled in proper audience etiquette by watching these shows. Day after day, millions of people watched as talk show audiences heckled and jeered the guests. They learned from these shows their job was to disrupt every time they didn't like something they heard.

A comic was treated like any of the chair-throwing, paternity test–failing lowlifes on TV, and their role as the audience was to weigh in like barbarians with each joke I told. I was convinced they were part of the reason my transition to starting sentences onstage with "I think" was met with such disdain.

We both needed a change. And indeed, changes were afoot.

Brian finally left *Maury* and landed a new job at CBS News on a magazine show hosted by Mrs. Maury, Connie Chung. He was excited; it was CBS *News*. A *news* magazine. At the Tiffany Network. He would finally do stories that mattered—about wage disparity, for example, or maybe go undercover busting a child labor ring.

Right?

Well, not exactly.

One of his first assignments in credible news was covering the trial of serial killer and renowned cannibal Jeffrey Dahmer.

So Brian was still part of the problem. He knew it, and so did I.

Little did we both know that soon he would become part of the solution.

The lease was up on my apartment, the rent was about to go through the roof, and Claire moved in with her boyfriend. But in the things-were-looking-up department, Christine had decided to try her hand in the film biz and had moved to New York. So Christine, The Chair, and I moved into a sweet little place on the third floor of a cheaper brownstone at 454 W. 20th Street. At just about the same time, a TV producer named Madeleine Smithberg and her husband, Jonathan, a singer-songwriter, moved into the apartment directly below.

Madeleine was a tall blonde with a can-do energy and a laugh that could cause a seismic shift.

Madeleine had been a producer for David Letterman for many years, and it just so happened that Brian did a college internship at the show while she was there. At the time we lived a floor apart, she was the executive producer of Jon Stewart's syndicated talk show. It was a small world.

It was 1995. I continued to toil away in The Chair, scraping together stand-up gigs, landing a few TV spots and some commercials, and still trying to bring my one-woman show to New York. Christine was working eighteen hours a day as a production assistant on a Meg Ryan movie called *Addicted to Love*, and so when we saw each other it usually involved her falling asleep on the couch in midsentence, holding a glass of wine. Our weekends were spent scouring flea markets with Madeleine and fending off stalkers. Not *our* stalkers, but the stalkers of a previous tenant. He moved out forty-five years ago, but while he lived in our building he wrote a crazy novel on a single sheet of paper called *On the Road*. His name was Jack Kerouac.

Every weekend, wide-eyed Midwestern dharma bums would come and ring either Madeleine's or my doorbell (there are varying accounts of whether the writer lived in my apartment or Madeleine's), asking if they could come in to see Jack Kerouac's place.

Because I lived near the corner of Tenth Avenue and Blow Jobs for Crack, I wasn't particularly amenable to giving strangers a tour of my home. Even my Minnesota Nice knew better.

In hindsight, these people were harmless and naive enough to ring the doorbell of a New Yorker and expect access. If they believed that was possible, they probably would have believed anything. I should have let them up for twenty bucks a pop and then made up a bunch of bullshit history about the place. "This was Kerouac's microwave, the one he made Cup Noodles in every day." (Pause for rapturous gasps.) "Oh, and this is The Chair he wrote in. For five bucks more I'll let ya sit in it." What a missed opportunity.

The irony is, whichever apartment it was Kerouac wrote *On the Road* in, it was in this building that I was given the opportunity to get "Off the Road."

A few months into living in the House That Jack Built, Madeleine came upstairs after work. The conversation went something like this:

"How would you feel about taking a break from performing full-time and coming to work for me?"

"Really? Doing what?"

"We need a guest segment producer. I talked to Jon and he thinks you would be great."

"Well, I have never really done it, you know."

"I know. But you are outgoing and have a quirky sensibility, and we need someone who can get fun stories out of celebrities, instead of the same boring ones we hear about their pets or their 'character.'"

I needed the money and loved Jon's show. Having some financial breathing room was just what the doctor ordered, and I could still do local stand-up gigs at night.

But there was one problem.

Remember how I bought The Chair instead of a computer? Well, I still never bought one. Which meant I didn't even know how to use one. I didn't even know how to type. I took choir instead of typing in high school.

I didn't tell Madeleine any of that.

Truman Capote famously said of *On the Road*, "That's not writing, that's typing." At least I wouldn't have to worry about that kind of slam of any of the work written by me. Just absolutely everything else.

I took the job.

I got to work on my first day and the little Mac Classic on my desk was already on, thank God. In the entire time I worked there I never turned it off.

Brian gave me computer lessons at night so I could learn the basics. I learned exactly as much as I needed to know: how to use the format to write a guest introduction and how to format my guest questions.

My tenure at *The Jon Stewart Show* was invaluable, but sadly short-lived. I got to produce a segment with George Clooney pulling a prank on Noah Wyle—they were both on the TV medical drama *ER* back in the '90s—and Jude Law was so nice, he scored me tickets to see *Hamlet* on Broadway starring his then-wife Sadie Frost (as Ophelia, not Hamlet). And every night there was an awesome musical guest. It was extra special when Soul Asylum and the Jayhawks came through town and appeared on the show. The Punk Rock Ghetto all started to kind of make it. We always celebrated with burgers and beers at a little bar in Greenwich Village called the Corner Bistro. And it was fun to see Jon again every day.

The team on this show was invigorating, and I realized how isolated I had become in The Chair. It was great to sit in the show meetings every day, tossing out ideas, having someone take an idea and elevate it to the next level and laugh.

We laughed a lot.

I started to enjoy myself and got into a groove learning a new skill. Then, just six months into my stint, it was over. The ratings weren't what Paramount wanted, so it pulled the plug and canceled the show. But some good came from it: I got to keep the Mac Classic.

Now instead of my going back to The Chair, Madeleine had a plan for us. Our bosses from *The Jon Stewart Show* had become the new heads of Comedy Central, Doug Herzog and Eileen Katz, so she suggested we come up with an idea for a show to pitch to them.

We cooked up a show called *The Network* about the world's worst television network. It was sort of a combination of *SCTV* and *The Larry Sanders Show*. We would see the inner workings of how crappy ideas get on TV, interspersed with scenes from the shows that made up *The Network*.

The only show I remember on this fake network was something called *Animal Friends*. It was like *Friends*, but they were New York pet friends. The Lisa Kudrow character was an Afghan; Matt LeBlanc was a black lab. It was supposed to be as stupid as it sounds.

We had our big idea ready to go.

But when we went in to sell it, the executives pulled the old bait and pitch.

They thought *The Network* was fine. But what they really wanted from us was a flagship show for Comedy Central. A show that was on daily and poked fun at the news. *Politically Incorrect* was moving to ABC, and they wanted us to fill the slot at eleven P.M. four nights a week.

Madeleine had the TV comedy production background, and now I had a short stint at *The Jon Stewart Show* and had seen some success with my writing and the Lizz 2.0 act I was doing. In fact, when Eileen was at MTV, she had booked me on some stand-up specials.

All that Chair time paid off.

I knew that if *I* saw the gold mine of comedy material provided by the news, someone in TV would eventually see it, too. I was so overjoyed, but tried to keep my cool.

They didn't know it, but they had just said to me, "We don't want you to do the show you pitched. We want you to do your dream show."

They just asked me to help create the show I had been wanting to do for years. Yes. Yes, they had.

Pinch me with the Jaws of Life. This was really happening.

So Madeleine and I plotted and planned until we came up with a format that had never been tried and was a whole new way of responding to the news.

We were not just going to make fun of the news and the talking heads that were everywhere. We were going to make fun of them by *becoming* them. We would operate as a news organization while acting like a comedy show.

It simply had never been done before.

We were sure we would have a hit if we used all the news conventions—the set, the graphics, the music, the format—all to expose the ways our media had elevated celebrity and scandal to an importance that used to be reserved for war and politics and corporate malfeasance.

We would have correspondents and send them to all the newsworthy events, blending in with the rest of the press corps, highlighting how ridiculous they had become. And the media landscape in 1996 was scorched-earth. The daytime talk topics had started bleeding—hemorrhaging—into prime time, and every night of the week there was a newsmagazine show, either *Dateline*, *Primetime Live*, *48 Hours*, or *Street Stories*. Each competed to score the "Celebrity Profile of the Week" or the "Ghoul of the Week." Sometimes they were one and the same.

And investigative journalism became a game of fear. It was a battle between who could scare the most shit out of you with stories like "Your Throw Pillows: What You Don't Know Might Kill You," or the unforgettable classic "Every Inch of Every Hotel Room in America Is Coated in Man Batter!" The feeling seemed to be, if we as a nation were not scared about everything we come into contact with, these shows were not doing their jobs. Fear and celebrity ruled the day.

In the past there had been shows I worshipped that had done amazing social criticism. Classics like *Laugh-In* and its predecessor, *That Was the Week That Was*, were more sketch-oriented than we planned to be. *Saturday Night Live* had "Weekend Update," but that was one segment on a larger comedy show. Michael Moore's *TV Nation* was also hitting great targets, but it was more of a magazine-style show that wasn't shy about its point of view. We wanted the entire show to be a *character*.

One big risk in trying this format meant no nodding, no winking, and no tipping our hand to the audience. We were going to give them credit that they were smart enough to be in on the joke. We'd play it straight; they'll know where to laugh.

We spent months coming up with a format and segments, a combination of news stories, entertainment stories, and oddball stories.

And to make it work, we needed the right team.

A host who could drive the ship, staying in a news anchor character as he delivered the comedy, and a set of correspondents who could round out the tone.

Jon Stewart was the first choice to be the host, but he had signed a development deal with David Letterman's company to create other projects and was tied up for two years.

So we began the search. It was harder than we expected.

Most of the comedians we auditioned were either too jokey, too set in their own comedic personas, or felt compelled to comment on the material instead of reading it like a broadcaster. We looked at features reporters from local TV news, but most of them were too wacky. We were coming up empty.

Doug Herzog was a big ESPN fan and had his eye on a blond-haired, blue-eyed ex-Minnesotan named Craig Kilborn, who had a sense of humor that was dry and compelling. He was a rising star at the sports network, so at first we assumed he was happy where he was.

Doug threw caution to the wind and called Craig's agent just to see if he would be interested. It turned out that Craig wanted to transition out of sports into entertainment, and he was game. So we had our anchorman.

Now we needed the rest of the team, correspondents who embodied the overblown sense of self-importance that had become the gold standard in TV news.

A. Whitney Brown was working at Comedy Central writing interstitials, small comedy pieces that ran on the network throughout the day, and the satirical commentary segment he used to do called "The Big Picture" on *SNL* was just the tone we wanted to cover politics. We found a hilarious comedic actress named Beth Littleford to be our version of the sycophantic celebrity interviewer. And as for the hard-hitting, investigative fear mongerer?

There was only one guy for that role, but it was going to take some convincing.

"C'mon, Brian, Madeleine and I think you are perfect," I told him. "You have worked with these types; you are imitating them all the time. They have given us a year commitment. No pilot. They know a show like this has to work itself out on the air."

"But if I come and do this, I will kill my career in news," Brian argued.

"Or you can finally take all your news background and use it for good. Shitting on what it's become."

Welcome to your new career, Brian Unger.

And of course, no news satire could be complete without the id of Andy Rooney. I was so excited to get my old friend Lewis Black onboard.

I was finally able to bring so many of my creative pals to a project—I mean down to the theme song. I called Bob Mould: "Hey, how about you do the theme song for this new project I am working on?" He jumped on it. It was something that seemed other people would get to do. I would go home every night to Christine and sob with joy. She usually tried to stay awake long enough to say, "I am so proud of you."

Now that we had the major talent in place, we had to face the daunting task of staffing and actually building the show. So far we had chosen the key players and developed a format, but now we needed to find a head writer to set the tone and find the writers who could pull off this task night after night.

It was then that Madeleine and Comedy Central may have taken their biggest risk.

They offered the job to me.

I was excited, naive, and terrified. I had never run a writing staff and had very little TV experience. Christ, I could barely type. But this was my dream show. The culmination of all I had been observing and writing about in my stand-up and stage shows.

This was the big one.

And it was my first one.

I had no idea what I was doing.

At least I finally knew how to peck on a Mac Classic.

Unfortunately, the show decided to go with PCs instead of Macs.

WHY DID MY DREAM SHOW HAVE TO BE MY FIRST SHOW??

This was crazy, but I had to say yes.

So, like the young parent of a first child, I made many mistakes.

And like a first-time parent, one of my biggest mistakes was that I was going to prove I could do this alone, often rejecting good advice. I thought asking for help would be perceived as a sign of weakness.

I was afraid at any moment I would wake up, be found out, and this whole wonderful experience would be over.

One thing I did have confidence in was my comedic instinct. And I had to rely on it completely until I actually taught myself how to do the job.

My gut hired the writers. I was allowed six of them. Most comedy shows had twelve.

My instinct told me that, since we were launching a show that from the beginning was going to run at half staff, I could not hire a single writer who did not live, eat, and breathe current events.

I knew a few writer-performers who would be up to the task.

Many of them weren't the guys who did topical material in their acts, per se, but they were the comedians I had conversations with about politics and the news who had me on the floor laughing with their insights. They were guys who were engaged in the world without getting paid for it. Guys who looked beyond the headlines and dug deeper. Guys who barely had two nickels to rub together, and when they did they would take one of them and buy a copy of *Harper's* with it. The news was in their blood, not just a writing submission tailored for the job. They didn't have a *Home Improvement* spec script anywhere.

But I knew only a few funny folks who fit that bill.

And they were all guys.

So then we put out the call for writing submissions. I received about 150 of them; only two were women, and I don't know how many were people of color. Out of those 150, I found two to round out the team. They were not the women or people of color. They were simply the funniest submissions, two print journalists who had written little comedy bits for the *Daily News*, the *New York Post*, and *Newsday*.

The writers were set, and the *Daily Show* staff reported for duty in Columbus Circle, in the former home of *The MacNeil/Lehrer News-Hour*. I scored Charlayne Hunter-Gault's old office and quickly removed her journalistic legacy when, on my third day as head writer, a very un-PBS-like situation arose. I had to wield my boss lady gavel for the first time by stopping behavior that was unacceptable while also offering a compromise to show my impressive leadership skills.

I gathered the writers in my office and closed the door.

"Guys," I said apprehensively, "I don't want to stifle your creative process in any way or have you think that I have become one of the suits." That was my biggest fear, that if I set rules, I would be perceived as a sellout, someone who would always toe the network line. "I want you to do what you need to do to get the best content out of you, *but* you can't invite your mushroom dealer up to the office for *any* reason." Then came my expertise in the art of compromise. "All transactions must be made at the diner across the street and without my knowledge. I would appreciate your consideration on this."

That was me putting my foot down. I thought that showed pretty good instinct.

There was some grumbling as they filed out, but it never happened again, although I heard a lot of "Hey, anyone need anything from the diner?" cracks after that. I guessed they didn't think I had turned into a suit.

We hit the pre-production ground running.

The field producers and correspondents hit the road, shooting piece after piece. We hired them, and then they were gone for weeks on end. I was hunkered down with the writers, creating short segments and playing with a structure to get all the written material in on time to make air each day. Brian was gone almost five days a week, and we both became so involved in our work that we forgot to remain involved with each other, romantically speaking.

One of the things people say is don't work with friends or partners because it could get ugly. For Brian and me, a unique problem arose. We couldn't support each other in a healthy emotional way outside work, as we were both buried under the weight of this huge undertaking, each with different burdens. We reserved the energy we did have left for each other for creative consult, and soon we both recognized we didn't have an ounce left over to keep anything outside of that alive. It was like we were each having an affair with the show, and when we sat down to break the news to each other about it, we both breathed a sigh of relief and gave each other the freedom to continue with our new loves.

One segment I came up with was a public service for *Jeopardy!* fans.

Yes, it was self-serving. But I figured so many viewers of our show worked full-time and would love to at least see Final Jeopardy at the end of their day. (This, children, was way, way, way before DVR.) Now, we couldn't pull the clips and air them, because *Jeopardy!* wasn't on until seven P.M. in New York City, plus it would have cost a fortune in licensing and clearance costs.

But I figured out a way to do it.

Jeopardy! was on at three P.M. in Minnesota. Of course my parents watched every day, so at three thirty, I had Mom leave the final question and answer on my answering machine at work. We built a graphic that looked like the Final Jeopardy card and would fill in the text when we got the info from her.

Simple enough, right?

Well, not for Mom.

Oh, no. She could not just leave the information we needed. She blathered on about what was happening in her life, such as my dad had been crabby because he hadn't moved his bowels for two days after eating that gumbo he insisted on making. Or that she didn't know what to do because Playtex had discontinued making the bra she had been wearing for the last thirty-five years. And when she did finally get to the Final Jeopardy part of her message, she didn't quite understand that accuracy was key.

Let's say the actual Final Jeopardy was something like this:

A. Aleksandr Solzhenitsyn wrote this nonfiction account of the Soviet forced labor and concentration camp system.

Q. What is *The Gulag Archipelago*?

A typical Mom dispatch would go something like this:

"Hi, dear. Today your dad was gone during the show, because I needed a new plunger. I did not understand the *Jeopardy!* final today, but maybe you will.

"Alexander Soldier-nitson, and do *not* ask me to spell it, wrote this fiction account of the non-Soviet labor and concentration camping systems. The answer is *Goulash Archipelago*. I guess it's a book; it sounds exhausting. No one will know this one. Let us hear from you now. Okay, bye!"

She was unintentionally hilarious. After a few of these, even I quickly realized that the actual Final Jeopardy clue wasn't nearly as entertaining as my mom. She was the star.

So we just aired the recording and slapped up the graphic when she got to the actual information. Or her interpretation of the information.

The segment was a hit with everyone—except for the lawyers at *Jeopardy!*

My lack of experience didn't really allow for me to think through the potential pitfalls of this segment. Apparently giving away the payoff of *Jeopardy!* every day was frowned upon by the folks at Merv Griffin Enterprises, the producers of *Jeopardy!*, so we got a cease and desist order.

But that did not deter us.

We dropped Final Jeopardy and turned it into a general quiz segment called "Trivial Compromise." We incorporated my dad into the act, giving Alex Trebek grief each day for making us drop the segment. Now the segment began with Dad saying things like, "Hey, Trebek, what kind of punk-ass prick picks on an old woman? Here's my wife, Ginny. This ain't *Jeopardy!*" Then Mom would ramble on until she got to the question.

Now both my parents were on TV.

Another thing I didn't think through.

A couple of problems arose. First, they became mini local celebs in Minneapolis. Everywhere Dad went, inevitably some hipster would spot him from his photo on the screen. "Holy shit, you're Wilbur! Fuck Trebek! You should get more screen time!" My dad agreed, saying things like, "I could go a little longer, you know, really stick it to them. I'll bet that Trebek didn't fight for this country in any war."

Um, he's Canadian, I thought to myself.

I often ignored his suggestions.

I had further added to his already bloated "Greatest Generation" ego. And Mom liked the attention, too, though I never really knew whether she'd figured out what she was doing.

The bigger problem, however, was when the segment ran its course. As a producer, I always just killed the segment. Except this segment involved my parents. I had to fire them.

Yup. It was my first big job in TV, the first time I had to fire anyone. And it was my seventy-five-year-old parents.

It sucked. I was gonna kill their fun.

WORST. DAUGHTER. EVER.

The good news was that the audience had taken to them and all of us agreed that if we found something else for my folks to do, they could stay. But we hadn't come up with anything, so the ax needed to fall.

I went home to Minnesota to do it. I figured I should break the news in person. I sat in the TV room to talk to them, and *Oprah* was on.

Before I started my spiel, Dad barked out, "Who reads this crap she shovels? Oprah's Book Club? I wouldn't join any club that would have Oprah for a member."

Thank you, Dad! You just saved your career.

Wilbur and Ginny review Oprah's book picks. So "Wilbur and Ginny's Book Club" was born.

I dodged a bullet.

And they got a raise.

BEST. DAUGHTER. EVER.

The *Daily Show*'s producers and correspondents spent their days scouring the newspapers and the wires for stories to shoot.

Yes, I just wrote "scouring the newspapers." Remember, this was mid-1996. There was no YouTube, no Google, no Facebook or Twitter. CNN was the only cable news network. Instead, we had forty newspapers delivered each day, an AP feed, and LexisNexis.

The production staff was divided into regions. The Florida and Texas producers seemed to have the best luck finding the inexplicable stories. Except during an election year. It was intense, and daily creative battles occurred in all areas of the show. We had ten hours to put on a new show every night.

It was a writing staff run by a novice who learned as she went along how to manage a group who had never been on a writing staff. Egos, chaos, and comedy operated at Mach 5. Sniping was a natural occurrence, but we all let it roll off our backs. We knew it was never personal. Besides, we didn't have time to take offense. Everyone was too busy.

The schedule was tight. Writers wrote from eight A.M. till 1:45 P.M. That was deadline. Pencils down. Whatever you turned in at 1:45 was what Craig would read at two P.M. in my office in front of Madeleine and all the writers.

At that meeting, everyone was edgy with anticipation.

I chain-smoked through the whole meeting, nervous. I wanted everyone to get something in the show.

The room was in violation of every statute of the US Clean Air Act. Not to mention an offense to the high journalistic standards of Charlayne Hunter-Gault.

Craig read the setups with each punch line submitted. I could feel each writer's eyes burning into me, as if they were trying to brand their jokes into my brain, laughing hardest at their own jokes, hoping I would circle one of theirs, which was the signal that it was a contender to use on the show.

Sometimes I wouldn't laugh because I was listening. Sometimes I would laugh and not circle. That made them nuts. Then they left and waited for the script to come out to see if anything they had written made it into the show. I knew that each day the stroke of my pen would singe some egos.

I would sign off on the jokes, the script would go out for approval to Madeleine and the network. The writers would be psyched but guarded that if they had gotten something into that script. Guarded because they knew each day, about thirty minutes after script delivery, I got the daily "You have to change that joke, it's too mean" call from the network.

In the beginning, I had a hard time with those calls.

And they came a lot.

The novice in me often allowed my anger toward our targets to take precedence over the comedy. Sometimes I couldn't judge the difference between hilarious and shockingly mean. My problem was I laughed at both. But as I grew as a writer, I began to notice that when the intention was cruel, the laughter was not cathartic; it made me feel sick. It was that same feeling of satisfaction-then-remorse I get after eating two bags of minidonuts, then washing them down with a bucket of cheese curds. (I really wish I were kidding here.)

Identifying this behavior was a slow process. Only through time and developing my own sense of purpose did I eventually gain the skills to shift the balance from cruel-funny to righteous-funny.

It was very frustrating for my bosses because they had to keep giving the same note: "Too mean."

At first I couldn't accept the note. I was skeptical of network executives. I didn't have the maturity to take a breath and hear them out, and see that often they were right. I had good bosses. They never said, "It's not funny." They always said, "You can do better."

It made me want to do better. I just had to figure out how. I hoped they would let me.

Eileen Katz was my network point person. She was the one who got the script and relayed the network notes back to me. I always dreaded five P.M. because that was when my phone would ring with notes and the scramble began because rewrite had to happen before our five-thirty run-through.

But then one day there was a five o'clock call that helped me realize a bit about myself and helped me learn to embrace the notes. The premise of the joke had something to do with George H. W. Bush somehow doing the bidding of Jerry Falwell. The punch line was, "Yet again we find our president with his head up the ass of the Christian Right."

The call from Eileen came in.

"Lizz, we can't say that. It's just too mean. You can do better."

Part of my problem was that I would get caught up in the fervor of the room, laughing hard, oblivious that shock value could cloud my creative judgment.

I repeated the joke to myself in my quiet, now-empty office.

"Yet again we find our president with his head up the ass of the Christian Right."

I got that fair-food feeling.

Eileen was right. I could do better.

It wasn't even a punch line. It was simply lashing out at both of them, a shocking thing to say rather than a clever insight about Bush bending over backward for Falwell to get the Christian Right's money and their vote.

"Can we do the premise?" I asked.

"Of course," Eileen said. "But be more creative, less mean."

I thought for a second about what would be funny and more creative.

"How about, 'Yet again we find our president tongue-darting the Christian Right.'"

"Great. Thanks. It's not so jarring."

Okay.

I wasn't sure if she knew what tongue-darting was (look it up, it's really naughty) or if she was really just that hip. Either way, it was a better joke. Clever, and not so "on the nose." And the best part was, it was naughtier *and* more to the point.

That exchange connected me to the fact that I was a creator. If an idea was killed, I had another one. Up to that moment, I had clutched a little too tightly to the material and defended it as if there were never going to be another joke coming out of me.

There was always another joke coming, either from me or one of the show's brilliant writers. I could let go. And letting go could actually make the show better. Realizing this fact made it much easier to get the five o'clock calls.

That day the writers didn't know I had gotten the call to change that joke. When we all gathered in the studio for rehearsal, Craig read it and the room erupted in laughter. The guy who wrote the original walked over and said, "That is a much better joke. Who wrote that?"

"I did."

"Hilarious," he said as he walked back over to the other writers. He wasn't angry; he was actually pleased. Pleased because as we developed as a writing team, we also developed a love of developing an idea to its best form. It didn't matter who initiated the idea. It only mattered that we made that idea the best it could become. We all learned the joy of the process.

Changing someone's work is always tricky, and when you are a head writer, it happens all the time. I tried to be judicious when I had to kill material. When there was time, I usually had the writer come in and we would rework the joke. Sometimes there just wasn't time. Sometimes I had to write something to replace it on the fly. That's where the democracy ends. But when it does, a bond can build.

I have found you retain writers' respect only if they know when you kill a joke, it's because you can write one just as good. And sometimes better. If you kill a joke for the sake of asserting your power or to put your own joke in, not because it's the best but because it's yours, you will alienate your team. Not to mention it's an inexcusable way to assert your authority. If you decide to go down that road, you will find it a very lonely place.

Having said that, the five o'clock call also meant defending material I believed in. I always fought hard if I thought it was worth it. This was not my most endearing quality to my bosses, as I was not always reasonable. But the writers I worked with knew I was in their corner. And that meant something—to them and to me.

They also knew I wouldn't win every battle, but the fact I was willing to fight was enough for them. They knew they had a champion. They deserved one.

Bonding with the writers was important to me. I like a homey work environment, in every sense of the word. I have found I get the best material out of writers who feel familial. I decorated my office with a harvest gold '50s modern living room set and a vintage bar. Some old black-and-white photos of Ed Sullivan were placed on the side walls, but the main focus was the eight-by-ten-foot show board covered with colored index cards indicating which segments would go in what show. My desk was an old barn table that hid behind the living room area as not to remind people we were doing work here. It felt like a clubhouse rather than an office.

It was also the hang-out spot. All throughout the day and sometimes long after the show taping, there was a lot of plopping down on my couch to open a beer and shoot the shit or toss an idea around. We were a weird little family. It was kind of like *Big Love*, except that we were all there by choice and there was very little sex.

Rob Fox and Hank Gallo were my sister husbands. Rob oversaw all the field segments with the correspondents and Hank ran the talent department. They were two guys who made me laugh every day. I was living in a world where I was so overwhelmed—with worry, uncertainty, and just hoping I got it right—I was so lucky to have the gift of two TV veterans I could bounce ideas off and share my vulnerabilities with. We trusted one another's talents and jumped into one another's areas only if asked.

It was such a relief to have smart people running each department.

I don't think I could have survived if I had had to micromanage these other two crucial parts of the show. One of the things that made that a reality was that from day one, Madeleine and I had spent so much time defining the tone and mission of the show for ourselves, it allowed us to make stealth hiring choices, so everyone could excel creatively in their own departments.

The bonus of that was to be able to go down to the studio each day and in rehearsal see an interview and a field piece for the first time and genuinely laugh. I rarely had to intervene in those areas. I got to remain a fan of my own show. I had fun every day.

Often in television the us-against-them mentality is mostly reserved for the network suits. But to this bunch, there was another group of "them," a prevalent dark force in the comedy world known as "the Harvard Guys."

It's a dirty not-so-secret reality in television comedy that a lot of the sitcoms you watch or the nighttime talk shows you fall asleep to are written by Harvard graduates—whose parents spent $200,000 in tuition for them to write for *the Harvard Lampoon* or the Hasty Pudding Club. They are almost guaranteed a job after graduation in some writers' room in Hollywood.

I wanted *The Daily Show* writing staff to be Regular Joe zone. Harvard writers may have dominated the TV landscape, but they didn't have to dominate *my* TV landscape. And they didn't. In fact, we had an occasional ritual called "the Burning of the Harvard Résumé."

I kept a Folgers can in my office, and a few times a year I gathered the writers together. On the coffee table I placed the Folgers can. We cracked a few beers, and then as I stood over the can I ceremoniously held the résumé of a Harvard graduate who did brilliant work at *the Lampoon* and who was looking for a job writing for TV, lit the résumé's bottom edge on fire, dropped it in, and watched it incinerate.

I rationalized this by saying, "Every other show in late night is lousy with Harvard writers. This program gives other writers a chance."

In hindsight, I can admit I felt inferior to those wunderkinds— me, a college dropout from a state school who might be found out if I hired someone smarter than myself. (I guess I just killed my chances of getting that Hasty Pudding award. Ah, well . . .)

Not that the writers I hired weren't smart. Oh shit, bring on the hate!

From the day we launched *The Daily Show*, our correspondents infiltrated events that up until now were covered only by the mainstream media. In addition to being head writer, I joined Brian and Whitney to form the first team in "Team Coverage." Even at the presidential and vice-presidential debates of 1996, we had our own area. Everyone wanted to talk to *The Daily Show*. Or else they heard "*The Today Show*" and didn't realize what they had said yes to.

My first journalistic ambush was Jesse Jackson. I wore my best lady reporter red suit, I joined his entourage, and asked, "Reverend Jackson, Lizz Winstead from *The Daily Show*. Can I get a comment from you?"

He said, "Yes."

I was stunned. My response was, "Really?" That was all the sound bite we needed.

Many of the politicians were good sports. Senator John McCain was being interviewed by our team at a debate in Hartford and he fell backward off the riser. He just kept talking, climbed back up onto the riser, and laughed as he said, "I meant to do that."

At the same event, A. Whitney Brown stunned the entire press gaggle when Mike McCurry, then press secretary for President Clinton, called on him and Whitney asked, "Would Bill Clinton support the death penalty if Kitty Dukakis were raped and murdered?"

We hoped looking like them and asking those kinds of questions gave them pause to think about reevaluating the kind of reporting they actually did.

But it was the "hard-hitting" Brian Unger who first introduced the world to the voice, the raised eyebrow, and the tone that has influenced so many *Daily Show* correspondents who have followed. On the very first episode, Brian filed a piece about a woman who had a cat named Princess Kitty. Kitty starred in a lot of TV commercials. But when Princess Kitty was tragically killed by a BB gun, her owner had a suit made for herself in Princess Kitty's likeness, channeled Princess Kitty through a medium, and then wrote her eulogy for Princess Kitty based on what the cat revealed from the grave. Then she delivered said eulogy in the Princess Kitty suit at a kitty funeral. Brian reported the story straight, in a tone that rivaled the way any news outfit would have covered the tragic loss of a child. It was perfect satire. And a comedy genre was born. It was also the day we learned Craig had a technique for holding his shit together. He pinched his own thigh hard and held it so the pain was greater than the comedy. We watched for the pinch, as it was our gauge of how much Craig liked a story. He loved "Princess Kitty."

Now someone from *The Daily Show* showed up everywhere the "legitimate" press was: elections, inaugurations, hurricanes, trials. And when we couldn't afford to go to some big events, we improvised. We couldn't get press credentials for the Olympics, for example, so we covered the Supermodel Olympics.

On the beach.

In the Hamptons.

If there was a big news story, we were there. Or at some facsimile of "there."

The press started asking, "Who are these people? They look like us, but they seem to be making fun of us."

The show grew almost immediately because the media just got bigger and bigger.

The same year *The Daily Show* launched, MSNBC launched, then Fox News launched, and our small little operation barely kept up. We needed more writers and more correspondents. We added two writers to the staff and some new on-air talent.

An amazing comedic actor named Stephen Colbert came to our attention doing lifestyle pieces on *Good Morning America*, and he seemed to be getting away with some things he shouldn't have. He seemed perfect for the team.

And as if I didn't have enough to do, I added movie reviews to my list of duties, teamed up with the hilariously flamboyant fashion writer Frank DeCaro, and dished on newly released movies.

It took time, but a machine was put in place. Old mistakes got ironed out as new ones emerged, and with each new problem I had that much more experience under my belt to fix it.

I had finally learned this job.

There are many jokes and pieces I remember fondly, but the one that sticks with me the most was my date to the prom.

Almost a year after *The Daily Show* debuted and I had regularly been on camera doing my pieces, I received a letter from a high school senior named Christian who lived in Ramsey, New Jersey. He was a super fan of the show. We did our first few weeks of shows without an audience, so we were kind of in a vacuum about who watched and how intently.

So the first day we added a studio audience, there was Christian, first in line, wearing a handmade T-shirt that read UNGER RULES. He pulled me aside at the show and quoted me all his favorite jokes. Smart ones, small subtle ones. He loved nuance.

He was one of those kids who had no idea that when the pain of high school was over, he would see the popular kids had achieved the greatness of being an assistant manager of the Muffler Hut and he would be cooler than all of them. I saw it right then.

Nine months later, he wrote me and asked me to be his date for his high school prom.

I was more receptive to the idea than you might think.

See, my hockey-playing ex-boyfriend from high school ruined my own prom by . . . oh, by not showing up. Yes, I was stood up for my own high school prom.

But now, thanks to a smart kid from New Jersey, I had my chance to reclaim the night.

I told *The Daily Show* staff my high school story, then read Christian's letter aloud to them. We all agreed: I would be Christian's date.

Not only did I accept, I accepted and took a camera crew with me. Our date would be on national TV.

I was thirty-six, he was seventeen.

Why not?

I poured myself into a red dress designed to scare parents. Christian wore a black-and-white two-toned tux, designed to scare anyone with taste.

It was prom. I went for it, and so did he.

I arrived at his parents' house. He gave me my wrist corsage and we had our pictures taken with the other couples we quadruple dated with in the living room. I must admit, we looked pretty great.

It was like so many dances I remembered from high school, except his parents pulled me into the other room, offered me a shot of whiskey, and said, "You're gonna need this, it's gonna be a long night."

So off we went to the high school gym. In a limo that matched his tux.

We walked into the school, and soon every cheerleader and football douche had the wind taken out of their sails when Christian walked in with a camera crew and a woman who looked like she knew something about sex. I clutched his arm very tight. I was his girl. This was his night, so I milked it.

We ate gelatinous chicken and danced to "Rock Lobster," and I saw girls in the bathroom pull out flasks of booze from nether regions that would shock dancers at a Bangkok brothel. We even slow-danced to "The Lady in Red." Christian kissed me on the cheek.

At the end of the night, I rode home with the crew in the van, and we sent the kids in the limo off to the Jersey shore for a bonfire and (I'm guessing) some of that secret girl drink. As we said good night, Christian said, "I know you could have ditched me and just gotten the camera shots you needed. I can't believe you hung out all night with me. It was the best night of my life."

I almost started to cry. I wanted to move the clock forward for him so he could see what an amazing life awaited him.

"Thank you for making this my best prom ever, Christian," I said. "I'm the luckiest girl here."

He is now almost the same age I was when we went to prom. I hope he pursued his dream of art school.

I didn't really know how to begin to write about my time at *The Daily Show*. Knowing how to end my story was even harder. I didn't know what people wanted to hear about it from me; after all, my tenure there was short, and it's continued on very successfully without me. But the story of how it came to be is one not often told and one that is mine to tell, and it definitely changed me forever.

The memories and anecdotes are endless. The people who helped and nurtured me were many. I came to the show with nothing more than a fuzzy sense of my own instincts and a skill to call out bullshit. I followed those instincts and helped create a framework and content that started a whole new way people get their news, and encouraged them to question the information they are given.

I left *The Daily Show* a few months before Jon Stewart took over, for complicated reasons that are far less important than my wonderful experience of creating and bringing it to life. And to be honest, when I left I had one nagging hope for it: that whoever replaced me to raise this baby would see that if they followed the lead of the media, picked their targets wisely, and kept giving the audience credit for having a brain, they would raise a gifted child. When I found out Jon Stewart was taking over as host, I knew he would. He nurtured that baby into a brilliant kid, and then a young adult, and now it's a Rhodes Scholar.

What I never could have predicted was how successful the show would become. Not because I ever doubted Jon, but because I never envisioned the news media would become so derelict.

During my time at *The Daily Show*, I learned how to make a TV show and I learned how in one of the most invaluable ways possible: I made every mistake I could. I can now hear almost any idea and say, "Yeah. I tried that, and here is what happens if you follow that through." Weeding out a bad idea before you have wasted time on it is one of the most useful skills to have in life.

I came to the show with only instincts, but I left it a writer, a producer, and a correspondent, and I learned I am a woman with a lot of ideas. Some good and some bad. But I hope neither end of that spectrum defines me, rather how I deal with reactions to both.

I SHOULD HAVE BEEN HAVE BEEN SENT TO FEMINIST GITMO

I had moved on from *The Daily Show* and developed more shows that provided a critical eye on the world. I produced a special celebrating Gloria Steinem and the twenty-fifth anniversary of the Ms. Foundation for Women, and a series for CourtTV called *Snap Judgment* that lampooned the legal system.

Brian Unger left *The Daily Show* a bit later, and we had such an amazing creative bond that we formed a production company called Payload Industries. We produced a pilot for Fox Broadcast, a takeoff on the television newsmagazine genre, and landed a few script and development deals. We had created a niche. We felt like we were on a roll.

Then came September 11, 2001.

Now, there were many types of 9/11 fallout far more devastating than the problems of two little people in this crazy world, but for those of us who made our livings as political and social critics, the attacks and the reaction to them had unexpected consequences. It also became the day satire came to a grinding halt.

Any television show that involved mocking the government or the media was an unwelcomed programming pitch. And when I say unwelcomed, I mean UNWELCOMED. As in Darwin-at-a-Tea-Party-rally unwelcomed.

Yes, immediately after 9/11, people, corporations, TV networks, everybody scrambled for airtime and announced they were going to become more thoughtful and serious. Or at least tone down the narcissism for ten minutes. They wanted people to know they were patriotic. Whatever that meant. Everybody got into the act with some version of "Look, look, we care, too! We are patriots, too!"

It was embarrassing. Then ridiculous. Then sublime.

VH1 released some sort of statement; the essence was the network was sensitive to the mood of the country, so they planned to bring a more understated tone to the Fashion Awards. Yeah, that's what people wanted: a subdued tribute to shallow-ass celebrity glamour. Anyone on the fence about whether they were going to watch surely read that statement and said to themselves, "Now that VH1 came out on the side of America, I will watch JLo win Best Lip Liner on the Red Carpet." Or whatever it was that she was nominated for that year. I'm sure she was dressed in a much more "understated" outfit that matched the mood of the nation.

I didn't watch.

It was hilariously misguided, and for me, vastly frustrating that I had no outlet to respond to this kind of "patriotism." I was a breed lost in the wilderness.

In the insanity of it all, I returned to my yelling at the TV from The Chair behavior. And thanks to the wonders of modern technology, I added yelling at the computer to my repertoire.

A year later, memories faded. I was living in Los Angeles, and people replaced the Rah Rah America flags on their cars with their Lakers pendants, and Brian and I finally sold a show we had been dying to do to the Oxygen network. It was a series that took on the cult of morning television called O_2Be.

It was part *Today Show*, part *Live! with Regis and Kelly*, and wall-to-wall funny (at least Brian and I thought so). Brian and I played the hosts, and Frank Conniff was our Gelman. We waxed on about the shallow dinner parties we went to and had "experts" on the show to dispense advice on a variety of topics. Two of my favorites: *Daily Show* alum Beth Littleford played a life coach who explained "how to be a wife and a mother *and* still balance your daytime drinking," and in another episode played a financial guru who advocated filling out every credit card offer you got in the mail in order to "stay ahead of your bad credit."

As shallow as our characters were, of course we each had vanity magazines. *Brian* magazine featured articles like "America the Bootyful" and "Sexual Harassment: 15 Alibis That Work," while *Lizz* magazine probed deeply into stories like "They're Called the Help, So Why Don't They?" and "Tuning Out: How to Smile Without Listening."

Most important, however, we took on some of the most taboo parts of the post-9/11 world. For instance, we exposed the hypocrisy of how the war had liberated the women of Afghanistan by doing a burka fashion show featuring, among others, a Burberry burka and a beach burka made of terry cloth.

The New York Times said about $O_2 Be$, "At its best, it's hysterical. It shows what happens when talented people are allowed to take their expertise and run with it." We were sure we had arrived with our next big hit. It was like nothing else Oxygen had on the network.

Apparently, that was not a plus.

After six episodes, the powers-that-be at Oxygen decided satire didn't work and canceled the show because the tone didn't fit with its 2003 branding strategy that included the phrase *Women with Weapons*. I kid you not.

The fate of $O_2 Be$ proved to be a microcosm of the general 2002–2003 media landscape, as MSNBC, Fox, and CNN started beating the "Countdown to the War" drums with more glitzy graphics and impending doom theme songs. So it seemed the zero-satire tolerance monsters had reared their heads yet again.

This was also the time that reality TV exploded. Our agents insisted we had to create the next *Survivor* to survive. We wondered if the satire blackout would ever end.

So Brian and I begrudgingly joined the lesions—I wish that were a typo—making the world a "better place" through reality TV. We landed at MTV, producing a spring break hidden camera show, ironically enough called *Burned*, concocted by two guys who had never worked in TV. We were hired to execute their vision.

The preproduction of the show was based in LA, and among other things involved interviewing dozens of bikini-clad twentysomethings trying to find three of them who fit the MTV criteria I dubbed BAIT: Beautiful, Approachable, Inconceivable Tits.

It was an exhausting, demoralizing casting process. To try to cleanse between each interview, I read the transcript of then Secretary of State Colin Powell's speech before the UN Security Council that proclaimed Iraq possessed "weapons of mass destruction." I wondered if anyone else in the building was doing this as well. Then I wondered if I could get *the New York Times* in South Padre Island, which was where we were going to film *Burned*.

I guessed "probably not" to both questions.

I was right.

Our casting led us to produce the following soul-charring show. You may hate me after you read this. Trust me, I hated myself more. Which was not as much as I hated this post-9/11 world.

Using hidden cameras, we rounded up frat boy "Playaz" on the beach, using our BAIT to lure them into a very elaborate hoax to see if they would act like sexist assholes or giant sexist assholes. We had the most luck finding guys who had passed out shirtless on the beach around four A.M. after a night of slamming down dozens of plastic horns full of shitty beer. We got to them around noon, and I think the only reason they escaped third-degree burns is that apparently the combination of sand and one's own vomit provides crucial protection from the sun's harmful UV rays. It may be the world's best natural sunscreen, but I'm no dermatologist.

Brian and I somehow talked Maggie, my roommate and a producer from O_2Be, to join the production. Maggie was another of the Punk Rock Ghetto gals, and in her former career she managed rock bands, so she knew how to coerce half-drunk idiots to do our bidding.

And so it began.

Mags and I, in our bathing suits, gathered up the targets. (I am both happy and saddened to report that drunken college guys respond to a female in a bikini even when said woman is old enough to be their mother, even before the media deemed that women in their forties were sexually attractive.) After trolling the beach for most of the day, we identified about a dozen guys who seemed like Playaz.

The only way to make this concept work was to get their friends into the act. So we played a good cop/bad cop routine. While Maggie chatted up our lothario, I hit up his friends to bring their Playa buddy to some potentially date-rapey spring break event that was happening later that night. Not because we wanted to foster a date-rapey situation, but because every spring break party had the stench of "This could go horribly wrong."

We sent in our three BAIT for Phase One.

Our hidden cameras captured our BAIT flirting with the Playaz. If they seemed like good targets, each woman invited her mark to meet her the next day at her hotel bar. This part of the show alone should have sent me to feminist Gitmo. I say this as a woman who also worked on *The Man Show*. And had fun.

You may want to make sure you have time for a shower before reading further.

Phase Two: The hotel bar. The meat of the show (so to speak).

We had the Playaz scheduled in forty-five-minute intervals. Each BAIT would go through a series of four guys, and then we switched them out for a new BAIT and four more guys.

Brian and I watched each scene play out in a luxurious, tiki-ish themed motel room stuffed with about eight network executives watching on monitors as below in the tiki-ish themed bar, our hidden cameras captured each BAIT charm the Playa to get him to reveal if he was all talk or all action.

At some point in the conversation, our BAIT excused herself to go to the bathroom. ENTER one of the Playa's friends. The Playa would download to his buddy how the date was going.

This is where the concept revealed a major flaw. (Okay, the whole show was a shit shack, but I am talking expected results.) The expected result was that the guy would be very sweet when talking to our BAIT, but when his buddy showed up, our hidden cameras would catch him talking smack about how she totally wanted him or how he was going to nail her—proof that would reveal he was full of it.

But when you have hungover guys who are not infused with the bravery of alcohol, most of them were boring or freaked out about talking to the BAIT. That could have been fine if they turned on the bravado when their friend showed up.

But instead, most of the conversations were real—which of course meant TV death.

From guy after guy we got a lot of "She seems nice" or "It's going okay." Or, worst of all, "I wanna get outta here and hit the beach."

This could not happen because it would have destroyed the payoff of the whole show.

The executives were more concerned that we weren't getting what we needed instead of worrying that what we were doing was legally dubious—eavesdropping on private conversations, recording them surreptitiously, then humiliating them publicly—all without their prior knowledge or consent.

So Brian and I directed the girls through earpieces and gave them lines that started out sweet and often devolved into things that would make even a politician in a rest-stop bathroom feel dirty. We were desperate to get the Playaz talking.

I felt like I was producing something akin to that Marion Barry[1] sting video, but with more attractive people. I couldn't mask the disdain in my face. There were a lot of variations of "Lighten up, Lizz" bandied about on the part of the executives.

We were running out of guys, but luckily—and I use that term in its broadest possible definition—we found two true Playaz who lived

---

1. For you children who don't watch *Jeopardy!*, Marion Barry was a former mayor of Washington, D.C., who in 1990 was caught on FBI surveillance video smoking crack in a motel room. Strangely enough, this behavior didn't deride his political career. After serving six months in jail for his crack-tastic video performance, he was elected to the DC city council in 1992, and mayor—again—in 1994.

up to the premise. We needed to get through one more phase to choose the lucky winner and subject him to "the Big Payoff."

It gets even more hideous.

The payoff was that our BAIT invited the guy who talked the most smack to his friend to be her date at an MTV party she was "invited to." He'd meet her there, they'd mingle for a while and have a few drinks, and then came the big surprise.

SURPRISE! Suddenly all the monitors in the bar started showing the footage of him. Every last gorgeous girl in the joint instantly turned to watch the insanity unfold. First came the scene of the Playa being sweet with the BAIT, and then it cut to him talking bullshit to his friends. There he was, busted in a room full of hot coeds, with TV cameras rolling. All of the women in the bar turned to him and chanted, "Burned, burned, burned" for five minutes straight.

He had been humiliated.

But not humiliated enough.

Oh, no.

As the chanting continued, now came the part where I asked him to sign a release form, and convinced him that being on MTV was cooler than having dignity.

It was at this moment I understood the power of MTV.

Our Playaz signed away.

"Go ahead, put me on TV!" they said. "I will be famous!"

Yes. It's better than anything else.

It gets EVEN worse.

Now here's the part of the story where you will weep for my humanity. And all humanity.

Of the two guy finalists we had to choose from, one was white and the other happened to be black. This is important to know, because MTV insisted that whoever was chosen, we close out the special with all three of our BAIT walking the biggest bullshitter at the end of a leash, shirtless, with the word *Burned* painted on his bare chest, through a gauntlet of hundreds of spring breakers lined up on the beach reprising the "burned, burned, burned" chant to finish off the already-scorching humiliation.

Brian and I raised the issue, then we raised our voices.

"Now what's the problem?" one of the executants snarked.

"We can't go with the black guy, it's not cool," Brian said with all the diplomacy he could muster.

The executive was puzzled. "Why?"

"Um. What part of the last hundred and fifty years have you missed?" I choked back. "Even the Klan would say, 'Whoa, that's harsh.'" We actually had to explain to these white executives that it is in no way, shape, or form acceptable to:

1. Drag a shirtless black man on a leash.

2. Down a beach.

3. In the South.

4. In 2003.

5. Or any other year.

6. While hundreds of white frat guys chant "burned" at him.

The executives could not believe we brought this up. They did not see a problem.

Let me repeat that.

THEY HONESTLY DID NOT SEE A PROBLEM.

They thought we were being oversensitive liberals who were looking for trouble where there was none.

It became a screaming match.

"You have got to be fucking kidding me!" Brian said. When he gets angry, he has a vein that pops up on his right temple. During this argument, it engulfed his whole forehead.

"How can you not see that in every way this is fucked up?" I chimed in.

I was willing to burn a career bridge with people this stupid. In fact, I burned it, and then I blew the fucker up.

"If you like both guys equally, let's pick the white guy," Brian said. "Because if it's the black guy, we quit."

We found no nobility in threatening to quit. We just refused to be part of anything that contained such sheer, ugly stupidity.

I think the only thing that saved us was that the executives had no more time and no more budget to get rid of us and start over again. And that gave us the upper hand. And they hated us for it. But no more than we hated ourselves.

Finally, the big cheese begrudgingly relented. "Ugh. Just use the white guy, then"—like we were fighting over which linens to use at a dinner party. I think Brian and I spoke maybe ten words to any of them after that.

We used the white guy and the network must have liked it because *Burned* got picked up for a series, and if I remember correctly, thirty episodes.

I am sure you will be astonished to discover that Brian and I did not continue with the project.

I have never felt so awful about myself. I tried to justify it, scraped the bottom of the cold comfort barrel for justifications like "I had to pay my bills" and "There is nothing else out there." But the only aspect of the whole nightmare that really gave me any consolation was that this content was still morally superior to anything on Fox News.

I still had not *officially* sold my soul.

I learned my limits, that even if I have to work to keep a roof over my head, I won't do that again. I am not proud of what we did, but I'm relieved that I understand my core values a bit better. And that I was willing to fight for them.

FINDING A
NEW VOICE

When I returned to Los Angeles from South Padre Island, I sunk into a massive depression. I simply couldn't make another show that put me on the moral ladder half a rung above the *Girls Gone Wild* guy. Or work for people who didn't know racial insensitivity when it was spelled out on the chest of a man on a leash.

I felt the way I had ten years earlier: like I was slowly drowning in creative quicksand. The only thing that saved me was my Sunday dinners. I am big on gathering friends in my home. I have been ever since I began to live on my own. Dinner parties, movie nights, game nights—I love bringing people together. I once had my astrological chart read, and the woman told me I was Leo/Taurus/Taurus. When I asked what that meant, she said, "You love to be the center of attention, but you hate to leave your apartment." Spot on.

The dinner crew in this part of my life consisted of anywhere from six to eight comedy writers and performers. The core group were folks who worked on O_2Be: Maggie, Brian, Frank Conniff, Kent Jones, Neil Kendall, and Mike Gandolfi. We had the occasional drop-in from Dana Gould, Sarah Silverman, and other funny types from LA or who were in town visiting from New York City. Even Michele Norris popped in one night while she was in Los Angeles on business to wax nostalgic about similar gatherings we had back at our old place in Minneapolis.

I never had a big place to live in Los Angeles. In fact, I was one of the few people whose apartment in New York was bigger than my place in LA. My apartment in California was cramped and hot, and we ate surrounded by every dirty pot and pan I had used.

It didn't matter.

We screamed and laughed about the shitty shows we were working on, the shitty shows we tried to get work on, or the shitty people who got the work on the shitty shows we tried to get work on. But mostly we talked politics. There were only two rules to Sunday dinner: Each guest must have a passion for politics and we must eat around a proper table.

I insist on having meals at a table. I firmly believe having big conversations involving everyone is essential, as it gives everyone a chance to hear the thoughts and opinions of the group.

I thrive on having lots to think about.

I also believe that, in some strange way, it helps people who have awful memories of family dinners to rethink that dynamic, re-learning that home-cooked food and discussion can be a loving, enlightening experience.

Sundays weren't a salon, per se, as the conversations were never planned. It was a given that everyone who showed up knew what they were talking about. They read *the New York Times* every day and watched tax dollars being spent on the news on PBS. They read books and magazines. Yes, in Los Angeles. With this gang you could count on the funniest download of the week's news. It was loud, insightful, hilarious, and often outrageous. We hung on one another's words.

One crucial part of life for comedians is something that people often overlook: For those of us whose career it is to make others laugh, we have to surround ourselves with people who make *us* laugh. And when we do? That's when we actually shut up and listen. When you add to that people who make us laugh while giving us something to think about, we laugh and learn. These folks are the best.

Each Sunday night, everyone around my table shared buried nuggets from a news piece that we may have missed or gave us a recap from that *New Yorker* article everyone was "meaning to get to." (The *New Yorker* person was usually Conniff. He was the only guy I knew who actually got to every article.) We went over the week's news and events—all of it—between bites of chicken potpie, spaghetti and meatballs, or pork roast. And of course dessert. Usually it was layer cake: coconut cream, German chocolate, or red velvet. The entire meal was a comfort food tsunami, and it fueled the conversation.

In addition to my proper table theory, I also believe that if you serve traditional American comfort food during a political discussion, conservatives will have a harder time calling you a commie.

It was Sunday night, so we wound down the evening counting the puns in *Sex and the City*. Sometimes we played games. By the end of each night, I was so satisfied, so happy and content, that all the laughs and the love became a lullaby, and I always fell asleep in a chair, waking up in the middle of the night draped in a blanket in an empty house.

Sunday dinners were a simple tradition that kept all of us sane as we did work we hated or struggled to find the next gig. Brian and I hadn't worked since my membership to NOW was suspended on South Padre Island. One afternoon in early July, he showed up looking like the cat that ate the canary.

"We need to talk," he said in a tone that was usually reserved for phrases like "I have cancer" or "Our relationship has become something else." Since we had had the "Our relationship has become something else" talk six years earlier, I panicked.

"You can't die on me," I barked.

"What?!" he said, taken aback. He never got used to my immediate overreactions. "I am not dying. Well, not in that way, at any rate." He paused and then sheepishly broke the news. "I just got offered a job."

"Oh, thank God!" I shrieked, relieved we were getting back in the saddle.

But then what he just said sunk in: *I* just got offered a job. Not *we*, *I*.

I couldn't get mad. We had talked about the fact that if either one of us ever got an opportunity to work solo, we couldn't turn it down if it was right.

"Okaaaaay, what is it?" I secretly hoped it was not something that would make me jealous. I wanted it to be a job that made me happy for him but that I did not want in any way, shape, or form. Like a surfing show on ESPN, or something to do with cars or space.

"I have been offered the host position on *Extra*."

Whoa. That was not what I expected to hear. And it was news that made me feel something I hadn't considered.

I was neither happy nor sad. I was concerned.

It was far from his dream job, I knew that. And it was something that I wouldn't want to do ever. What surprised me was that I never expected that he'd want to do it, either.

I didn't know how to react.

"How do you feel?" was the best I could come up with.

"Well, now you understand my dying comment," he said. "I just can't turn down work. It will keep us both afloat."

I hated to think of Brian taking a job that I knew might kill him. I loved him for taking a job for both of us. The "something else" that led to our relationship ending? He had become my brother.

I made him take me to lunch, where we talked it over.

When I got home, I cried, because my partner in crime was moving on to commit a crime without me.

Fuck. I was lost.

A few days later, my phone rang. It was a man with a beautiful baritone voice. The following dialogue is as close to accurate as I can remember.

"Hi, I am looking for Lizz Winstead."

"You found her."

"My name is Jon Sinton, and I am launching a national progressive radio network out of New York City with Al Franken, and I got your number from him. He suggested we find a Lizz Winstead type to help create programming and thought you might have some suggestions."

Well, that introduction rendered me speechless.

A Lizz Winstead *type*? I had no idea I was a type. Wow. What was a Lizz Winstead type? Did he want someone exactly like Lizz Winstead, only less Lizz Winsteady? What would that be—me, but with a more soothing demeanor? That would certainly be a "type," but not a "Lizz Winstead type."

And then my instincts kicked in.

Ahhh, I thought to myself. *You want Lizz Winstead, but younger.* That's what all these showbiz types always wanted. Or worse, Lizz Winstead but a guy version.

They got *a lot* of work.

Or the very worst, a Lizz Winstead who could reach a "broader audience," which was code for "Lizz Winstead Lite."

Lizzilla was instantly on the prowl, because I had heard this executive rap again and again. Asking for a "type" was a new one to me, but having network execs pretend they wanted to do political satire when they really didn't was routine.

Dealing with networks was a Kabuki dance of ideas that boiled down to "Lizz, what we really want is a show that is like *The Daily Show* but doesn't make too much of a point or doesn't ruffle feathers and isn't really about politics and is more focused on celebrities."

"Soooo, not at all like *The Daily Show.*"

"Exactly."

Got it.

Before I settled into a seething rage of contempt at this man I'd never spoken to in my life, I remembered an important part of what

he said: *a national* progressive *radio network* with *Al Franken, and I
got your number from* him.

I backed away from the lash-out ledge.

This was an Al Franken project, *and* he used the word *progressive*
without a caveat.

Thoughts of working with Al Franken ran through my head like a
marathon. I must have been silent for ten seconds.

"Hello, did I lose you?"

"I'm sorry, you just kind of threw me."

It was true. What else should I have said?

I wanted to believe this was awesome, but I still had a reasonable amount of skepticism, so I proceeded with a tempered caution,
the type I'd used before to suss out a guy selling a bed frame on
Craigslist.

"So what are you thinking with this progressive radio station?" I
asked. He proceeded with his soothing voice to explain his vast
radio background. I was half listening, still seething about the
"type" comment. But then he started in about how infusing satire
with issues was going to be the foundation of the network. This
brought me back into the conversation.

He wanted to develop shows that combined comedians and
broadcasters, both of whom who were passionate about progressive
ideals. He made his case about how our media had been hijacked,
how the voice of truth was nowhere on the TV dial except on Comedy
Central. He floored me with the fact that the ratio of diverse points
of view on talk radio was 91 percent conservative to 9 percent progressive. He spoke of the need for bold opinions mixed with humor
and people who cared about the facts.

On the other end of the phone, I was drooling like a dog under the dinner table; I was starving to make a difference. It sounded like he was describing Sunday dinner on the radio. With less cleanup to do.

"How about the *actual* Lizz Winstead?" I said, hoping that would be an amenable alternative type.

He shot back without hesitation. "Really? Even better."

I just stole a job from all those Lizz Winstead types out there. Whoever they are.

I immediately called Brian, who was just starting at *Extra*. He was happy for me. And I think a little sad *his* partner in crime was moving on to commit crimes without him. And moving back to New York to do it.

I had never worked in radio. I had never launched a network. Now I had a job doing both. Here we go again. After a few phone calls, I was made senior vice president of entertainment programming for a yet-to-be-named progressive radio network, and would also cohost a midmorning show from nine to noon. I had to help staff eighteen hours of programming and find some cohosts for the show I was going to do. I do have a pretty good knack for picking talent, so I hoped my TV experience and instincts would help me out.

Step one was easy. Before I even moved back to New York, I got the comedy writers in place. First I roped the Sunday dinner crew into coming aboard. Half of them moved to New York and a few couldn't make the trek, so they telejokemuted.

The one I really wanted had to pass. He was the host of *Extra*.

I picked up the rest back in New York. It was an easy sell, and within a week I had assembled my team. We had some former *Daily Show* writers mixed with the $O_2 Be$ writers. I added a few great stand-ups and one first-timer who was about to become very intimate with the term *trial by fire*.

Another *small* piece of business also happened before I got back to New York, but since no one was making a big deal about it, neither did I.

The station changed hands before it was even a station.

It was originally owned by a husband and wife team out of Chicago, but was sold to a pair of guys who had a radio station in Guam. But Jon was still there, and Al Franken was committed to the project, so I didn't question anything about putting my career into the hands of two guys from Guam no one ever heard of who had at one time owned a radio station in Guam.

It was probably the best station in all of Guam.

I just kept packing up my stuff for my move across the country to work on this massive radio network now owned by two guys from Guam. And so were a lot of my friends.

Did I mention they were from Guam?

What could go wrong?

I got back to New York City in September of 2003, a month ahead of the writers. I had to meet Shelley Lewis, my compatriot on the news side, so we could get to the daunting task of actually staffing up the station so the creatives could get to work.

Shelley was a radio veteran who had moved to television news and had left her most recent post at CNN to come over to the yet-to-be-named-progressive-radio-network-owned-by-two-guys-from-Guam. I was excited because of all the accomplishments on her résumé; the one that impressed me most was that for years she produced the overnight cult favorite ABC's *World News Now*.

Shelley was the greatest gift out of my AAR experience. "I left

CNN to come and make a difference," she told me at one of our first dinners. "Plus, my husband is an artist, so I always have the security of that to fall back on." Her dry sense of humor got me through challenges at every turn—challenges that I had never encountered in my entire career.

First, we had *a lot* of bosses.

There were the two Guamanian owners. They had some ideas.

There was a CEO, a president, an executive vice president, and all kinds of senior vice presidents of this or that. I had a hard time remembering who was whose boss. I knew that most of them were my bosses. They all seemed to act like it, anyway.

Some of them had radio backgrounds but knew nothing about progressive politics. Some were progressives but had no experience in radio. None of them had ever worked in comedy. All of them had extensive backgrounds in having an opinion. Jon Sinton had both a background in radio and politics, so he had to make the dynamic work. Sisyphus wept for him.

We were to launch March 31, 2004. We had seven months to pull it together.

At first I naively thought it would be fairly easy to do. A lot of the talent was in place or identified as potential talent to bring on board. Al Franken was ready to do his show from noon to three P.M. and had snatched away Minnesota Public Radio favorite Katherine Lanpher to be his partner.

Janeane Garofalo had signed on just about the same time I did. She had a show idea with comedian/writer/director Sam Seder. I knew Sam from his stand-up and films, and we played in the same poker game on occasion, so I thought, *Perfect.* Funny, smart, brave. We were cooking.

Janeane suggested the brilliant Marc Maron for morning drive time and Marc was game, so we teamed him up with Mark Riley, a veteran of New York City talk radio, and Sue Ellicott, a former BBC correspondent. Mornings accomplished.

Randi Rhodes was a powerhouse talker in South Florida who had a very hot afternoon drive time show, often beating Rush Limbaugh in her time slot, and who was itching to come to New York and go national. Perfect.

Marty Kaplan, director of the Norman Lear Center, was hired to do an arts and culture show between Al's and Randi's programs.

It was starting to look like a real network.

The Guamsters had secured a spot on the dial in NYC on AM 1300 WLIB (pure coincidence) and had also purchased five stations. We would stream live on the Web for the rest of the country.

Our studio in New York City was the top floor of a building on 33rd and Lexington, at the corner of Nowhere to Get Lunch and the Shitty 6 Train. The office space was a few floors below and we had taken them over from the staff of "Showtime at the Apollo." The walls were lavender and chartreuse, and the original color of the carpet was some other color than the gray it had become.

The staff came on in stages. First it was the development team, which was basically Shelley and me, and our many, many bosses. Then the writers and producers, and finally the on-air talent.

My concept was to create a bank of evergreen comedy bits that dealt with the environment, corporate malfeasance, politicians, the media, you name it—to have at the ready when we launched. The goal was to produce pieces that could be a companion to any news that broke. If a corporation did something hideous, we had a funny gag ready to hammer it home. A politician fucks up, we had a mini bio of his life to button the story. We wrote hundreds of bits. Once we were on the air, teams of writers were assigned to each show, and they helped write the comedy that sprang from the news of the day.

We wrote so much material, everyone who worked there at the time did a character or a voice. The CEO of Air America brilliantly voiced a satirical travel guide for each of the fifty states. Our chief legal counsel was an incredible mimic; Jon Sinton, our president, and even our man Reed in ad sales lent their voices. Shelley was hilarious, recording parodies of those sugarcoated 1950s corporate industrials, except we skewered the likes of Blackwater, Dow, and Monsanto. We covered every base there was.

So up until launch, after a full day of work putting the mechanics of a radio station together, we spent almost every evening in a recording studio with takeout food, beer, and three-quarters of the AAR staff, laughing, rewriting, and recording comedy pieces. We were working eighteen-hour days, but it seemed right because we were doing something that mattered. Writers, assistants, producers, and executives all came together with one idea: to create a national progressive radio network. It gave everyone who had never worked with comedians and comedy writers a much greater understanding of just how hard the business of comedy was.

I was so proud that the comedy helped foster such respect. It energized me in a way that I never knew something could. We chugged along, existing on adrenaline and fear of the unknown. We were a team. We valued one another. The bosses who didn't participate never really learned that.

I believe the camaraderie we built in those months prior to the launch created a bond that kept us from drowning. But remember, passion is an amazing flotation device. Eventually adrenaline wasn't enough, and the reality of making this work on a day-to-day basis seemed daunting.

Some things changed while others stayed the same. For example, as the staff grew, office space did not. There were seven and a half offices for eighty employees. From what I had read about Guam, these were typical working conditions—minus the sewing machines and PR department.

The chaos was just beginning.

The writers had been comedy machines, but up until now they had desks and computers. As more and more staff arrived, everyone was being moved around like a radio refugee camp. Offices were taken over by shows and people were shoved four or five to a room. Any room.

Shelley and I gave up our office to make room for the midmorning show crew. She was brave and turned a tiny storage room into her office. Her privacy needs were greater than mine. Plus, I always thought it smelled like supply closet sex.

I moved out to the couch in the lobby; it was the only unclaimed piece of furniture left in the place. I sat there hours on end, editing comedy bits. I had trained in The Chair, so it seemed fitting. Now we had more people than we had desks. And phones. And computers.

The space problems led to a bit of a morale issue, which is to be expected when you have a lot of people and little infrastructure. It was as if the Guamen didn't see what was happening to the offices, like those people in denial on *Hoarders*. Everyone was caged like capons in a corporate chicken farm. Shelley and I were made to feel like divas when we demanded, "Everyone here needs a computer and a desk" or "We need a Staples account!"

Some of our many bosses recognized the working conditions had become untenable and tried to intervene, but the Guamala-madingdongs would respond with, "Why can't the writers share computers?" or "Just get what you need for supplies and we will reimburse you."

I finally just donated my two personal laptops—yes, I now was computer savvy—to the cause and put my credit card down at Staples so that we could stay stocked with toner and copier paper. It remained "the Staples account" until I left.

The Guamaniacs were very excited when they finally came up with a space "solution" for the writers. The office next door was rented by penny stock traders and had a bunch of empty chairs. I suspect but don't know that they slipped them some cash each month so our creatives could set up shop in there. So sharing space with the traders screaming on the phones and playing Nerf basketball, and having no Internet access, the writers for our radio shows were expected to be creative.

And grateful.

I complained yet again. I was quickly becoming in the eyes of the owners the person who would never be happy, I'm sure. I didn't care if I was happy. I just wanted the writers to be happy. But the relentless chaos and creative exhaustion led me to slowly start losing my ability to make anyone happy.

It was really a brutal situation, and we started working weekends in the office just so we could finally get some work done. The Guamereiners saw this as a great solution rather than the satire sweatshop it had become.

Those kinds of "solutions" should have been red flags to all of us, but there was so much to do and I was so overwhelmed and so tired that someone could have taken a red flag, tied me up with it, and taken another red flag and shoved it up my ass and I wouldn't have noticed.

Maybe now would be a good time to tell you the owners never hung out at our recording sessions.

Shelley was busy hiring newscasters, producers, and researchers to fill out the production teams of each show. After one excruciating day of meetings in her closet, she staggered out, plopped down next to me on the couch, and sighed. "You know what's amazing about all of this? People are flocking to come and work at a place that looks and feels like an airport full of people stranded during a blizzard."

She always made me laugh. And it was true: The sheer volume of people who wanted to be part of this network was staggering.

There was one tiny order of business that needed to get resolved. It was sort of an important one. Hiring the third person to cohost my show. The nine to noon slot.

One piece of amazing news was that hip-hop legend Chuck D had signed on to be one of my cohosts. In any other circumstance I would have been so excited and freaked out that five days a week I would be sitting next to Public Enemy's Chuck D that I would not have been able to think of much else. But I was so buried in preproduction that I didn't even have time to process the fact. Or the fact that I was going to be the lead-in show for Al Franken. And three months before our launch, I still didn't have that big-brain progressive to fill out the show.

When the reality of this sunk in, I started to fear I might not find the right person, my show would suck, and they would resume their hunt for that "Lizz Winstead type." Our bosses were adamant that we make this a priority. The ones who knew very little about what a progressive was were pushing for hosts like Gloria Allred or Jerry Springer.

"Gloria Allred?" Shelley laughed. "If I went home and opened my refrigerator right now, Gloria Allred would be in there with her latest client giving an interview."

I reviewed the other piece of bad idea theater.

"I refuse to go on air with a guy who as mayor of Cincinnati got busted for writing a check to a hooker," I said. And that was the least of his moral transgressions.

"He is a liberal and he really wants to do radio" was the big argument made in his defense.

"He also makes millions exploiting people on TV," I shot back. "It's not happening."

Our radio overlords didn't seem to understand that calling yourself a liberal or a progressive and living like one are two different things. We had a bit of a strained relationship.

One thing I knew in my heart was that if we launched a network that was going to call out hypocrisy, we couldn't give the right a big, gaping target that immediately illuminated our own. Shelley and I knew that we couldn't keep saying no without options of our own to bring to the table. We started scrambling, listening to demo reel after demo reel that had been piling up. No one was working for us.

We had hired Laura Flanders, a progressive rabble-rouser I loved on Internet radio and thought might be the answer, but she was more interested in doing her show on the weekend and felt she was stronger solo than part of a team. Great news for the weekend programming, bad news for Chuck and me.

Time was not our friend. Nor were patience or sleep.

We were now in the Christmas season. Still no third host.

I got home one evening and opened my mailbox. Among the sea of red and green envelopes was a small padded package postmarked from a town in western Massachusetts. It was from my dear friend Paul who fled New York City a decade ago for Turners Falls, MA, to teach photography. He had harangued me for years to come and visit him and meet his amazing friends, but I am not one of those "Let's go to the country for apple picking and hiking!" people, so I hadn't made it up for a visit.

I opened the package thinking it would be a holiday mix CD featuring cool renditions of Christmas classics like Patti Smith doing "We Three Kings." It was a CD, but not of music. The note accompanying it read, *I have a friend who hosts a morning radio show here in Northampton. I know I have talked to you about her. She is great, and I think would be great for your network. Give it a listen. Now that you are back in New York, you need to come up and hike! Merry Ho Ho, ya big ho!*

I tossed the mail on the dining room table, ordered Chinese delivery, and fell asleep before it arrived.

As I walked out the door for work the next day, I saw the CD peeking out behind the unopened cards. I grabbed it and hoped for a miracle.

When I got to the office, I walked into Shelley's closet. "Shelley, I got this from a friend. I have no idea who this woman is. I make no promises. She could be a shit chef."

"If she owns one less pink suit than Gloria Allred, we are hiring her," Shelley said.

We started to listen. Wow. This woman was smart, funny, and engaging. She went to Stanford and was a Rhodes Scholar. And she was openly gay.

"I'll call her and see when she can come down to meet us," Shelley said as I left to grab a cup of coffee. A few minutes later I walked back into the closet and Shelley said, "She is getting on a bus from Northampton right now and will be here this afternoon."

Huh. Is the fact that she was able to come *right now* a good thing or a glaring problem?

Since we now know how well I could spot a red flag, who knew? I guess we will find out shortly.

Shelley and I gathered the rest of the team to meet her, and that afternoon in walked Paul's friend, a charming woman who loves politics, music, and dogs. We talked about prisons, gay rights, women's rights, music, and booze—just about everything you could think of. She was terrific. We offered her a job that day. In the news department. Shelley wanted her in the news department.

Poop. I wanted her for my show.

Rachel Maddow, welcome to the yet-to-be-named-progressive-radio-network-owned-by-two-guys-from-Guam.

Rachel lasted about two seconds in the news department, as it became apparent we connected on so many levels from the get-go.

"Shelley, Rachel and I would be a great team. Let's put her on our show and get someone else to fill the news slot."

"I agree. You want me to find out if she has written any checks to hookers?"

The shows were finally complete and the full staff had now arrived. The Guampaloompas found it in their hearts to procure a bit more office space two floors down, so the bosses and the IT folks moved downstairs. That was about the extent of the improvement in infrastructure. They also had room for the writers down there. This was good on the one hand because they were released from the stockyard and were once again able to access the Internet. The bad news was, because my office was the couch, I had no phone, so anytime I had a question, I had to run up and down the stairs. It was great cardio, but lousy efficiency. Don't even ask about the elevators; they were the least efficient things about this place.

Amid all the chaos were two documentary crews roaming freely. One was filming Al, and one was filming the rest of us. They followed me around for weeks, filming meetings, filming me at home and at writing sessions, and the final product was an HBO documentary called *Left of the Dial*. Look for me in the last twenty seconds of the film in the studio with Chuck and Rachel. *Left of the Dial* was some people's version of the story of Air America Radio.

Yes. The network finally had a name. Air America Radio.

We were in the final prelaunch stretch. The writers were assigned their shows and practice runs began. Rachel, Chuck, and I had a great chemistry. Chuck was more of a public gentleman than a public enemy, and Rachel was a brainful of joy.

The shows retreated to their own pockets of energy and chaos, each of them working it out in spite of the house of cards we were all operating in.

Then came launch day, March 31, 2004. We were all nervous. The first day kicked off with Al's show *The O'Franken Factor*. Flowers and fruit baskets poured in, leaving zero floor space in the gulag.

Now our offices looked like a funeral home episode of *Hoarders*. All the bosses paced, nervous and in the way.

Brian Unger had sent the writers a HoneyBaked Ham, and at one point I looked over and witnessed our CEO pick up the whole ham and gorge on it without comprehension. He didn't drop a single pork shard on his signature layered polo shirt that peeked out under his dress shirt topped with a navy blazer ensemble. Impressed, yet dumbfounded, I exclaimed, "What are you doing?"

He looked at the ham. "I don't know what I am doing, I am so nervous."

"Just put the ham down and back away slowly," I said.

"I just don't know what to do with myself."

"I suggest you go wash your hands."

Finally it was noon, and Al hit the air and the first day of Air America Radio began. The website overloaded. That day we had more people streaming than any other program that had ever streamed on the Internet. It was blowing up.

Air America was on the air.

We launched the next day with the full slate. *Morning Sedition* with Marc, Mark, and Sue, and then us. We called our show *Unfiltered*.

"Welcome to the premiere of *Unfiltered* on Air America Radio. I'm Rachel Maddow, here with my cohosts Chuck D and Lizz Winstead. Joining us today for our first broadcast are Arianna Huffington, author Christopher Hitchens, and from *Harper's* magazine Lewis Lapham. . . ."

All the shows were works in progress and slowly found a groove. The audiences were building. The writers helped define each show.

My groove was more like a lurch. I got up at four thirty A.M., walked the dogs, and started my reading: newspapers, magazines, and the Web. I got to work at six, went on the air from nine to noon, then worked on the next day's *Unfiltered* show till I headed home at around four. I spent the next three hours looking over comedy bits for the other shows, maybe ate dinner, then fell into bed at nine.

But as the shows fell into a rhythm, the pressure let up and I could step back a bit. The irreverent tone was set, so I could give more comedic leeway to the head writer and producers of each show. Shelley oversaw their day-to-day needs, and I focused more on my show and dealt with the daily tasks of trying to manage the writers' schedules and morale. This was the goal I tried to reach.

But because the pressure never really let up, it often got to me. Sometimes I killed morale more than boosted it. Lizzilla often won more battles than Lizz.

But in spite of Lizzilla, *Unfiltered* developed nicely. Rachel, Chuck, and I connected. I loved our show because we all were happy in our skin. Rachel had the skills to drive the show, and her wisdom set up my humor. Chuck brought a hip-hop and cultural perspective that, combined with his extensive international travel, gave us a first person insight of how the rest of the planet views America. He truly is a citizen of the world.

Our show was equal parts serious, silly, and touching. Rach and I could barely get through our regular dramatic interpretations of the Concerned Women for America website, an actual website founded by such "concerned women" as Lynne Cheney and Beverly

LaHaye, wife of Rapture enthusiast and tolerance enemy Timothy LaHaye. To close out each show, former *Daily Show* writer, O_2Be producer, Sunday dinner companion, and now Air America staffer Kent Jones did a hilarious Walter Winchell homage called the Unfiltered News. But Fridays were my favorite show day because the talented chanteuse Ambrosia Parsley would sing us out to the weekend by recapping the week that was.

We had the privilege of befriending Paul Rieckhoff, a young Iraq War vet who made his radio debut on *Unfiltered* to talk about the plight of US service people. Because of him and his organization, the Iraq and Afghanistan Veterans of America, we talked to and met countless heroes fighting for the rights of the men and women who fought for my right to be a loudmouth. Paul became our de facto little brother. Chuck, Rachel, and I learned together and reported about Abu Ghraib, Halliburton, and children being left behind. We tried to relay the information with facts, outrage, and humor. I like to think that I was as funny as Rachel was smart, and vice versa.

I can't speak for the other shows, but the dynamic among everyone who worked on *Unfiltered* was genuine. We cared about one another's lives off air as well.

If I had an important stand-up gig, I could always count on Rachel, after spending an already chaotic ten hours with me at work, to attend and laugh the loudest. For one big Comedy Central special, Chuck switched two plane flights to try to make it, missing me by fifteen minutes.

As Chuck planned his daughter's sweet sixteen party, he asked our advice about picking the caterer, the hall, when the father-daughter dance should take place in the course of the evening. And

as the three of us rallied with the thousands of homeless and struggling New Yorkers at the Poor People's March during the 2004 GOP
convention, Chuck gave a speech that inspired me to work harder at
being an advocate for the have-nots.

We wept with our listeners when John Kerry conceded to George
W. Bush while we were live on the air.

I couldn't write about *Unfiltered* and not mention the listeners.
They were engaged, sharing, blogging, correcting me via the website. We stayed connected all three hours of the show on every level.

But one of my fondest memories of my time at Air America was
renting a bus and driving with about twenty of the women on the
network staff to the March for Women's Lives in Washington, DC,
joining hundreds of thousands of Americans as we stood up for
women's reproductive rights in the nation's capital. Rachel and I
proudly marched as we carried our Air America Radio banner surrounded by so many women who had become the heart and soul of
our network.

P eople love to dwell on the failings of Air America Radio. I like
to remember the successes.

It is true that at the end of the day, the Guambats turned out to be
wolves in creeps' clothing. But even as their questionable financial
decisions started to come crashing down around us, the network's
talent, writers, and producers forged on. We woke up each day and
put shows on the air.

Sometimes we didn't get paychecks.

Some of us paid our staff out of our own pockets to get through.

There were a lot more George Baileys than Mr. Potters at Air America, and that is something that can't be emphasized enough. It was a place full of good people doing good work.

When the first Air America implosion—or, as I referred to it, the Fall of SaiGuam—finally happened, there was massive unrest. Yet again, it switched ownership, and they brought in new bosses with different ideas about what the network should be.

On my last day, Rachel and I were interviewing Timothy LaHaye, the hideous author of the Left Behind series, who told us the poor were predestined to be poor, so he didn't believe in charity. He also basically told Rachel that no matter what, she was going to hell. He was counting down to the Rapture and we were clearly not gonna wind up on the good end of this when it happened. At the end of the interview, Rachel, who rarely loses her cool, even with the biggest hate slingers, matter-of-factly asked, "So, Mr. LaHaye, when the Rapture happens, can I have your stuff?"

Dial tone. We burst out laughing and quickly had to close out the show. We laughed all the way downstairs.

Jon Sinton met me in my office. He was uncomfortable and just said what he had been charged with saying.

"Lizz, we are gonna have to let you go."

I was stunned. "What? Why?"

"The new management doesn't see comedy as a priority in delivering the progressive message. I'll walk you out."

I collected my things and Jon gave me a big hug and put me in a cab. There wasn't anything either of us could say.

That is how many radio stories end. One day, you are just done. I was crushed.

So *Unfiltered* sputtered out. Chuck went to the weekends, Rachel went to five A.M., and I went and closed out "the Staples account." This made way for the new bosses' vision: to replace Rachel Maddow, Chuck D, and Lizz Winstead with Jerry Springer.

I will let you draw your own conclusions about how this was received. And how I felt about losing my radio show to Springer.

But the band played on, every day fighting the fight.

Despite Air America's difficulties, I believe that we had developed a network that put passion and ideals over all else, and that should never be considered a failure. And Dad turned out to be right after all: Having an opinion and being clear about why you believe what you do is something to be proud of. I was reminded of it every day at Air America, *The Daily Show*, and onstage. I helped develop a network that bore some pretty awesome fruit: Rachel Maddow, now one of the purest voices in cable news, and Al Franken, now one of the purest voices in the United States Senate. This is nothing any other radio network still in existence can claim.

So there.

DIELARITY

When they took Dad to the hospital for the last time, he called me from his room.

"Lizzy, the paramedics asked me if I was on any medications. I told them everything but Viagra. Then they put the oxygen mask on me."

Those were the last actual words I heard him say.

It was a hot August day, and it was my birthday. I was celebrating it in Coney Island with my sister Ann and her family. The cell phone service was shitty and the call went dead.

"Fuck Sprint," I said to the group.

I told them the Viagra story and we laughed. It was typical of Dad: dark, inappropriate, and funny.

"We'll call him later. Let's go see the sword swallower," I said.

We talked to my sister Linda that night and she told us Dad was scheduled to leave the hospital on Monday. He would then go for a week to the place he had come to call "the Lutheran Abu Ghraib," which was more colloquially known as a rehab center.

Linda called back the following morning. We were all in the elevator of my loft, as we had just come back from the dog park.

"You need to come home," she said in a voice that sounded like a little girl who had snuck away from the babysitter and called her parents because she was scared. "Dad is dying."

"How long does he have?" I said. I don't know where those words came from and couldn't believe I asked them as though I were talking about someone I didn't know. Ann looked at me, the elevator stopped, and we all walked out into my apartment.

"Maybe a day or two, so you need to come home now," Linda instructed.

"'Kay, I'll tell Ann. I love you."

I didn't have to tell Ann. She knew. We both just started sobbing.

Ann's husband, Tim, kicked into gear while we both stood in the middle of my apartment and wept. "I'll book your tickets so you two can leave tonight," he said. "The kids and I will come tomorrow."

To this day, I don't even know if I thanked him.

As my brother-in-law arranged our travel, I started packuuming. Then I stopped myself, realizing I needed help. This was not the time to show up in Minnesota with six pairs of cutoffs and three bathrobes.

"Ann, can you help me? I don't pack well under pressure."

Since Ann only had to repack what she brought, she started going through my closet, pulling out sensible items, like pants and shirts. Then she went back and forth, hanger after hanger, in a desperate attempt to find something she was sure was there.

"You don't have a black summer dress," she said incredulously.

In my family, not owning a black summer dress is like not having indoor plumbing or a copy of *Rubber Soul*. I couldn't believe it myself.

"I don't have a fucking black summer dress?" I was as stunned as she was.

"No," Ann said. "But you have a black fucking everything else!"

I needed a black summer dress. Thank God I lived in the capital of black dresses. I must leave now to go get a black dress. I must drop everything and get that dress. It was a task I thought I could manage.

I shock-walked out of my apartment, like a soap opera actress who had been drugged and somehow escaped the attic and made it onto the street. I weaved and bumped into the endless flood of Europeans who smugly bought up the whole of NoHo.

I lived in downtown Manhattan, right at the intersection of Washington Place and German Tourists with Banana Republic Bags. Whenever I walked out my door it felt like I lived above a mall. If I turned right, I would hit McDonald's, Gap, the Vitamin Shoppe, and Foot Locker. This day I turned left and bypassed Canal Jeans, a bookstore, American Apparel, and finally wandered into French Connection.

I spotted a black linen shift on the sale rack. In my fog it seemed appropriate from the front; sleeveless, boatneck, black. But the back was riddled with strings and hoists. I didn't trust my judgment that it was appropriate, but since it was my size and $19.99, I walked it up to the clerk at the counter for advice.

"Can I wear this to my dad's funeral?" I asked.

"Hm." She looked up from her phone and gave me a half assessment. "I don't know. The back is sort of sexy."

Well, "sort of sexy" was going to have to do, considering the time constraints I was under.

"Great," I snapped. "It's a sexy funeral."

She stared at me as if I had just started playing with my own poo. I ignored her as she was all of twenty and was more concerned with texting than helping me, so I just handed her my credit card.

Plus, I couldn't resist the wisecrack. Dad would have expected a snide remark from me. I convinced myself I was doing it for him. (Aren't rationalizations a wonderful thing?)

Honestly, I didn't care what I picked out. Back in Minnesota everyone in my family thinks I dress like a freak, anyway. No matter what outfit I wear, some Scandin/aggressive will say, "Oh, your dress is so *different*. I wouldn't be able to think of a single place I could wear that."

To which I usually replied, "Thanks, Mom."

"This is a final sale," this retail zygote reminded me in a tone she thought might jar me out of buying a sexy dress for my dad's funeral.

"Well, then," I concluded, "I hope it's sexy enough."

I signed my slip, grabbed my bag, and walked out. That evil little exchange had a silver lining, as it made me feel something other than numb and momentarily snapped me back into the real world, and I celebrated my victory. "I went shopping in a state of shock and found a dress in seven minutes. I love New York."

That detached euphoria lasted the entire length of my three-building walk home. *The next time I walk up to my building,* I thought, *Dad will be dead.*

It was a long elevator ride back up to my apartment.

I n his own way, Dad had tried to prepare me for this day. A few months before his death, he had sent me a card and had asked me not to open it "till after I'm gone."

Of course I opened it immediately.

The front was a photo of the Manhattan skyline. When I opened it, it simply said, *I love you. You are my favorite. Please don't tell the others.*

The sentiment evoked a range of emotions in me at the time. It made me feel elated that I did something right. Then it made me feel bad for my brother and sisters. Finally, I felt horribly guilty for opening it.

I taped it open inside my jewelry box so I would see it a lot, and as I went to grab my pearls, my last item to pack, I glanced at it, and at that moment I was selfishly grateful that Dad and I shared this important secret.

Ann and I flew to Minneapolis and went straight to the hospital from the airport. As we walked toward Dad's room, the sound of laughter got louder. The hospital had put him way at the end of the hall, next to the family area. Probably because before Phil Spector, the Winsteads were responsible for constructing the original Wall of Sound. The hospital had allowed my dad's big double room to become a de facto hospice/party space. When we walked into the room, there was Dad, lying on his back in a heavy morphine paradise, the bedside table littered with a pizza box and pop cans.

Mom was sitting in the chair next to him, holding a piece of pizza in one hand and Dad's hand in the other. She was not going to relinquish either.

My brother, two sisters, and sister-in-law were all sitting in a row on the extra bed in his room with their legs stretched out. Tears were streaming down their faces as they laughed. They looked like little kids who were still too small to have their feet touch the floor.

Dad couldn't speak, but he could hear everything. His stomach was bouncing up and down, as he was laughing, too.

"What did we miss?" Ann asked desperately. "I hate when I miss any laughing."

"The meat! The gas station meat!" my brother said, choking through what I like to think of as dielarity.

dielarity: /dī-'ler-ə-tē/ n. *The dark humor created in the environment of or at the expense of someone dying.*

Ahh, the gas station meat. The crown jewel in the pantheon of Dad's many "deals."

Dad loved getting a bargain. He loved driving through the city, discovering deals in every neighborhood. He found them in the good areas and the ones where the only reason you would be there was if you were scoring meth. He usually stumbled upon his "deals" in the latter, and it was always stuff that no one wanted, never mind wanted to get a "deal" on. And I suspected that sometimes it may have belonged to someone other than the "salesman."

He mostly liked gag gifts, like the footstool with humanlike legs wearing tube socks and sneakers. Or the sixty-five-pound brass elephant phones we each got for Christmas one year. When we asked him where he got them, he said, "Some Indian guy downtown had a store loaded with lamps, scarves, and some kind of pipes. It looked like the Garage Mahal."

"What were *you* doing there?" one of us inquired.

"Buying these phones," he stated matter-of-factly. There is some logic you just can't argue with, so we just left it at that.

Throughout his years of cruising for "deals," Dad had created a whole world for himself. There was a diner he discovered where he raved about the onion rings, and the Vietnamese restaurant he frequented because he liked the sign: I DIDN'T COME 9,000 MILES TO COOK YOU ORDINARY FOOD.

His cruises eventually turned into specific routes for specific things. One of his routes involved a place he called "the Institute." It was a barber school he frequented about once a month that trained guys just out of prison to cut hair. He could get a hot shave and a cut for eight bucks.

"I could get the basic shave for six bucks," he informed us, "but I get the works for eight. I spend the extra on the guy who is just about to graduate. When you're doing something that involves a razor and a guy just out of jail, you don't want to do it on the cheap."

His criteria for what to do "on the cheap" were wildly inconsistent. Which brings us back to the gas station meat.

I chimed in immediately. "I remember we were in Beanie's"—my brother Gene's nickname—"backyard, eating these beautiful rib eyes Dad had just grilled."

Ann interrupted—as you have learned, you can't tell a Winstead family story without being Winsterrupted. It's how we do it.

"And Dad, you were so excited to tell us about the 'deal' you got on them."

I then Winsterrupted Ann.

"First he told us about the gas station he found twenty miles away that was three cents cheaper than the gas down the street."

Then Beanie Winsterrupted. "I could never figure that out, Dad. It cost you five bucks in gas to drive there and you saved seventy-five cents."

By then Dad's stomach was in full bounce. We were all laughing. I sat on the end of Dad's bed and Ann squeezed onto the extra bed with the other four.

I Winsterrupted Beanie. I also grabbed Dad's foot as the ribbing continued.

"I will never forget being halfway through my steak when you got to the part," I said as I continued in my best Dad baritone voice. "'I was filling up the tank and notice this fella's got a station wagon there with the tailgate open. And the guy says, "You want to check out my meat?" And at first I thought, Who is this weirdo who wants to show me his meat?'"

"Dad, you are so bad," Mary said, more as a chime-in than a full-fledged Winsterruption.

Dad was so proud of that dumb joke, his belly was in full force. Then the story reached its climax with each of us Winsterrupting all over the place.

"That guy had half a cow in an old cardboard box in the back of that station wagon."

"That came from God knows where!"

"Or *when!*"

"And Dad bought all of it!"

"For forty bucks!"

"We were eating black market roadkill."

Mom finished her pizza and weighed in. "The ribs were really very good."

We swapped stories for a few more hours until the dielarity exhausted us all.

Dielarious laughter is different from regular laughter, as it drains you of every emotion inside you. It is an exhausting release of all the pain, fear, love, and loss that you have been holding in until your body can no longer physically take it. I freely let it happen, because if I didn't, if I had left even an ounce of energy in me, I would have spent it reminding myself that my life was about to change forever.

Dad's spirit was humor—his and his family's. So ipso facto, if there was still laughter, he would continue to exist. That day, sitting in that hospital room with him and my mother and siblings, I wanted to laugh myself to sleep.

I looked at Mom gently rubbing his hand. She was eighty-four and had survived three heart attacks, but somehow she never seemed stronger.

"I need to go home," Mom said to the room. "I think tomorrow will be a long day."

She turned to my dad and kissed him on the forehead. "Night, Wilb, see ya tomorrow." Her tenderness inspired a comforting confidence that we would have Dad tomorrow.

The rest of the family had already been there for twenty-four hours and needed sleep. I think they had exhausted themselves enough to finally get some.

Ann and I decided to stay overnight with Dad. We climbed into the spare bed and tried to make it work. Let me say that two grown women trying to sleep in a hospital bed reaches a restfulness level that is just above two people on a dollar-store lawn chair. Ann and I were so spent, we remained fully dressed—too weary to take off anything but our shoes, so as we tossed and turned we kept buckle-stabbing each other. When we both found comfortable positions, just as we thought we'd fall asleep, the oxygen machine kicked in with a foreboding lullaby. We must have slept some, because when I woke up from an unconscious state Ann was sleeping in the chair next to Dad and I was sprawled all over the bed.

I sat up to look at Dad and Ann stirred.

"Everything okay?" she asked.

"Okay as it can be, I guess."

At this point I wasn't sure what okay was. I just knew I was coated in a thin layer of travel gravy and unease. Dad was on his side, sleeping or morphining or whatever you call that state of being where you are on a continuous IV of paradise up until the moment you slip away from your loved ones forever.

Later that morning the family filed back in and reassumed their positions. Mom was on the chair next to Dad, the kids on the extra bed; we rotated in to lay next to Dad. The day was long. It consisted of nurses coming in and turning Dad every hour to a different side. His stomach-bouncing was minimal today.

We didn't know what to do. We just sat, waiting to feel worse than we already did. That seemed almost impossible. A hospice worker stopped by to talk to us. She suggested we each take some time alone with Dad to share our private thoughts.

And so that process began. His room was next to a family gathering suite, so as Mom began her time with Dad, we kids went next door. While we waited for our individual turns, we watched a series of judge shows on TV. I stared out the window into the parking lot, watching people come and go, and wondered how their visits to the hospital were going to end.

Mom came into the suite and suggested we say our good-byes in birth order, which meant that I would go last. I tried to figure out what Mom had said. How do you talk to your spouse of fifty-eight years in his final hours? What is the last thing you say? The stakes seemed so high. She never told me what she said, and I never asked. I hoped it was everything she needed to let him know.

As each of my siblings walked back into the family suite, they were swollen-faced, yet looked somehow peaceful. Finally, it was my turn.

At first I felt a bit afraid of being alone with him. His breathing pattern started sounding finite. Each inhale was a jarring gasp that seemed to come in ten-minute increments. When he exhaled, it sounded like a January wind whistling through a small crack in a window. I learned later that is what is fondly referred to in hospice circles as a death rattle.

I climbed into bed with him and grabbed his hand. I put my lips right up to his ear and spoke in my normal voice.

"Dad, squeeze my hand so I know you can hear me." He squeezed back. I wanted him to squeeze it off.

I didn't know where to start, so I started with apologizing for opening the card.

"Dad, I opened your card. I couldn't wait. I hope you are not mad. It made me feel so special."

He didn't squeeze my hand, but his belly started to bounce. Right then, that felt better than a squeeze.

"You know I love you, and you are my inspiration to go out and make the world a funnier place."

Squeeze.

"I know you let me win at *Jeopardy!*"

Squeeze.

I wanted to say every single thing I ever felt, but I was in a verbal freefall, so I just wanted him to laugh. I wanted to be funnier than those guys on BET.

"Dad, I am who I am because of you, and that includes the bad parts, mister!"

There was a knock on the door. It was the hospice worker.

"The priest is here for the sacrament of the sick."

"Okay, just a minute," I said, and then continued into Dad's ear. "You couldn't have done a better job of being a dad. Love comes naturally to you. I hope you are proud of me. I love you."

Squeeze.

I kissed him on the forehead again and went to open the door.

Everyone filed in and took their places.

Uh-oh. The priest looked like a Jesuit—bearded, Birkenstocks, his collar tucked into a rumpled shirt. He looked like he just came from an antiwar protest. Dad would have hated him. I felt like God sent him on my behalf.

Father Liberal seemed to be on his death rounds, sort of like Last Rights Express. He had an Extreme Unction travel kit he carried in kind of an over-the-shoulder-sacrament-holder that had just enough room for the oil and the prayer. I wondered if he used it as a man purse when he wasn't lubricating people up for their trips to heaven. I started thinking about Jesus trapezes and wondered if he would laugh if I told him that story.

I just couldn't listen to what he was saying.

Now I started having a private moment of dielarity, laughing and crying softly (so it looked like crying) as I remembered sitting with Dad a few years back in the TV room at Club Meds. We were watching the endless coverage of the Vatican deliberating on a new pope when Dad got up from his recliner and walked into the kitchen. He had been rummaging around in there for about ten minutes and I finally got up to see what he was doing. He stood, waiting for me to discover him, with a FedEx envelope on his head and holding a wooden spoon like a scepter.

"What are you doing?" I asked.

"I got sick of waiting around for a new pope, so I decided I should just take the job. I'm Pope Wilbur the First. I absolve you of all your sins."

That memory was all the last rites I could handle.

The priest finished and stayed a bit to talk to Mom. Then, soon after he left, a nurse came in and checked on Dad again. She put him on his back and turned to us. "It is time," she informed us. "Your dad will pass within the hour."

By now, many of the grandkids had arrived and we were about fifteen people gathered and sitting on Dad's bed. His breathing became so shallow, so slow, that as a family we all tried to breathe for him. As a group we inhaled with him and painfully watched as he choked out an exhale, like he had breathed in a box of tacks. It was the worst thirty minutes of our lives. Each of us wanted his pain to end, and we took turns assuring him that he could go, that we would all be okay.

Finally he took his last breath. We all exhaled with him like a very unsettling yoga class. His jaw slacked and my brother gently took his two fingers, closed Dad's eyes, and removed the oxygen tubes from his nose. We hadn't seen him without those tubes in years. My father used to say, "Next to your mother, this oxygen tank is the longest relationship I've ever had."

He looked rested. Yellow, but rested.

We didn't know what to do. We just sat there, wept, and stared at our dead dad. I always wondered what this would feel like and what the first thing would be that would come to my mind. I had never been in the presence of a dead person. I really thought I would freak, but it all seemed natural. Before I could even form my first thoughts, I looked over at Mom.

She was still holding his hand.

"He loved you kids so much; you were his world. He always hoped he told you enough. It's why he sent you kids the cards to open after he died, so you would always have a reminder."

"I keep mine open in my jewelry case," I said in an attempt to let her know we knew how much Dad loved us.

Then I thought, *They all got cards?* I had heard that people prepared for their own deaths by reaching out to their loved ones and getting their emotional house in order. I loved that Dad helped prepare all of us in his own way with a special thought for each of us.

"Oh, you opened it?" Mom asked knowingly. I guess he told her he was sending us cards, but did he reveal our secret to her? I couldn't imagine he did.

"And did the rest of you open your cards, too?" Mom asked.

Suddenly I felt horribly guilty. "Oh, please tell me I was not the only asshole who went against his wishes and opened the card."

Everyone smiled and nodded. They were all clearly shamed, but you could read in each person's face how much Dad's special words gave them peace. No one would be judging anyone today. He had given everyone something lovely to think about.

"Dad wanted you to open those cards after he died, and since you all went against his wishes and already have, I would love to hear what he wrote to each of you," Mom said.

Oh, no, Mom, I moaned to myself. *Not now. This is so not the time.*

"I would like nothing more right now. Lizz, you start."

This cannot be happening. My father has been dead for five minutes, and I am about to make people feel worse than they already do? So much for no judging anyone today.

I didn't know what to do. Deny my mom's first wish after her husband of fifty-eight years had just passed? Do I lie? Yes, I would just lie. I would say the card said, *You will always be my baby and I love you.*

Wait, I can't lie. The first thing I do after Dad is dead is to lie? I don't think so. I haven't even had a decent cry yet.

"Mom, maybe now is not the time," Linda said, to my over-whelming relief.

"Let's just focus on Dad and you," Ann added.

Crisis averted. No one wanted to read their cards, either. I felt relieved, and now I am not the bad guy who denied Mom.

"Lizz, you start," Mom repeated. She was not letting this go.

The only person who could make this stop was lying there not doing anything.

Oh. Fuck. *MY DAD IS DEAD!* Finally, I started crying because I was helpless to everything surrounding me.

"The card said, 'I love you. You were my favorite. Please don't—'"

And before I finished, everyone said in various tones of unison, "—tell the others."

Mom had a smile on her face that put the Cheshire Cat to shame. The room erupted with convulsions of dielarity. Dad had pulled off the greatest gotcha moment of his life. And at his death, no less.

He knew we all would open that card the second we got it. And he knew how we would all believe what he wrote. And relish it and find some smug superiority in it. But more than anything else, he knew how hard we would laugh when we found out, having to laugh at our own ridiculousness and remembering that he made us laugh, even after his death. He knew that this moment would be more precious than ever feeling like the favorite.

His greatest moment of hilarity and he couldn't take a bow. Not physically, anyway. But in our minds, he graciously appreciated our standing ovation.

Bravo, Dad. Bravo.

LET ME TELL YOU WHAT I THINK ABOUT WRITING THIS BOOK

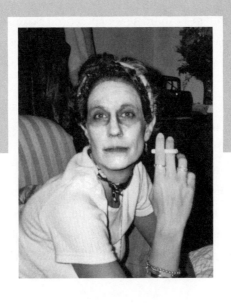

I had a really hard time finishing this book. I started writing it at the end of 2009 in conjunction with my 2010 touring schedule. The thought was, I would perform two shows a month and spend the rest of my time writing these essays.

Well, 2010 came screaming in, fulfilling a political satirist's wish list that surpassed anything I have seen in my twenty-seven years of doing this. First came the largest environmental disaster in this country's history, which occurred because meth-snorting government workers were too busy having orgies to remember to change the batteries on the blowout preventer—never mind an oil industry that swore there would never be a blowout using a drilling rig that needed a blowout preventer. And then there was the moronathon of political candidates ranging from ones who ran on the platform of ending all government programs as a rallying cry to land them a government job, to a candidate who practiced satanism while railing against masturbation in an economic climate where masturbation is the only form of entertainment Americans can afford anymore.

It was comedy overload, and I was trying to keep up as I hopped from town to town doing a one-woman show that each week was full of fresh outrage.

But while my comedy shows were writing themselves, this book was not. I wrote in fits and starts. I finished a few essays, and just when I was on a roll, *bam!* Rand Paul said he thought private businesses have the right to discriminate against people of color. I'd start another essay and get derailed by some fake Christian screaming on cable news that if a couple of gay folks she didn't know were allowed to get married in a state she has never been to, it would destroy her "normal" marriage. The stupidity was volcanic, and I could not be pulled away from it to write the book, so I took a drastic step.

In late November 2010, I decided to take a hiatus from touring, packed up my two dogs, some clothes, and my computer, put them all into a rented SUV, and drove halfway across the country to the outskirts of Minneapolis to focus on my book in the snowy seclusion of my sister Mary's home.

I thought I needed quiet, no distractions. But in the age of cable, the Internet, and Twitter, there was no such thing as seclusion.

And then 2011 arrived, as if to say, "Hey, 2010, is that all you got?"

I again struggled to write my book as Hurricane Tea Party grew to a level 5.

These 115-mile-an-hour windbags started knocking down Planned Parenthood, science, climate change, and humanity. Facts were officially Public Enemy Number One.

The pied vipers were leading an unwitting flock. Choosing who should be the 2012 Republican nominee was like deciding who is the smartest Kardashian. The assault on logic was as constant as the tide.

I couldn't just stick my fingers in my ears and pretend all of this wasn't happening. And I don't know why I thought I wanted to. So there I was, in front of the fire in my sister's house in Bachmann country, the Land of Ten Thousand Flakes, being cozy and watching the snow in a perfect writer's environment for everyone but me. I was bad at this.

Being away from people made me linger on social networking

sites longer. A lot longer. I felt lonely as I read tweets about where all of my pals were having sushi, or the shows they were performing in New York and LA as I fake-romanticized my "six-month writing sabbatical" in Minnesota.

I was not inspired. I was stuck.

Oh, dear.

So I sat at my computer eighteen hours a day. An essay page here, thirty tweets there, another essay page, Facebook rants, etc. As the old saying goes, "Everywhere you go, there you are, on Twitter."

I was in a creative catch-22. If I tried to ignore the news, it blocked my writing of this book because I felt guilty not being informed. And if I paid attention to the news, I would write material for blogs and anything *but* my book.

I had to do both somehow.

My solution: I didn't have one.

Then life dealt me a shit-soaked curveball.

In May of 2011, a week after I spent four months writing the essay about my father dying, Mom fell ill. Within two weeks she had passed away. I had dredged up all the emotion of losing Dad, and now I had to relive it again fresh with Mom.

For a week I couldn't find the inspiration to get dressed or shower, never mind write anything. Somehow I had to write a eulogy.

Recalling her life really helped. And the obligation I had to honor her publicly, with my siblings counting on me to do it right, brought me out of that hole. I couldn't let them down.

I thought about her totality and what was important to her, and I tried to capture her spirit with love and humor.

The day of her funeral, I delivered my tribute.

Here are a few of the jokes:

"I remember walking into her apartment one day and she was watching a show on the Catholic Channel called *Catholicism 101*. She didn't need the primer; she was fact-checking."

"It was important for our family to remember our mother at a place she attended religiously for thirty-five years. Unfortunately, Walgreens was unable to accommodate us, so Father Dale most graciously invited us here to Christ the King church."

I was writing a book that addressed how humor had pulled me through some difficult times, and this was one of those times. Through her death she got me laughing again, and I got my siblings laughing again.

But I found out something about myself writing that eulogy, something important. I discovered that I could write through the pain and find clarity and hilarity.

It was time to go home and finish this beast.

So after six months of fits and starts, I went back to Brooklyn. I had momentum, but I also needed to keep it going, which meant reconnect with my comedy audience. So I decided to do that on my drive back. I packed up another SUV, loaded the pups, my computer, and all of my stuff, and I drove across the country to New York, doing comedy shows along the way. But not just any shows: I did a stand-up tour—six cities in ten days—that benefited Planned Parenthood. I connected with people who needed a laugh as the world seemed to be running on the fumes of sanity. Each night after I concluded my act, I gave a reading of my messay "All Knocked Up." It was a risky move, as I had no idea if the essay was any good, or if anybody even cared about what had happened to me all those years ago. The response startled and humbled me. Women of all ages thanked me. Actually thanked me. Many of them had similar stories, and these women told me that I had inspired them to start telling them.

It was then that I started to get the feeling that maybe my goofy experiences were relatable to somebody outside my family and that they might help readers know they weren't alone. I had more stories to tell, and I was now truly excited to write them.

Throughout my career as a TV writer and producer, I always preferred writing collaboratively rather than by myself. I love taking an idea and tossing it into a room of trusted compatriots. It grows and develops into the best material it can be. I love the process.

But with this book, I didn't have that option. I was back in the metaphorical Chair. I couldn't toss my life into a group and say, "Let's take this life and add whatever we want to it, to make it the most interesting life it can be." Nope, I had to rely on the life itself and my own skills as a writer and a storyteller to make it worthy of the read.

I hope I didn't disappoint.

ACKNOWLEDGMENTS

My mom and dad didn't live to see this book come out.

I hope it would make them proud.

I would be shattered for any outcome shy of that.

They brought me to this place. And not a day goes by that I am not thankful for their love and support, even when they vehemently disagreed.

My siblings, Linda, Gene, Mary, and Ann; through love, encouragement, endless shit-giving, and cold hard cash you have been there. You never judged me in the struggle and helped me celebrate in my successes.

Seriously, each of you scraped to bail me out at some point to help me realize my dream.

Have I paid you all back?

How is it even possible?

You are why I get up every day.

And an extra shout out to my sister, Mary, and her amazing husband, Peter—you invited me into your home this past year, a year that was one of the coldest winters on record, literally and emotionally. You kept me alive with your unending support and love.

I could not have gotten through this without you.

To Hank Gallo, who has been a friend, colleague, a shoulder, an advocate, a financier, and often times my wordsmith. You are such a treasure.

To Jo Miller, whose brevity and brilliance was instrumental in this process.

Maggie Macpherson, who unlocked her heart and her home and our memories to help me recapture some amazing moments in time. Mags, I thank you, and Buddy and Edie thank you. You are goodness personified.

To Jake Morrissey, who saw me through this process with patience, inspiration, and a gentle pen. You are a fine American.

To Riverhead Books, for taking this book on and working so hard to bring it to life.

To Kate Ritchey, who made it look like I have a clue about grammar.

To Kirby Kim, my agent and friend. Your encouragement and calm allowed me to thrive.

To Brian Unger, because your love is limitless.

ACKNOWLEDGMENTS

Oh Darbi Worley, you are heaven sent.

To Doug Herzog, Eileen Katz, and Madeleine Smithberg, who entrusted a young, inexperienced, opinionated loudmouth to help create a show that meant so much to you.

To Jon Stewart and *The Daily Show* staff past and present. Because you cannot be recognized enough for everything you do.

To Rachel Maddow and Chuck D. You made me smarter.

To Shelley Lewis, Jon Sinton, David Goodfriend, and Mark Walsh, who made history, and all the Air America Radio staff and on-air talent, especially Vanessa Peel and Jen Hodgkins, who hung in during the worst of times, putting the message above yourselves.

To the Shoot the Messenger team:

Aaron Kheifets, Amy Kantrowitz, Anne Teutschel, Baron Vaughn, Barry Lank, Benari Poulten, Bruce Cherry, Carol Hartsell, Dan Borrelli, Dan Houle, Danielle Mazur, Darbi Worley, Daric Snyder, Dave Hickey, Eric Seader, Erik Kraus, Erin Judge, Gabi Moore, Geoff Lerer, Hank Gallo, James Manzi, Jeff Kreisler, Jim Colucci, Jo Miller, Joe Moore, Jonathan Light, John Marshall, Josh Simon, Kevin Janus, Lani Levine, Leah Biel, Livia Scott, Lucas Held, Lee Papa, Mark Manne, Matt Gorman, Mindy Tucker, Sean Crespo, Shannon Manning, Shawn Wickens, Shelley Lewis, Than Hussey, Tom Gilroy.

Your story is not yet written, but your talents inspire me every day.

ACKNOWLEDGMENTS

To Sarah Silverman: You have had my back and front. *Mwah*.

Helen Martineau and Ann Gastler: Because it's been 30 years of a sisterhood.

To those who had lovely things to say about this book: Roseanne Barr, Lewis Black, Arianna Huffington, Julie Klam, Patton Oswalt, Paul Provenza, Sarah Silverman.

To my friends and colleagues whose love and support touched me at so many points in my life: Caroline Hirsch, Sara Nelson, Lani Levine, Corey Pandolph, Kent Jones, Suzanne Fagel, Katherine Lanpher, Rob Fox, Beth Littleford, Sue Remes, Joe Blake, Kim Tillman, Susan Griak, Melissa Mosedale, Matt Mahoney, Joe Minjares, Josh Weinstein, Ambrosia Parsley, Dave Ayers, Brian Balleria, Joan Bechtold, Chrissie Dunlap, Steve McClellan, Bill Sullivan, Jim Boquist, Marc Perlman, Scott Hansen, Jeff Cesario, Joel Madison, Louie Anderson, Dudley Riggs, Lucien Hold, Jim Walsh, Jean Heyer, Rita and Tony Pucci, Jim Peterson, Molly Roth, Jennifer Roth, Ed Schultz, Joy Behar, Mo Gaffney, Dana Gould, Norn Cutson, Elon James White, Baratunde Thurston, David Bender, Cara Stein, Jimmy Griggs, Karen Glass, Frank DeCaro, Jim Colucci, Bobby Grotenhuis, Kevin O'Neill, Paul Teeling, Tom and Martha Casey, Michele Norris, Dan Murphy, and all my friends who have reached out, offered support, and stayed with me during all those hard times when it probably seemed unbearable to do so.

I can't thank you enough.

ACKNOWLEDGMENTS

To all the comedians I have had the pleasure of working with throughout the years. Thanks for making me laugh.

To regulars of Sunday dinner in L.A. and New York:

Mike Gandolfi, Bruce Cherry, Barry Lank, Kathleen Roll, Neil Kendall, Josh Perlman, Frank Conniff, Pam Griffiths, Ray James, and Brian Unger.

To all the women who are facing an assault on their reproductive freedom, I will fight with you every day so you too can stay healthy and make the choices to become the women you dream of becoming.

My countless Twitter and Facebook friends, especially #TeamGinny

The following are just some of the Minneapolis bands whose writing and music I admired and admire. Keep writing, you helped me find my voice whether you knew it or not:

Soul Asylum, the Gear Daddies, Hüsker Dü, the Replacements, the Jayhawks, the Hypstrz, NNB, the Suicide Commandos, Man Sized Action, the Suburbs, Slim Dunlap, Curtiss A, John Eller, Rifle Sport, Run Westy Run, Trip Shakespeare, Sussman Lawrence, and of course, Prince.

I know I will have forgotten to acknowledge many who have been on this journey with me. I love you and I hope you can forgive me.